D0792546

TOWARD A NEW CATHOLIC MORALITY

BY JOHN GILES MILHAVEN

IMAGE BOOKS

A Division of Doubleday & Company, Inc.

Garden City, New York

Grateful acknowledgment is made to the following for permission to reprint their material.

AMERICA (NATIONAL CATHOLIC WEEKLY REVIEW)
"Loyola Opposition in the Church" by John G. Milhaven, April 30, 1966 issue. "The Importance of Being Roman Catholic" by John G. Milhaven, June 28, 1969 issue. "Be Like Me! Be Free!" by John G. Milhaven, April 22, 1967 issue, under the title, "Becoming Free." All originally published in *America*.

AMERICAN ECCLESIASTICAL REVIEW and CATHOLIC UNIVERSITY OF AMERICA PRESS
"Sharing God's Dominion" by John G. Milhaven, January 1970 issue, and in part in "The Distinctiveness of Christian Ethics" from *Bases of Ethical Insight* edited by George McLean, *Catholic University Press.*

COMMONWEAL PUBLISHING COMPANY, INC.
"Creative Activism" by John G. Milhaven, October 1969 issue, under the title, "Exit for Ethicists."

CORPUS INSTRUMENTORUM, INC.
"Thomas Aquinas and Exceptions to the Moral Law" by John G. Milhaven, June 1968 issue, under the title "Moral Absolutes and Thomas Aquinas" from *Absolutes in Moral Theology?* edited by Charles E. Curran, copyright © 1968 by Charles E. Curran.

CRITIC
"Sin" by John G. Milhaven, March 1970 issue, under the title, "A New Sense of Sin." "A New Catholic Morality" by John G. Milhaven, June–July 1968 issue.

HOMILETIC AND PASTORAL REVIEW
"Homosexuality and Love" by John G. Milhaven, May 1968 issue, under the title, "Homosexuality and the Christian."

THEOLOGICAL STUDIES
"The Abortion Debate" by John G. Milhaven, March 1970 issue. "Criticism of Traditional Morality" by John G. Milhaven, June 1966 issue, under the title, "Towards an Epistemology of Ethics."

THOUGHT
"Responsible Disobedience in the Church" by John G. Milhaven, Autumn 1969 issue, Vol. XLIV, No. 174.

Image Books edition 1972 by special arrangement with Doubleday & Company, Inc. Image Books edition published February 1972

For Anne, Rege, Ed and Katie

CONTENTS

INTRODUCTION

Gustave Weigel once remarked, "All men are divided into two classes: those who divide all men into two classes and those who don't." Being, like Father Weigel, of the former class, I divide all living men into two classes: those who believe we are at a turning point in the history of the Church, and those who don't. In the lively discussion among Christians on innumerable questions, two biases consistently emerge: an *a priori* inclination to look for a new answer (not totally discontinuous with the old) and an *a priori* inclination to look for an old answer (appropriately modernized). The polarization is not always obvious. Many who are in fact searching for something new feel the need to look for it in the Bible or the *Summa* or the writings of Martin Luther. Many who in fact cannot let go of the old feel the need to express it in the words of Karl Barth or Teilhard de Chardin or Vatican II. The polarization is further obscured by the influence of a third bias, found principally among men trapped in positions of authority, namely an *a priori* inclination to treat the first two inclinations as essentially the same thing.

Subject, as I am, to the first bias, I have written essays over the last four years charting the new direction the Church is turning into as far as Christian ethics or moral theology is concerned. The present volume is a collection of those essays, revised and correlated. I have found a direction which is so unified that I do not hesitate to speak throughout the essays simply of "the new morality" despite all the variations that must come under this label. The phrase, "the new morality," is used today with many different meanings. I mean by it no more and no less than what the book presents as the new direction we Catholics are taking in our moral thinking.

The use of the word "Catholic" may surprise some people in this highly ecumenical age. I do not mean that I am speaking of a morality which, after reaching full growth, will be of the genus Catholic, rather than Protestant. But I am speaking of a *Catholic growth*. In the title, "Catholic" should modify "toward" rather than "new morality." Ecumenical experience makes clear, as I argue in the thirteenth chapter, that the importance of being Roman Catholic is that this is where the Roman Catholic is "at." He can only move from where he stands at the moment. His way, at least in the beginning, will be a Roman Catholic way. In our time, the paths of men of different faiths and churches are drawing so close that one feels no need to make them identical. Moreover, their closeness makes it possible for a man to learn from the ways of others while following his own. Hopefully, Protestants and Jews reading this book will profit as much as I have from reading ethicists such as Eugene Borowitz and Joseph Fletcher.[1]

Whether that dusty pilgrim, the Church, is at a turning point in its trek is a matter of historical fact. It either is or it isn't. If historical evidence shows that it is not, the contents of this book are false. There are, however, those who, not on historical evidence but on theological grounds, would deny any turning point and reject in advance the contents of this book. The Church *cannot* turn in its teaching. The role of the theologian is simply to pass on, perhaps in new words, the accepted truths of Christian tradition. In reply, I borrow the words of Avery Dulles:

> The theologian should not be content to defend officially accepted views. He must also keep the inherited body of doctrine under constant review, questioning what is really questionable and denying what he believes to be false. Only if theologians are honest is there any hope of keeping Catholic doctrine abreast of the times. A Church in which candid questioning was forbidden would rapidly stagnate and become obsolete.

Much of what passed for Catholic doctrine some ten or twenty years ago was inadequate for our times. John XXIII, calling for an "updating" of the Church, remarked that the substance of an ancient doctrine is one thing, and the way in which it has been formulated, quite another. And John Courtney Murray, in what was perhaps his last public statement before his death . . . added that Pope John's statement should not be simplistically interpreted as if only words were at stake. What is demanded is a creative re-interpretation of the ancient deposit of faith.[2]

Despite pioneers like Robert Johann and Charles Curran, much remains to be done by Catholics today to creatively reinterpret Christian faith in action, alias moral theology or Christian ethics.[3] Do the following pages contribute to the new interpretation? They should, at least, be read in the spirit expressed by Father Dulles:

We cannot predict the limits of future change. But to fear and resist change itself would betray a lack of confidence in the Holy Spirit, who continues today, as in the past, to fulfill Christ's promise (John 16:13): "He will guide you into all truth."[4]

1 NO ABSOLUTES

The "new morality" is not as new as it once was. But while its novelty is rubbing off, more and more Christians, Protestant and Catholic alike, seem to be taking it as coin of the realm. The question often arises, "Can a Christian adopt the new morality?"

That kind of question can be answered only by first answering a number of more precise and limited ones. The first question I would like to take up is an exclusively practical one: To what extent does the *practice* of the new morality conflict with the *practice* of traditional Christian ethics? Or, more positively, to what extent could a Christian, remaining faithful to the Christian tradition, adopt some of the *practice* of the new morality? The question does not touch any philosophical or theological underpinnings of the new morality, but centers simply on what the new trend means in actual practice.

In a comparison of the practice of the new morality with that of the Christian tradition, one must avoid caricaturing either. On one hand, the Christian tradition has never held that the individual Christian, as he faces commonplace moral decisions, should be able to apply *absolutely* certain principles in an *absolutely* certain way and thus make *absolutely* certain moral judgments on what to do. The tradition maintains that sometimes a man can do this, but many times he cannot. Thomas Aquinas brings this out when he discusses the virtue of prudence.[1] Even those who show little sympathy with the modern trend (for example, Pius XII in condemning the new morality of his times) admit—in fact, underline—the place that tradition has always granted to a certain moral relativism.[2]

On the other hand, the new morality—at least in its present American form—is not the lawless caricature that some critics imagine. Hardly any contemporary follower of the new morality rejects all moral principles. The man of the new morality does not respond simply and exclusively to the unique situation before him. When he tries to assess a situation he sees, like any man, a certain value in the general principles with which his own experiences and those of his community have provided him.[3] Like any man, he holds that the state should generally protect the lives of its citizens, that infidelity is generally bad for married life, that parents should generally show love for their children, etc.

But even with caricatures set aside, there remains a genuine conflict between the practices of the new morality and the practices of traditional Christian ethics. The man of the new morality sees his practical moral principles only as general, never as absolute. That is, they all can suffer exceptions in certain situations. The only absolute the new morality recognizes in practice, the only thing a man has to do always and in all situations, is to love. A given kind of action may be in most cases right or in most cases wrong, but it is always possible that in the situation before him it is the opposite of what it has been before. Exceptional situations do come up where love dictates that the state should *not* defend the life of a particular citizen, that a wife should be unfaithful, that a parent should not here and now care for his children.

Many Christians are disquieted by the new position that *no moral law holds in absolutely all cases except the law to love*. It certainly conflicts with the concrete practice of the Christian tradition. For example, adultery is always wrong *versus* adultery is sometimes right. But to assess the extent of this practical conflict, one must understand fully the approach of the new morality. Its denial of absolutes follows from a more basic practical attitude.

The basic practical approach of the new morality is seen more clearly in its contrast with the approach most commonly found in opposition to it today. Just as there are men who think out their problems of practical ethics along the lines of "the new morality," perhaps instinctively and spontaneously without having heard the term or formulated a precise ethical theory, so there are men who think out their practical ethical problems along certain lines of thought which are radically opposed to those of the new morality. I call the latter approach that of the "citizen." I am borrowing the phrase, though not the exact meaning, from H. Richard Niebuhr.[4]

For the man with the "citizen" mentality, the irreducible and first fact about the world he lives in is that it is a world of authority and law. If he is a religious man it is, first and foremost, a world where God *rules* and *governs*. If he is a Christian he lives in the Church and that is for him, above all, God's kingdom where God's laws, interpreted and applied by constituted authority, hold sway. When the "citizen" has to decide on a course of action, the one absolute, irreducible practical norm, the first thing to which he refers is the particular law that applies to the situation. Perhaps it is God's design manifested in the nature of creatures. Perhaps it is God's will passed on and given concrete form by God's community, the Church. Only when he is sure he is within the limits of the law will he proceed to any further examination of the alternatives before him.

On the other hand, when the man of the new morality has to decide on a course of action—the one absolute, irreducible practical norm—the first thing to which he refers is not a law, but what love demands. What he means by "love" should be made clear. The "citizen" too, if he is a true Christian, acts out of love. But his is a love first and foremost of law. He loves God and God's laws. He loves his fellow men and that implies the nature and the purpose God decreed for them. For the man of the new morality, however, love means something else. His is a love, first and foremost, not of law, but of good experiential consequences.

As an example, let us look at a situation in which many Americans today practice the new morality without knowing it: should the husband be head of the house? The "citizen" answers the question by looking at God's design. He concludes that God intends wives to be subject to their husbands. And that's that. But many Christian husbands and wives feel that, on the contrary, God intends only that they grow in love, i.e., living together harmoniously, respecting each other and enjoying the other's unique self. They feel that it is up to the two of them, gradually and through experience, to work out what is the best course of action when they cannot agree. Without thinking much about it they may have come to a working arrangement where, let us say, the wife has the final decision in some matters, e.g., the care of the children, the husband in others, e.g., in what is connected with his work and in larger financial matters. Or perhaps they treat each situation separately, feeling out which of them is taking the matter more seriously or who is more tired and under pressure at the moment, etc. Note that the "citizen" and the Christian of the new morality may end up with the same practical conclusion. A wife once said to me, "It's absurd that I should obey my husband because he is a man and I am a woman. But I have found that I am the sort of person who is happier when somebody who loves me makes the big decisions for me." With the new approach, she came to the same practical conclusion as a "law-abiding" wife.

Take another example. An engaged girl comes to a priest or older person for advice. She and her fiancé, in expressing their love, have gone beyond what is permitted for unmarried people. Despite renewed good resolutions, they fall again and again. She is humiliated, ashamed, losing confidence in herself and her capacity to live out her ideals. What counsel should she receive? The counselor who is primarily a "citizen" will reply gently but firmly that God's law is still the most important thing in any creature's life. Undoubtedly she and her fiancé are to some extent victims of their passions and therefore not fully responsible for what they do. God made the passions and they are good, but He wisely forbids them to be given outlet outside of marriage. God understands their present weakness and forgives their sins each time. Let them, however, keep trying to observe God's law, especially by avoiding occasions of sin.

The counselor who follows the new approach will react differently. He will not soften the truth that the engaged couple are sinning. At the very least, they are going against the tradition and authoritative teaching of their Church as well as against their own consciences. But he will point out that the more important thing is their growing love for each other. The girl should be proud that more and more she is loving as a woman loves a man, with her body and feelings and heart. God sees her weakness and regrets it. But he also sees her love maturing spiritually and sexually. He rejoices in this; He is proud of her. She, too, should rejoice and be proud.

Until recent years, the subject of sexuality seems to have been dominated by the "citizen" mentality in the Church. How often the Catholic in the pew has heard the preacher describe and condemn the various violations of God's law for sex. How rarely, if ever, has he heard the preacher describe and urge the good experience of a full, healthy sex life for married couples. For instance, we seldom hear a preacher remind wives of their serious Christian obligation to respond fully, psychologically and physically, in their sexual experience with their husbands, in order that the sexual experience may truly be of "mutual help." Should a preacher speak of these things? If he feels free to speak of sexual transgressions, why is it out of place for him to speak of healthy sexual experience? But I agree. The sooner the married people take over the public discussion of sexuality from celibates, the better.

Here is one more illustration of how the hierarchy of values for the Christian of the new morality differs in practice from that of the "citizen." On a given summer evening, the Christian of the new morality feels angry and depressed and guilty because half a million human beings in his city are condemned because of their race to live in crowded, sweltering, primitive rooms in an atmosphere of ostracization and frustration. He feels that he must do something about it, or else he will be unworthy to come to the

Sacraments of his Church. The "citizen," too, regrets this situation and knows it is wrong. But he becomes angry and determined to do something only when store windows are broken, property looted, and general order breaks down. It's not that he's in sympathy with the storekeeper or the insurance companies. It's the fact that law and order are violated which disturbs him most profoundly.

What characterizes the basic practical attitude of the Christian of the new morality in our three examples? He reacts, first and foremost, with love. But it is a particular kind of love. It is a love of good, experienced consequences: the harmonious living-together of the husband and wife; the free, growing love of body and soul on the part of the engaged couple; the end of the heat, smells, discouragement, isolation, boredom and hatred that people are feeling in Harlem.

Why do the two practical attitudes differ, one giving law the first place, the other favoring experienced consequences? I submit that the difference flows from an even deeper difference of spirituality. The Christian "citizen" sees himself, above all, as a *child* of God. Like any child of a loving father, he has great freedom and love and peace in his father's care. Like any child of a loving father he is protected by wise laws as well as surrounded by things which belong to his father and which he is not to touch without permission. It is better that way. Ultimately, the child is not responsible for experienced consequences. He is responsible only for obeying his father. If he obeys, his father will see to it that the experienced consequences are not harmful, but good.

The Christian of the new morality does not find this picture displeasing. He simply finds it false, unChristian and not worthy of a man. In his eyes the Christian is, before God in Jesus Christ, not a child, but a man or woman. God, his Father, watches him with pride and love, encourages him, but leaves him on his own for the concrete decisions. The man is responsible for the experienced consequences. God does not save him from them. This is the only way he and God judge the man: through the experienced consequences he has chosen to bring about. God's saving love in Christ bears him up and gives his life its ultimate meaning, yet in his particular moral judgments and decisions he stands alone, free, responsible.

But this stance has an inescapable logic. According to the new spirituality, a human being is a man or a woman, not a child, and therefore, among other things, he is a father or mother. As a father, his sole responsibility toward his son is love. If he loves his son, he does not worry about what his "obligations as a father" might be. He worries only about what is experientially happening to his son. Is his son happy? Healthy? Doing well in school? Getting along with his friends? If not, he feels somehow guilty. He is responsible. This is his only morality in regard to his son. There are no holds barred, because he knows there are no rules to the game and no guaranteed happy ending. Suppose his son becomes fatally ill. He is warned by doctors that his son faces nothing but weeks of agonizing pain and mental distress. His son will experience no more peaceful human moments. In fact, he will be capable of no more human choices or reactions. Our man has no sense of God's laws and no sense of human existence being sacred and belonging to God alone. He has only love and responsibility for the experienced life going on in his son. If he sees that the experience his son is going through is horrible and not worth living, he will be inclined to kill his son. His love moves him to do this. We see how the basic practical spirituality of the new morality, which perhaps in many ways wakens sympathetic chords in many of us, seems to lead inevitably to conflict with practical absolutes of the Christian tradition, such as the prohibition against euthanasia.

Let us take a closer look at the general conflict in practice. First of all, what are the absolutes of the tradition that the new morality cannot accept? The word "absolutes" can mean many different things. It can, for example, mean principles such as, "Do not murder," or "Do not steal." But tradition admits that these principles cannot be applied simply as such. If you want to find out whether the action being contemplated is really murder or stealing, you need other principles. When a starving man takes a rich man's food, is it stealing? When a judge condemns a criminal to death, is it murder? The problem is, as the tradition has always known, that words like "murder" and "stealing" contain in their definition a moral judgment. Murder means to kill a man *unjustly*. Stealing means to take some property *unjustly*. To say these things are always wrong is obviously true, by their definition. But it doesn't tell me whether a particular action is *unjust* killing or *unjust* taking. "Absolutes," in this sense of the word, offer no conflict with the new morality.

The tradition also employs another kind of principle which is more concrete and practical. One would not call principles of this type "absolute." As the tradition admits, they only hold for the most part; they admit exceptions. St. Thomas' example is the general principle that one should return to a man what belongs to him. Ordinarily the principle, as such, can be applied. The book belongs to the library, therefore, I should return it. But there are exceptions. The exception Thomas gives is up-to-date. I should not return a fatal weapon to an insane person. The weapon belongs to him, but I should not return it to him. Since principles of this sort permit exceptions, they offer no conflict with the new morality.[5]

What, then, is the kind of absolute principles which *do* conflict with the new morality? They are the principles which clearly identify an external action and affirm that it is always wrong. The word "adultery" has a definite meaning: a married person has sexual relations with someone to whom he or she is not married. For the tradition this is always wrong. There are no exceptions. Obviously, absolute principles like this can be applied directly to human conduct. There is a clearly recognizable sort of external action and it is always, without exception, wrong. It is this kind of absolute principle that the new morality refuses to accept, and it is what we will mean by the words "absolute principles" or "absolutes" in the rest of the chapter.

We hear a great deal about this conflict: the new morality denies there are any absolute moral principles and the traditional morality claims there are some. It can come as a shock to realize how few principles of this sort the tradition does actually claim. The absolute principles claimed by the tradition are mainly certain prohibitions in the sexual domain and prohibitions against certain types of direct killing. The prohibitions are obviously important, but in the vast complexity of moral judgments a Christian must make, most of them are not relevant. Take the father and mother of a family. In the twenty-four hours of a day, the absolute prohibitions of the tradition may be relevant now and then. Certainly not often. Yet, on the other hand, how often will the father and mother be called upon to use Christian love and Christian prudence in order to discern, in a particular situation, how to deal with each other, with their children, with their neighbors. No absolute principles apply here, but there is a great need for moral insight and discernment. This is the traditional view, and not an innovation of the new morality.

Many today who point with alarm to a modern breakdown of morality seem to be referring principally to this small number of prohibitions. There may well be a breakdown on these points. But why don't they point to the buildup of morality in other areas: mounting concern for psychological health, for personal maturity and responsibility, for racial equality, for the diminution of poverty, for peace, for the rights of the citizen before the police, for the experience of community, for the full experience of worshiping God in Christ Jesus, etc.? This is morality, too, and in our time we see a growing sensitivity and responsibility toward it. One gets the impression at times that all moralists are divided into two classes: those who are concerned about *un*born babies and those who are concerned about *born* babies. Those who are concerned about what happens to unborn babies in hospitals do not seem too concerned about what happens to the ones born in India and Vietnam and Harlem. And vice versa.

My first point, therefore, is that there is a genuine conflict in practice between the new morality and traditional Christian morality in the area of moral absolutes, but that this area forms only a small part of traditional Christian morality. The reason I am talking so much about moral absolutes is because I wish to say that we should talk much less about them. They are important but, confronted with the practical approach of the new morality, we realize that we can exaggerate their importance. Tragically, we may let the question of absolutes block from our view the far vaster and more important task of discerning the relative principles, the empirical general principles which hold merely for the most part, but upon which Christian love, whether traditional or new, depends to achieve its ends.

Traditional moral theology has always recognized the importance of relative principles, but the modern mind, with its empirical bent and practical skill and knowledge, emphasizes them in a way a man of the Middle Ages or the sixteenth century could not have imagined. Is there something here in modern culture that the Christian moral tradition could organically and fruitfully assimilate? What kind of general principles does the new morality arrive at with its empirical, pragmatic approach? Not all proponents of the new morality elaborate specific principles. Some seem to be as exclusively absorbed in attracking the traditional absolutes as certain traditional moralists are in defending them. Nevertheless, I submit that those who go with the momentum of the new morality come to a great number of principles, objectively valid, though permitting of exceptions.[6]

For example, a mother who loves her teenage son and simply desires good consequences for him in his experience has to face certain facts of life. She has to face the fact that if she does not give him more freedom and responsibility as he grows older, if she plays a domineering and possessive role in his life, then certain consequences are likely to occur. Her son is likely to be missing, at least at this time, the experience of growing into manhood; he is likely to be unhappy and emotionally unsettled. It is also likely that his future life and experience will be badly affected. The likelihood of these bad consequences is a recognized general principle of adolescent psychology. It is not absolute; it has exceptions. The particular boy may be so exceptionally independent of character that his mother's attitude has little effect on him. But if a mother truly and maturely loves him, will she run the high risk of hurting him? Obviously not. She would rather respect this and other general psychological principles concerning adolescence. Yet how would she know the principles? Not by her own experience. Most mothers have not dealt closely with many adolescents. She could know these laws mainly by drawing on the experience of the community, i.e., by talking to a teacher, by discussions with other parents, by reading something, by hearing a lecture or sermon.

The point of this example is that the purely empirical, pragmatic love of the new morality must by its very momentum turn to the community's experience for general principles, and that these principles, in effect, are as binding on the Christian as an absolute principle based on a law of God. The man of the new morality finds these empirical principles everywhere. His love drives him to seek them out —often to his own discomfort. A man working with juvenile delinquents, if he loves them, will look into the experience of the community—perhaps the personal experience of others in the field, perhaps published empirical studies—to see how best to improve the lives his boys are experiencing.

A husband feeling estranged from his wife, a teacher feeling that he could be teaching more effectively, a person in authority who feels he is not helping those under him, a man who finds himself subject to growing moodiness—all these, if they truly love, will seek out the experience of the community to find principles which might help them improve the situation. For instance, the man whose marriage is going to pieces may learn from a marriage counselor something he did not know or had forgotten: to keep a marriage going, a man and a woman regularly need times when they get away from the children and routine concerns and are able to talk in a relaxed, informal way with each other. Is this a *moral* principle? For the man of the new morality, it is. He has a grave obligation to seek out practical principles of the community's experience and set up conditions in which he and his wife can start relating to each other again.

Of course, it is not only from the community's experience but also from his own that an individual will find practical principles which he must respect if he truly loves. He may find that, for him personally, if he loses his temper or takes a fourth martini or goes out with a certain woman, nine times out of ten the consequences are experientially harmful to him and to others and he regrets it afterwards. The consequences may be so harmful that one of the most serious obligations in his life will be to obey his own private law prohibiting fourth martinis.

This is how the man of the new morality goes about discerning his moral responsibilities. He does nothing but love. But this means that in practice he wants to do nothing but find the means to bring about, in himself and others, a rich, happy, mature life of human experience. However, this means he must find out the empirical principles which indicate ways that are likely to be effective. He finds no absolute principles, but if he is honest and open, he ends up with far more general principles and far more concrete obligations that he must respect than the man of the Middle Ages or the man with the "citizen" mentality. I would suggest—and this is my second point—that traditional Christian morality could profitably adopt the practical approach of the new morality in its search for empirical principles.

A final question remains. Would it make a great practical difference if one used this empirical approach precisely on the questions with which the limited number of moral absolutes mentioned above have traditionally dealt? To answer with any assurance one would need more empirical data than is currently available, especially in the area of sexuality and marriage. Nevertheless, I would suggest that the empirical general principles that the new morality seeks out can come close to the moral absolutes of the tradition. For example, there is no doubt that the prolonged, agonizing deaths of some human beings are such that anybody, not just a man of the new morality, would desire them to die as soon as possible. The man of the new morality, unlike the traditional Christian, might be inclined, at first, simply to kill the suffering person. We described above the case of the father and his incurable, suffering son. Yet, according to the new morality, the man must ask further questions. Will it have good experiential consequences in the community if any individual can decide when it is good to end a person's life?

Consider, for example, the permanently disabled and aged who wish not to die but to keep on living. What would be their experience if, knowing they were a burden to others, they also knew it was socially acceptable for them to consent to a "mercy death"? The empirical line of thought could lead the man of the new morality to a general condemnation of euthanasia, paralleling the absolute condemnation of it by the tradition.

Remember, the man of the new morality does not consider the physical life of man to be "inviolable," but he does value it highly. He is more likely to oppose war or capital punishment than the Christian of the "citizen" mentality. For him, physical human life is precious because it is the necessary prerequisite for that conscious, experienced love which is the only thing absolutely worthwhile on earth. His condemnation of euthanasia would not be absolute. He would always admit the possibility of exceptions. But there would be no reason why the Christian community of the Church could not step in here and, by its authority to direct the lives of the faithful, universalize the condemnation of euthanasia.[7]

However, it is not likely that all the general principles which the new morality might work out with modern empirical methods would coincide with the absolute principles of the tradition in the matter of sexual morality and certain kinds of killing.

Traditional Catholic moral theology, as formed in the Middle Ages and in the sixteenth and seventeenth centuries, often had the same practical approach as the new morality, and not that of the "citizen" mentality. But it was not clear about its own methods. It was weak in empirical inquiry. It did not consider certain possibilities that have come to light in subsequent centuries. It legislated for a community that was more used to authority making decisions for them. As a result, even if the new morality is, as I believe, a consistent development of the tradition, it is likely to come to principles that are more subtle and therefore partly different from the tradition.

In evaluating empirically the consequences of adultery as

of euthanasia it would come, I think, to prohibitions not much different in practice from those of the tradition. But an empirical inquiry from the new point of view would hardly take masturbation or premarital sexual pleasure in all cases as seriously as has the tradition. Could the Catholic community learn something here from the new morality and change its sexual morality in particular details? At least it is a question we should put to ourselves.

The comparison of the practice of the new morality and that of the traditional Christian morality leads me, in conclusion, to two practical suggestions:

1. In the matter of the traditional absolute prohibitions, I would suggest that (a) if the only reason a Christian can see for observing a prohibition is the authority of his Church, he should recognize the obligation to obey, but realize, too, that obedience has its limits and can, at times, be outweighed by other Christian virtues, such as charity and justice; (b) since the prohibitions form only a small part of Christian morality and one where there may be changes in moral teaching, we Christians should not give undue time or importance to presenting them as part of Christian living; and (c) by our own reflection, experience and discussion, and by scientific study and experimentation, we should try to work out a set of prohibitions in this area which will respect the same values as did the tradition, but may well be in part different because they are empirically more sound and more effective.

2. My second suggestion is, I think, more important: that in all the areas where a Christian decides and acts, we should work out together, again by reflection, experience and discussion and by scientific study and experimentation, the *positive* empirical principles that can lead us as human beings to experience a free, happy and long human life—the black man, the doubting intellectual, the bored housewife, the juvenile delinquent, the anxious religious, the elderly—all of us in terms of our limitations and problems. In the 1970s this is a responsibility each of us has as a member of the Christian community. It is going to be a slow, difficult and demanding business.

2 SHARING GOD'S DOMINION

Its rejection of absolutes has won the new morality a *succès de scandale*, but this is peripheral to it as, hopefully, the preceding chapter has made clear. I would like to probe further into the dynamics of the new morality, contrasting it more centrally with traditional morality. Consider certain shifts of emphasis which are taking place in the Catholic Church. One hears less of the obligation to fast before Communion and more of the obligation to participate actively in the liturgy. Less of the obligation of the unmarried not to give themselves "venereal" pleasure and more of their obligation to develop interpersonal relationships. Less of the obligation not to take or damage the property of another and more of the obligation to help blacks to grow in their sense of personal dignity. Less of the obligation not to procure an abortion and more of the obligation to aid disturbed children. Less of the obligation not to divorce and remarry and more of the obligation of married couples to grow in openness and understanding.

None of the above obligations of which one hears less were taken as absolute. According to traditional moral theology, proportionate inconvenience or harm could excuse one from the law of fasting. The principle of double effect could justify, under certain conditions, the causing of venereal pleasure, the taking or damaging of property and the procuring of an abortion. Not unconditionally forbidden were the sexually stimulating reading of the medical student, the eating by the starving man of the rich man's food, the therapeutic abortion to remove a damaged uterus. The Church, representing God, authorized divorce and remarriage in certain cases.[1] Understanding the kind of thinking that is downgrading these and other "relative" obligations may cast further light on the novelty of the new morality.

In the five contrasting pairs of obligations listed above, the obligations of which we now hear less have certain traits in common. One could sum it up by saying that they make good laws. For a law to be good, it has to be so formulated that the average citizen and the average law-enforcer can easily see what he is supposed to do or not to do. It holds true of the five obligations and many others whose importance seems to be waning today. Catholics had little difficulty understanding what it means to fast before Communion, to masturbate or pet, to take or damage property, to procure an abortion, to divorce and remarry. In regard to all five, as has been noted, exceptional cases arose that forced moral theologians to qualify the application of the law. But, on the whole, these five obligations, like most of the others stressed by the older moral theology, could be easily recognized by a Catholic in the concrete circumstances of his life, and therefore made good laws.

For the same reason, the obligations have another common trait: all five are negative. Traditional moral theology is often criticized for being predominantly negative. The charge is true, but unfair as a reproach. Because it was mainly concerned with making good laws, it had to be mainly negative. Traditional moral theologians saw their task as that of taking general moral obligations (such as "Be just" or "Be chaste") and translating them into effective laws. As they themselves have pointed out, positive obligations are, by their nature, hard to pinpoint sharply enough so that they may be readily applied in a wide range of cases.

The difficulty can be overcome often enough with human laws, whether ecclesiastical or civil. One can prescribe effectively positive obligations such as attendance at Sunday Mass, the wearing of a headcovering in Church, Easter duty, baptism of babies, sending children to Catholic schools, etc. Human laws are usually intended not to determine what is in itself good or bad but to designate one effective means, out of a number of possible ones, to assure the achievement of some end. If a law turns out not to be a good law, the legislator can alter it or the subject can apply the principle of "epikeia" or excusing causes. But when the moralists endeavored to determine laws of objective morality they were looking not for human laws but for laws of nature and God. Even though some moral theologians conceded that the divine Legislator could intervene miraculously to dispense one from certain natural laws, or all moralists agreed that the content of the law was more subtle and restricted than the layman might think (and therefore did not apply to cases such as those noted above, of marriage, indirect abortion, etc.), still they were trying to determine an existing obligation that was, on the whole, eternal and universally applicable as well as easily discernible to the average Christian. I am not sure why it is so, but if one tries to spell out an obligation of this type, one almost always finds it easier to give negative formulations rather than positive ones. Concerning venereal pleasure, for example, it was and is easier for a moralist to specify the conditions under which one may not cause it, rather than those under which one is obliged to.

The same epistemological truth explains inversely why the obligations about which we hear more nowadays do not make good laws. Since the new trend sees moral obligation primarily as responsibility for good experiential consequences, it looks for positive obligations. But it is not easy to pinpoint positive obligations in a generally practicable, readily applicable form, i.e., as a law. Another illustration would be the obligation of a wealthy man to give to the poor. What must he do? What form should the charity take? To whom? How often? How much should he give? Could he give the money to another good cause? It is not merely impossible to lay down general laws. Even if one knew an individual man, it would be impossible to identify concretely any one thing he had to do to satisfy his positive obligation to the poor.

In brief, the obligations about which we hear less nowadays are, on the whole, the readily identifiable, negative kind of obligations that make good laws. The obligations we are hearing more of are, on the whole, positive and make poor laws. The five listed above obviously oblige us to take positive action. They make poor laws because for each it would be hard to say clearly and concretely what one has to do. What exactly should I do to help these black neighbors grow in pride in themselves or to aid this disturbed pupil? Nor are those who urge the obligations interested in reducing them to laws. They recognize, of course, the necessity of human laws, civil and ecclesiastical. But, concerned primarily with positive responsibilities, they see the importance of law as secondary and limited.

To some Christians, the nonlegality of the new moral trend is scandalous. But it flows from a theological understanding of man's relationship with God. God is no longer seen as a sovereign Legislator with man as His subject relying on God's law in order to know how to act in his present situation. God leaves it up to men to decide what ought to be done. As Dietrich Bonhoeffer wrote,

> And we cannot be honest unless we recognize that we have to live in the world *etsi deus non daretur* [as we would even if there were no God] . . . God himself compels us to recognize it . . . God would have us know that we must live as men who manage our lives without him.[2]

Not that God is made remote or irrelevant. The "God who forsakes us" is still the "God who is with us." It is "before God and with God we live without God." We Christians derive our strength from "Christ our hope." Only because Jesus Christ lived, "has life a meaning for us." Christian life is a transformation of human life into a "participation in the being of Jesus," in particular, "His being there for others." The formulae call for theological scrutiny, which we shall attempt subsequently, but there is no doubt that the new perspective places God in the center of human life, "in the middle of the village."

To return to the theme of the present chapter, however, God leaves man to decide by himself what are his specific moral obligations. The older moral theology, like every theology, had to rely on human models to envision God and His relationship with men. For historical and sociological reasons, it chose the model of the legislator promulgating his code. The current moral trend also uses human analogies, but of a more intimate, interpersonal sort. As was suggested in the preceding chapter, the new morality compares God to a father who has entrusted his grown son with his business. He watches all that the son does, but lets him make all the decisions. The father's presence means a great deal to the son and motivates his labors in various ways, but never by telling him what to do. It is in an analogous way that "before God and with God, we live without God." God has shared His dominion of the world with men. "Shared with" in the sense of "delegated to."

Thomas Aquinas did not, I believe, view the moral life in this manner (despite certain texts that are cited to this effect). But in another area of theology he showed a similar conception of God sharing dominion with man. According to the Arab occasionalists, creatures could have no actions of their own, since it would detract from the sovereign power and dominion. Thomas replied that the contrary was true. The greatness of God's power and dominion was seen precisely in His ability to share so much of it with His creatures. The greater the creature was in itself, the greater the Creator must be.[3]

With an analogous conception of the divine dominion, Bonhoeffer and many others today go a step further and say we make Christ "really Lord of the world" only when we see Him letting the Christian "belong wholly to the world," i.e., not with God to solve his human problems for him, but by himself "living unreservedly in life's duties, problems, successes and failures, experiences and perplexities."[4] He has to decide for himself what his duties are, how to solve his problems, etc. Dietrich Bonhoeffer judged himself obliged to return to Germany in 1939 and eventually to join the plot to assassinate Hitler. He did so not by deduction from any moral law laying down the conditions that make assassination obligatory, but by long, agonized reflection on his personal situation, concluding that this was the way he had to go on being a man for others, like Jesus Christ. Christ, his hope, empowered him to do what he had to do, but Dietrich Bonhoeffer alone decided what it was he had to do.

What engenders the new moral emphases these days, therefore, is a modern interpretaion of the verses of Genesis, recounting how God made man to His image by sharing His dominion with him.

Then God said, "Let us make man in our image, after our likeness; and let them have dominion over the fish of the sea, and over the birds of the air, and over the cattle, and over all the earth, and over every creeping thing that creeps upon the earth." So God created man in his own image, in the image of God he created them. And God blessed them, and God said to them, "Be fruitful and multiply, and fill the earth and subdue it; and have dominion over the fish of the sea and over the birds of the air and over every living thing that moves upon the earth."[5]

In the eyes of contemporary man, God's giving man dominion means that He gives man sole responsibility for what goes on in the world. Responsibility has to be, of course, being there for others, as Jesus Christ was. But what that means concretely in here-and-now action, man alone decides. He has to discover something that befits the situation. As a Christian he knows he is where the buck stops being passed. He is responsible and so he has to do something. The concept of God's sharing His dominion with men inevitably leads the Christian to stress positive obligations, leaving him relatively unconcerned about making good laws.

Keeping the focus of the present chapter on the practice of the new morality, and not yet examining further its generative theological vision, one notes other novelties. Inasmuch as he recognizes few clearcut laws, it is easy for the individual to rationalize his way out of obligations or simply to put them out of his mind. If the Church were ever to extend its claim to exercise the divine authority of granting divorce and thus narrow the force of existing laws, it is likely that many marriages would end tragically in divorce that otherwise would have stayed intact and been ultimately successful. Similarly, the new morality makes laxity and failure more easy.

On the other hand, if a man believes that God has shared

dominion with him, he soon faces more obligations than he had before. He may well stagger under the responsibilities and wonder how he got into so rigorous a position. As was seen, sharing God's dominion means it is up to man to do something about what's going on: not just about events on a large social scale, like suffering in Biafra, bombing in Vietnam, hate in the American ghettos, but about private happenings: the loneliness of his senile mother, his own waning religious practice, the anxieties of his charges. Thinking along new lines, he lacks certain "outs" possible under the old morality. He cannot evade his responsibility by saying it is not clear what exactly he is obliged to do. If he does not know what that something is, then it's up to him to find out. *That's* what he's obliged to do right now.

Neither can he excuse himself on the grounds that, although it is clear what would be a helpful course of action, it is not *certain* that it *is* obligatory. He lacks the principle of old time probabilism, "That in cases of doubt as to the lawfulness of any concrete action, if there exists a really probable opinion in favor of liberty, i.e., of disregard of the law, although the opinion in favor of the law is more probable, I may use the former opinion and disregard the latter, and in doing so, I am acting with complete moral rectitude."[6] Reasonable doubt about a law or its application can free one from the obligation of the law. Reasonable doubt does not free one from responsibility, as any parent with a sick child knows. One often has well-founded doubts that a given way of dealing with someone's problem (a patient or student or member of the family) is going to work out successfully. Nevertheless, being responsible may mean that I have to choose this promising, but uncertain, means of success.

A curious phenomenon is connected with the trend to view God as sharing dominion with men. Critics of the view reproach it for the same thing for which its advocates praise it, namely, that it is a morality for the mature. They expose the nerve of a crucial question, perhaps the most important practical question arising from the new morality. Is it consistent with Christian faith and the goal of salvation to present human maturity, not as a counsel or ideal, but as the central obligation that the Christian must strive to meet and on which his whole moral life must be based. Does it lead to an elitist morality irreconcilable with Christian faith? Does it lead to an elitist morality *demanded* by Christian faith? Current discussion has not yet given adequate attention to the question.

The new trend poses another question of practice that needs further discussion. What do secular ethics contribute to the moral understanding of the Christian? Or, in a more personal form, what role does the secular experience of the Christian play in his making of moral judgments? If God has turned over to man His dominion over the world, man is totally on his own to determine what to do. What can he turn to except human knowledge and experience, his own and that of the community? And yet, as contemporary theology accentuates, the Good News of Jesus Christ is God's entrance into history, freely relating to man and transforming the meaning of each human life. How can the news not affect all the decision-making of man? Today in ethics, as in other areas of theology, the dilemma arises: the Christian imagines himself as totally secular and totally Christian. How can it be? *Can* it be?

The question has not yet received an answer which is universally acceptable to proponents of the new morality. I would like to sketch one answer offered, or at least implied, by many Christian ethicists. I incline to make it my own without claiming to be able to solve all the problems it creates. Some Protestants find this implication characteristically Catholic, and they may well be right. Discarding the teleology of the natural law tradition, it contains the same intrinsic humanism. In order to discern human values and obligations, one need not know God's eternal plans and purposes, nor turn to His revelation. The first reason for a man to take up the responsibilities of the earth is not the dignity of God and His law, but the dignity of life on earth. The first reason for a man to love is not because human love is from God, but because human love, no matter how imperfectly realized, is good in itself. The first reason for killing being an evil is human life itself—its worth and dignity. This humanism by no means denies that man is a heart restless for God, a sinner needing Christ. But the first and decisive reason that should determine human action is simply humanity itself: human love, however pathetic, the confused joys and sorrows of the earth, the unimpressive individuality of, let us say, a peasant caught in an attack on his village.

In short, any Christian ethics must rest on a secular base, man's experience in the world, his experience, for example, in marriage. The secular experience is irreducible; it cannot be altered by religious faith or theological understanding. All the values, responsibilities and obligations the Christian recognizes—except those pertaining directly to God, such as prayer—are forged first of all in this human experience. The "first of all" need not be chronological. But the definitive form any value or responsibility possesses in the mind of the Christian must be the one that emerged from the Christian's secular experience.

This thesis underscores the secular quality of Christian ethics. Without yet inquiring how such an ethic can still be Christian, one has to admit that the history of the Church reveals a persistent openness to the secular values and obligations of the particular time.

> The ethical teaching of the early Church, we have seen, falls into a scheme of practical precepts for everyday living, a scheme based upon a realistic recognition of the structure as it then was, and following in general outline the patterns of ethical teaching which were being set forth by teachers of other schools.[7]

The noted scripture scholar, C. H. Dodd, is speaking of the Church at the time of the New Testament. In subsequent centuries, the Church continued to echo the great Stoic moralists.

> When someone asked him whether women should engage in philosophy, he began to teach that they should engage in philosophy. For, he said, women have received . . . the same intellect as men, the intellect which we use in dealings with each other and according to which we

reason about each matter and judge whether it be good or evil, noble or base. Women likewise have the same senses as men: seeing, hearing, smelling, and so on. Both sexes likewise have the same bodily parts, and neither has anything more than the other. Furthermore, desire of and affinity for virtue are found not only in men but also in women. For, no less than men, they naturally take satisfaction in noble and just deeds and reject contrary ones. Since this is the case, for what reason could it be fitting for men to seek out and to examine how they would live nobly, which is what philosophizing is, and for women not to do so? Is it because it is right for men to be good, but not for women?

But it is necessary for those who are not licentious nor evil to think that only those sexual acts are just which occur in marriage and which are accomplished for the begetting of children, because they are accomplished in accordance with law, and that those acts which hunt for mere pleasure are unjust and unlawful, even though they occur in marriage. Of other unions, those involving adultery are the most unlawful, while those between men are just as intolerable, since their enterprise is against nature. Those unions with women that do not involve adultery cannot include procreation in accordance with law, and so all of them are shameful, since they are entered into because of intemperance. Thus no one with self-control would undertake to approach a prostitute or a free woman outside of marriage or, to be sure, his own slave. The unlawfulness and unbecomingness of these unions is a great shame and rebuke to those that seek after them.

The essence of marriage is the community in life and in procreation of children. He said that the husband and wife must be united to each other in such a way as to live with each other, to act together, and to regard all things as common between them and nothing as private, not even one's own body. For great is the procreation of man which this union accomplishes. But procreation is not sufficient for the person marrying, since it could be done without marriage by other forms of mating such as animals have. But in marriage it is necessary that there be a shared life and a mutual care of the husband and wife for each other in both sickness and health and in every season. It is to obtain this as well as to beget children that each person enters into marriage. But where this loving care is perfect and the married couple give it to each other completely and each strives to surpass the other, then the marriage is as it ought to be and is worth emulating; for such a shared life is a noble thing.

One could not find a community more necessary and more desirable than between men and women. For what comrade is so gentle to his fellow as a beloved woman is to her husband? What brother is so gentle to his brother? What son is so gentle to his parents? Who, when absent, is so longed for as a man is by his wife or a wife by her husband? Whose presence would do more to lighten sorrow or to increase joy or to amend misfortune? To whom have all things been judged common, both bodies and souls and possessions, except to husband and wife? For these reasons all men regard the love between man and wife as pre-eminent over all others.[8]

The words might seem to be the words of Christian philosophers, but the voice is the voice of Musonius Rufus writing during the first century A.D.

The penchant of the Church to learn its morality from the best secular ethics of the time is particularly evident when it does so tardily. Since World War II, Church leaders have been prodding the people of God to open themselves to the values of the contemporary world.

This blindness on the part of many Catholics has caused great harm to Christianity. Every era has its own sensitivity to values in the realms of art and literature as well as ethics. When, however, Christians reveal no openness to the values pursued by their contemporaries, a dialogue between Christianity and the world becomes impossible.[9]

The Louvain theologian, Albert Dondeyne, wants primarily for the Christian to make a contribution to the historic changes taking place in the world. But this assumes that the Christian appreciates the concrete values coming to light in modern times, especially the epochal values connected with the evolution of science, the development of democracy, and the rise of the working class.

Professor Rogier, of the University of Nijmegen, in one of his lectures, used a striking figure to make us realize that absence of the Christian community from what is taking place in today's world: "The Church," he said, "has become a sort of reservation amidst a de-Christianized community; whereas it is her task to impart God's blessing to a world in its journey to eternity." If we want to realize how true that is, we have only to recall the three great events that are at the origin of our time and that still continue to determine its specific character. These events are 1) the formation of modern science through Descartes and Galileo, and later through Darwin in the field of biology; 2) the dissolution of the Old Regime and the birth of the democratic regimes of freedom; 3) the social break-through in the latter half of the last century. When we consider these great upheavals, we must confess to our shame that the Catholic community reacted very slowly to them, that it showed hesitancy and fear, and that it had its eyes riveted more on the past than directed to the future.

It is quite evident that this hesitancy of the faithful to take part in those changes has affected the prestige of Christianity, especially because, as we have pointed out, these movements which still dominate our times, contain authentic moral values. For a long time, the Catholic community seems to have had little appreciation of those great moral values.[10]

If the words of Dondeyne, written before the Second Vatican Council concerning the European Church, apply less to the American Church in the 1970s, it is because of the fruit of similar prodding by leaders of the Church to bring the Christian people tardily to learn from the values and obligations recognized by the world about it. When Vatican II affirmed religious liberty, John Courtney Murray could observe that the Church had only caught up with the world.

In the history of the Church, individual Christians have often been not tardy, but in the lead in defending or advancing human values, e.g., in the 1930s in the United States in the face of racism and laissez-faire capitalism, and in Germany in the face of Nazism, in the 1940s in the face of aerial destruction of whole cities, in the 1950s in the face of French torture in Algeria, in the 1960s in the face of the unending list of Vietnam casualties. The individual Christians shared vision and labor and peril, not with the mass of people or the hierarchy (who only years after gave approval and praise), but with atheists and agnostics at their side.

The thesis that Christian ethics is secular in content, therefore, receives support from the historical fact that the Church has regularly learned from secular ethicists, that the Church has tardily joined massive historical movements, that individual Christians have held common cause with agnostics at the forefront of moral protest and progress. It would be difficult—to my mind, impossible—to find a single human value or obligation that the Church endorses which has not been also fostered independently in a non-Christian milieu. When the new Christian moralists try to share the best secular humanism of their times, they are doing nothing new in the Christian tradition.

Nor are philosophical explanations lacking in the secularity of Christian ethics. In *Man and the State*,

. . . M. Maritain recalled the surprise of many that the proponents of sharply diverse ideologies could agree upon a list of the "Rights of Man" to be included in the International Declaration of Rights, published by the United Nations in 1948. The philosopher did not deny the incompatibility of much that these ideologies contained, nor did he question the sincerity of their proponents' theoretical views. Instead, he pointed out that the practical agreement substantiated the proposition that growth in moral knowledge and moral feeling comes to man as much from "the natural work of spontaneous, pre-scientific and pre-philosophic reason," which is common to all, as from the particular philosophical systems and logical bases that are held by individuals.[11]

But philosophical explanations do not answer the theological question raised by a secular Christian ethic. Like the earliest Christians, like Justin, we, the latest, must bring to bear the theology of our time to understand that, though in many and various ways God has spoken to unbelievers, He still says something new to us through His Son.[12]

3 CREATIVE ACTIVISM

The man who fondly consents to forecast the state of ethics in the Church in the year 2000 would not seem to have to look far for the plank to walk.[1] The procedure for making a fool of himself would appear simple. He needs only to take up ethical questions one by one and conjecture, wildly or tamely, the position of the Church on them thirty years from now. The questions would be familiar ones concerning war and weaponry, abortion, euthanasia, sexual behavior, etc., as well as new ones appearing now for the first time, such as those concerning organic transplantation and genetic manipulation.

However, the revolution presently sweeping through Christian ethics is in the process of transforming its nature both as an ethic and as Christian. Men are starting to propose not so much new answers to old ethical questions, as new *kinds* of ethical questions. Those whose ethical inquiry has a Christian dimension are starting to ask something different when they say, "What does the Church hold?" A less airy procedure of prediction would be, rather than taking up individual questions one by one, to try to elucidate these two new general developments and extrapolate them to the year 2000, introducing particular moral questions by way of illustration. In this chapter, I will try to do it principally for the first development, the transformation of Christian ethics as *ethics*. Toward the end of the book, I deal with the development of the Church as *church* and some of the ethical repercussions of this.

The new ethic that will have evolved by the year 2000 should still be continuous with its past. It should still be the human attempt to answer the question, "What ought I to do?" Men will still recognize that there are things they "have to do," whether they like it or not—things that are "of obligation." If they do not do them they will have failed, have missed the mark, be guilty, be ashamed. It is when a man in a given situation is not sure what the necessary actions are that he raises the ethical question, "What ought I to do?" Thus Moses and his people, Socrates and the hemlock, Kierkegaard and Regina, Bonhoeffer and Hitler. Thus also Christians in 1970 and 2000.

What is beginning in our day and will presumably reach completion by 2000 is that men—not for the first time in history—while continuing to raise the question concerning their "oughts," are altering its more specific meaning. For centuries, when a Christian has asked what he ought to do in a given situation, he meant, "What does the law say?" He might be thinking of the natural law of either Catholic or Protestant variety or of the prescriptions of the Bible or of "what the Church says." It is public knowledge, respectively lamented and cheered, that the number of Christians posing the ethical question in this sense is presently decreasing. One could presume it will be minimal in 2000.

Without claiming unusual foresight or expecting to surprise anyone, I could already draw one conclusion about 2000: the traditional moral theology that solved cases of conscience through application of the law, will no longer be in demand. Its practitioners will have undoubtedly found other employment. As will be discussed subsequently, Christians will still recognize the moral relevance of principles, but not as solely decisive factors. There will no longer be a role for the specialist who, given a few key details of the case, e.g., of a medical operation or a type of sexual behavior, can announce certain things that should or should not be done.

There is no point discussing here, for the thousandth time, whether ethical thinking, in shedding the concept of the obligation determined by absolute laws, is progressing or regressing. It would be more fruitful and revealing of the future to bring into focus the incoming understanding of "obligation" and "ought," frequently and aptly labeled the obligation of "responsibility." The question, "What ought I to do?" is coming to mean, "What is the responsible thing for me to do in this situation?"

The word "responsibility" is very much in use and is being used with a multiplicity of meaning. Proponents of older ethics have seized on it to stand for traditional moral concepts. However, the use of the term in any moral sense is recent. To use it for the new concept of *obligation*, one does not have to try to communicate a new meaning with a term having old associations, as contemporary ethicists have to do with "love" and "obedience to God." H. Richard Niebuhr, one of the first American ethicists to use the term, has ably defined "responsibility" in the new moral sense: "For the ethics of responsibility, the *fitting* action, the one that fits into a total interaction as response and as anticipation of further response, is alone conducive to the good and alone is right" (the italics are Niebuhr's; "fitting" is the operative adjective throughout the ethics).[2] It is evident that the essential components of "responsibilty" are not new to Western thought nor to Western ethics. What is new and portentous is that the concept now occupies the center of ethics. It, and it alone, determines the content of moral obligation. It, and it alone, characterizes the things men have to do to avoid failure and guilt.

The contrast of the old and new meanings of obligation appeared in two visits I received one morning while working on this paper. Both men had been referred to me as a "new moral theologian." They were married, middleaged, educated in Catholic colleges and evidently of intelligence and moral integrity. They both wanted to do something that the Catholic ethics they had learned had forbidden. They were asking whether it was now permitted. For one man, it was a vasectomy. For the other, masturbation. At the close of each visit, I realized I had not communicated with my visitor. We did not speak the same language. More literally, we were not asking the same question, though we used the same words, "What ought he to do?"

What each of my visitors was asking was whether his action was forbidden by moral law. On learning that there were grounds for thinking there was no clear and certain prohibition, his moral questioning was over. Mine began. To judge whether the operation or the masturbation could be a responsible act, a fitting response for the man, one had to assess the concrete circumstances to see whether the action could "fit into a total interaction as response and as anticipation of further response," e.g., how the desire to do the action arose from the life he shared with his wife and how it was likely to affect her and their future life directly and indirectly. Of course, a further reason for our inability to communicate was that with their query they were looking for the decisive solution given by traditional moral theologians, whereas my kind of questioning precluded that I, an outsider, could give a definitive answer. Only they could weigh all the concrete factors to judge whether the action could make up a fitting response. All I could do was to start them along lines of reflection likely to lead to a well-grounded judgment.

If the two men are of a vanishing breed and the new concept of moral obligation determines the decisions of more and more Christians, the moral life of the Christian community in 2000 will be a strenuously active one. Not merely does the new norm channel the individual's sense of obligation into neglected areas (such as the experiential intimacy of husband and wife) while easing prohibitions in others (such as vasectomy and masturbation). It is, by its nature, an activistic norm, demanding positive action far more often than could obligation under law. In whatever situation one is in, one must respond. Usually, though not always, that means doing something—smiling or applauding or singing or kissing.

But, given the human condition, the action called for is often of one kind. Key to most human situations are the needs of the persons involved. The fitting response is well expressed by the final line of a scene in Bertholt Brecht's *Furcht und Elend des dritten Reiches*. A woman weeps uncontrollably over the death of both her sons in the Hitler-led war in Spain. Her husband pleads, "Don't cry, Maria. That doesn't help." She ceases to weep, stares at him silently for a moment, and cries out, "Then do something that helps!"

In the play, written for German-speaking people watching the growing dominance of the Nazis, Brecht brings the curtain down leaving the cry ringing in the ears of the audience. It is no accident that pioneers of the new ethics, such as Barth and Bonhoeffer and Thielicke, reared their ethical syntheses out of similar experience. Before the growing terror and misery of the Third Reich, they and their countrymen had asked, "What ought I to do?" The traditional moral laws gave little light, in fact often forbade what was necessary, e.g., the lying and deceit and disobedience needed in order to rescue Jews. Yet their conscience urged inexorably, "Do something that helps!"

The same cry rings in the conscience of the Christian who shares today the new ethical feeling and thinking. It is his inner reaction to the needs of men and women of his time—the poor, the racially oppressed, those involved in the Vietnam war, those involved in broken marriages, those researching new biological and chemical instruments of war, those bored by liturgies, the mentally retarded—to select examples exclusively from wider social life. *Do something that helps!*

Some are responding by publicly and illegally protesting, destroying files, sitting in, shouting down, etc. The suavity with which Catholic intellectuals like myself discuss protest, balancing appropriately appreciation and criticism, can conceal its novelty as a widespread phenomenon in the moral life of the Church. The instincts of the Catholics who snarled at the priests marching in support of the Catonsville nine were unerring. Something foreign, and therefore threatening, was invading their Catholic life.

The novelty does not lie in the conscious violation of law. The old morality permitted the violation under certain conditions, just as the new morality condemns it under certain conditions. Nor can one explain the novelty by diagnosing the psychological makeup of the individual protesters as sick manifestations of a sick modern society. Both the old and new morality condemn rash judgment. Nor are the protesters to be distinguished from their critics by their greater moral energy. The new morality can concede that studying to get into medical school has a genuine moral value and is, in the long run, more arduous than persistently occupying other people's offices.

But one thing that is new with the Catholic protester and distinguishes him from his Catholic critic is, I submit, his understanding of moral obligation. The protester feels it is up to him personally to do something about blacks in ghettos, soldiers and civilians in Vietnam and future victims of chemical and biological warfare. The Catholic, still thinking along traditional grooves, may view with concern what is taking place, but does not see it as his obligation to try to do anything about it. Concerning the Vietnam war, one can think of exceptions, e.g., many of the men fighting in Vietnam. But they *are* exceptions, and in the case of the suffering of black Americans or of the future of biological and chemical warfare, rare is the critic of protest who feels obliged personally to do anything about it. He may be a moral man, trying to live by a demanding code, but it is not a code that includes obligations of this sort. The difference between the two moralities lies not in the reply to the question of *what* the average American citizen should do about the development of biological instruments of war, but *whether* he should do anything about it.

Conceivably, the new trend is an elite morality or an ethics proper only to intellectuals. Conceivably, the majority of any community, for reasons not necessarily discreditable, will always conceive moral obligation in legal terms. If that were true the premise of this chapter would be false and the forecast invalid. But if one continues with the hypothesis that the new trend will characterize the ethical thinking of the general Christian community, one can still ask whether the protester is typical of what will be the average morally-concerned Catholic in 2000. The answer, I believe, is: in his moral imperatives, yes; in his actions, no. Illegal protest is appropriate only for the small minority endeavoring to alter the moral judgment and conduct of the majority. It staggers the imagination to think of what Christian life will be, individually and socially, once the new thinking penetrates and reforms the genuine moral sensitivity and energy of the

Catholic mass and brings them to bear universally on the needs of members of the community.

It may sound too good to be true, and perhaps it is, for one reason or another. In any case, it does not follow that Christians will be any better than they are now. They will be what they always have been: sinners. They will continually need Christ's forgiveness and grace. There is no reason to think that their efforts to live morally will be greater than they have been in the past. But, inasmuch as they do try to meet their basic moral obligations before Christ, they will have no choice but to go into action and respond to those in need. Like the concept of responsibility, the idea of helping out is not new to Christian thought. The Christian who strove for the higher, more perfect Christian life strove to imitate Christ in his active care. But in 2000, it will no longer be a matter of counsel or of a more perfect way or a secondary obligation, but the central duty of Christian life. It is hard to imagine what that will be like.

Being, therefore, activistic, an ethics of responsibility demands a different kind of methodology than an ethics of obedience to law. To be *obliged* to a fitting response, normally in some form of positive action, is to be inevitably obliged to *create* a response. A creative methodology is required. "Creative" is an "in" word, and it is not in to be in. But creativity does aptly characterize an ethics of responsibility. One can see this more clearly envisioning concrete cases than by abstract analysis: I am trying to be a responsible father, to be a responsible teacher, responsibly to entertain the friend of a friend. Or, more particularly: I discover that the woman I love is given to moods of anxiety; an acquaintance down the hall shows that he wants to become my friend; two of my employees begin to show jealousy of each other. In each case, I spontaneously ask, "What ought I to do?" In each case the answer, a fitting response to the situation, is clearly something that I will have to create, small decision after small decision, in the coming days and months. If I meet my moral obligation, I will inevitably create a history of responses that never existed before.

That the traditional moral theologians rarely, if ever, discussed the last five of the six cases signals how radically the new ethical inquiry differs from the old. Just as characteristic and more substantial is the methodology called for by the creative kind of answer, looked for in each case by an ethical question. A further analysis of the creative response, with the above six paradigms kept in mind, can explicate this.

It is impossible to imagine that in any of the above cases I could find only one possible fitting response or series of responses. To start off I have to choose, almost arbitrarily, where I will look for possible fitting responses. I could start by exploring the possibilities of spending more time with my son, or of delegating to him some of my authority and responsibility in regard to the younger children, or of giving him more freedom, or of conversing with him in a new manner, etc., etc. One could well consider more than one of these possibilities, but rarely would a man feel obliged to explore all. Within the chosen area one rarely comes to the end of conceivable possibilities, e.g., ways of father and son spending time together. Moreover, none of the possibilities have ever been duplicated before. There has never been a man like me or a boy like him or the complex of concrete realities that make up our lives. Finally, in carrying out the response upon which I have decided, I never find that it progresses as conceived. I have regularly to readjust my project, and even then the final outcome is something of a surprise. When a man who has tried consistently to be a responsible father reflects at his son's marriage on the plans he had for his son at birth and over the intervening years he will assuredly smile with a certain pride and satisfaction at his ever-changing resolutions and projects.

A traditional moralist could, I believe, understand that the continuous response of father to son was creative and, as a human being, he could recognize drama and value in it. But as a moralist, he would find the "cases" uninteresting. He would find it hard to see how the planning and replanning of the father had anything to do with the methodology of moral theology or ethics. The difficulty is understandable.

The methodology of the old ethics was modeled on the science of lawyers and doctors. The methodology of the new is, as Jean-Paul Sartre suggested, best understood by comparison with the evaluative judgment of the artist, and, derivatively, the aesthete.

The work of art, like the responsible human act, is a creation. Nothing like it existed before. It proceeded from the vision of the artist; he saw, dimly at least, what he "had to" do. But he was not copying some preexisting model nor simply applying general rules nor had he acquired his vision from another man's mind. The vision itself, the original conception of the sculpture or novel or sonata, probably evolved and changed as the artist labored and took final form only at the completion of the work. Yet the value and greatness of art is not subjective or relative. It can be objectively evaluated and criticized. The vision Picasso has as he takes up his brush is, in the real order, far superior to any I might have. His finished work is objectively great art, objectively surpassing the work of lesser painters. The judgment Picasso had of his project and the judgment he and other men have of his completed work are true, objective judgments which reflect reality. So, too, can be the judgments of the new ethics.

But as the new method of ethical reflection becomes clear, it may make new, as well as old moralists, uneasy. After the new moralist fends off any application of absolute law to the case, what more can he say? What moral wisdom could Joseph Fletcher or I (I know he will pardon the pairing) write down that incipient fathers, launching on the ethical methodology described above, could read with profit? Could any general principles be of use to them? The planning will be, for each father, so personal, concrete, creative and unique that no one, it would seem, can make statements generally relevant to it.

Here again, the analogy with aesthetic evaluation is useful. The free creativity of the artist finds its concrete reality only in a medium that has its limiting constants. Certain results, and only they, can come from a given kind of musical instrument, stone, paint, human voice, etc. Nijinsky could pause only so long in flight. Only out of thorough knowledge of the medium can the creative vision arise. Human behavior and its constants are the medium in which ethical responsibility must create fitting responses. Though less regular and less easily detectable than those of stone and paint, the constants of human behavior determine the possibilities of creativity; the ethical judgment must take them into account. A married man would not need much experience to know that his excessive drinking is likely to create a history of unfitting responses between him and his wife. With some knowledge of psychology, he might be able to see that his drinking is his cowardly and effective way of getting back at his wife and that he and she are both dimly aware of it.

Since they more reliably and extensively bring to light constants of human behavior, the behavioral sciences, and any professional or trained experience, will more and more give answers to the new kind of ethical question. The question looking for a fitting response in the situation always centers on a "How can . . ." question. How can we bring peace to these nations? Not: is this war unjust? How can we appropriately reenact Jesus' last meal? Not: what are the pertinent rites and rubrics? How can we lessen anti-Semitism in this vacation resort? Not: may a hotel legitimately refuse guests on the basis of race? How can this university senate work more effectively? Not: do students have a right to participate in administration? How can one encourage a healthy appreciation of sexuality in one's community? Not: what is pornography and should it be banned?

The "How can . . ." questions, demanding knowledge of the pertinent sciences and/or possession of the pertinent specialized experience (e.g., of the professional diplomat in regard to bringing about peace), move moral questions out of the range of competence of the general moralist, old or new. Ford and Kelly could ably field the old kind of questions concerning war, sexuality, medicine, alcoholism, confidentiality, etc. But what single man is professionally competent to answer the five "How can . . ." questions just above?

Richard Porter, President of the Catholic Economics Association, expressed shock at the decline, recorded by his poll, of encyclical courses in Catholic universities.[3] The decline, I suggest, illustrates the shift in the nature of the ethical question and consequently in ethical methodology. In the economic sphere, the ethical task is no longer only to establish and correlate rights, e.g., of individuals to private property, of workers to a just wage, of everyone to material subsistence, of citizens vis-à-vis the state, of the state to care for the needy, etc. The ethical question now is practical: what measures can be taken to direct our economy so as to contribute to the greatest good of the citizens?

The science of economics does not establish what is good for the citizen, but neither do men of good will dispute about it (e.g., good working conditions for miners, respectable jobs for the victims of racial discrimination, recreational facilities for children, good housing, security of medical care, etc.) Nor is the purpose of ethical questioning to prove that these goals are good. The ethically-concerned man raises an ethical question usually to force himself or somebody else to face the necessary means, painful though they be, to achieve the goals he has always theoretically endorsed. Thus the ethical question can be purely a question of economics and an economics course may, appropriately, replace the encyclicals. My experience as Lecturer of Medical Ethics at Georgetown Medical School brought me to draw a parallel conclusion and to urge the authorities to discontinue my lectures. Good medicine was good morality, and vice versa, and the medical professors could cover the pertinent points in their regular courses far better than could philosophers or theologians.

In the original publication of the present chapter as a *Commonweal* article, the preceding paragraph, especially the last sentence, seemed to provoke the strongest opposition. Perhaps I can pacify some of the opposition by clarifying my point through an illustration. To ethically channel experimentation on human beings, medical men have worked out guidelines, e.g., the code of Claude Bernard, the Nuremberg Code, the Declaration of Helsinki and the Code of the British Medical Association.[4] Individual institutions have hammered out more detailed rules. The "Statement of Policies, Practices, Procedures for Clinical Investigations and

Research on Man at Georgetown University, Washington, D.C.," regulates researches and clinical investigations in the Georgetown University Medical Center and Georgetown affiliated services.[5] The statement details the protocol the investigator must fill out for his project, the reviewing bodies to approve his project, and the procedure he must follow in obtaining the informed consent of the participating subject. The statement is "good medicine," not merely in a technical sense, but in the sense of the humane, moral, dedicated practice of medicine that is the ideal of the good doctor.

In creating good medicine, medical men can and do profit from consultation with laymen, whether they be ethicists, lawyers, clergymen, social workers or the patients themselves. It can be useful or even necessary that laymen sit on committees and have a deliberative voice in determining regulations for delicate areas of medicine, e.g., the treatment by a private hospital of the drug addicts that come to the clinic. Coming from outside the medical milieu, a layman is likely to make a different contribution, whether it be as a negative check or as a presentation of other viewpoints. But the basic competence to decide on concrete rules or judge on concrete cases normally requires trained experience, e.g., of experimental procedures, possible developments in them, psychological reactions of the patient to them, etc.

The human values at stake are not difficult to discern: the good of men advanced through medical discoveries, the life and health of the patient, the personal dignity of the patient, the image of medicine in the city. One need be neither ethicist nor doctor to recognize them. But one does need scientific experience and knowledge to answer the ethical question: how can the values be incarnated in the day-by-day practice of the hospital? How should a new drug be tested before use? Who, in the institution, should make the final judgment as to whether or not the risk involved in a lung transplantation outbalances the possible gain? Who gives the informed consent on the part of a patient who is a minor? Or mentally incapable? What must the participating subject be told in order that his consent be properly informed? Under what conditions should the subject remain free to halt the experimental procedure once it has begun? Plato's Socrates would be as valuable in a medical center as he was in the *agora*. But he would not be good at legislating ethics in a hospital just as he would not have been good at legislating ethics for a kingdom. Which is a pertinent modern footnote to Plato.[6]

Particularly difficult to predict for 2000 is the ethical impact the behavioral sciences will have in areas where they have made little progress at the present date, e.g., human sexuality. Ethics will probably be as absorbed with sexual conduct in 2000 as it is now. Man's sexual life should be for him as fascinating and explosive and as far-reaching in its repercussions as it is now. But to understand what human sexuality concretely is and how it can be matter for the creation of a fitting personal and interpersonal life he will, in keeping with the new ethical methodology, turn in the year 2000 almost exclusively to sciences such as psychology or sociology. At the present state of those sciences, we have little certainty as to what he will find there in thirty years. The admittedly limited and defective Kinsey study is still being used by professional people because, on the whole, nothing any less limited or defective has been done.

The sociologist Ira Reiss, surveying the findings of scientific research into sexual behavior, emphasized that the research was in its initial stages:

> Probably no other area in the social sciences has as poor a pedigree as the study of the human sexual relationship. The approach to this area has been blurred by impressionistic approaches and deadened by moralistic tirades. Just as it has taken years to achieve objectivity in the study of labor problems and of race relations, so it has taken even longer to approach impartiality in the area of sex. One's fingers and toes are more than enough on which to count the number of objective, impartial, researches carried on in this area. . . .
> In the post-war period, good quality social scientific research on the human sexual ralationship has gradually emerged. In fact, one can probably say that with the ex-

ception of the Kinsey reports, the vast majority of the important research in this area has occurred within the last ten years.[7]

Moreover, as Lester Kirkendall, specialist in sex education and family relations, pointed out, a good deal of the research is focused on the physical forms of sexual behavior rather than on "what happens to persons within the context of the interpersonal relationship in which they find themselves."

The historical preoccupation with sex as an act has also been reflected in the character of sex research. Until recently it has concentrated on incidences and frequencies of various forms of sexual behavior. Some of the more pretentious studies broke incidences and frequencies of the total research population into smaller groups, e.g. Kinsey. He looked for possible differences in sex behavior in sub-groups distinguished by such factors as religious affiliations, socio-economic levels, rural or urban residence, adequacy of sex education and similar factors. This analysis, of course, took into account situational factors which could and do influence interpersonal relationships. Strictly speaking, however, the research still remained the interpersonal relationships framework.[8]

Kirkendall offers a useful report of fifteen or so studies of the interpersonal aspects of sexual adjustment. But suggestive though the studies for ethical evaluations may be, they are too limited to ground any scientific generalities, much less moral principles.

Thus one cannot exclude the possibility that in the year 2000 the ethical judgment on homosexuality may be the reverse of what it commonly is now. As we shall discuss in the next chapter, the prevailing opinion of psychiatrists and psychologists is presently that homosexual behavior reflects an emotional sickness or retarded growth. But there is reason to think that this is true only because those who take up homosexual behavior do it in the face of strong social taboos and therefore are likely to be the victims of compulsions or unadjusted drives. The present scientific evidence does not exclude the possibility that those who took up homosexual behavior in a permissive society might be generally healthy from a psychological point of view and capable of integrating their sexual conduct into a fitting interpersonal life.

However the science of sexuality, or of economics, or of medicine, progresses, and whatever they and other sciences uncover, it is clear that their findings will enter into the moral judgments of the future. One foresees the exit of ethicists and moral theologians. If there be need for a specialist for the concrete ethical question, it will be the man of scientific and professional experience in the matter at hand. For the rest, ethics will be simply the creation by the Christian community and its leaders of its ethos, its potent complex of ideals and goals, and the creative planning by the individual Christian of experience for himself and others. In the present evolution of the abortion question, we see the phasing out of the last debate where the ethicist and moral theologian can speak out with authority and be listened to. Those of us still alive in 2000 will be able to tell youth of the eloquence and pathos of those great debates by the specialists of absolute right and wrong. The young will, I presume, listen respectfully, showing wonder and appreciation and perhaps some regret. Then they and we will get back to work.

4 HOMOSEXUALITY AND LOVE

A couple of years ago, ninety Episcopal priests of the New York metropolitan area expressed agreement that the church should classify homosexual acts between consenting adults as "morally neutral" and acknowledge that in some cases such acts may even be a good thing.[1] Public discussion of the morality of homosexuality was flaring up at the time, and was reflected in popular periodicals and TV panels.[2] Eventually the public excitement subsided, but Americans and Christians continue to question what their fathers felt was unquestionable. One form of their question is: "If a Christian has strong impulses to homosexual behavior, what should he or she do? What does Christian morality say about it?"

First of all, "Christian morality" does not say anything about homosexuality or anything else, because there is no such person named "Christian morality." At least, not that I know of. There is nobody named "Christian morality": there are just Christians, we who are the Church, are Christ's Body, are God's people, us. How, then, do Christians answer the question: "What should the Christian do who has strong impulses to homosexual behavior?" Nowadays, Christians go about answering the question in different ways.

Some Christians turn to the Bible. They read, "No homosexual will inherit the Kingdom of God." For some Christians no more need be said. God's Word condemns all homosexual behavior. No Christian, therefore, may ever act homosexually. Among the Christians who answer the question in this way, simply by reading the Bible by themselves, there are, I believe, more Protestants than Catholics.

Other Christians turn to natural law. They look for God's

creative purpose as inscribed in the nature of things. One purpose of God that some Christians find inalienably inscribed in man's sexual nature is that every single sexual act be ordered to bring new life into the world. God, through nature, forbids that a man ever act sexually in such a manner as to render impossible the procreative purpose. For some Christians, no more need be said. God's Law condemns all homosexual behavior. No Christian may ever act homosexually. Among the Christians who answer the question in this way, simply by reading in nature God's precise purpose for every sexual act of man, there are, I believe, more Catholics than Protestants.

But there are Christians today who cannot adopt either of the two approaches. The approaches go toward the right sources, of course. The Christian, facing an ethical decision, must turn to God's Word as recorded in the Bible, and he must turn to God's purpose as manifested in the realities He created. They are *the* two sources of light in which a Christian lives. But the two approaches we have described do not go far enough. To listen to God's Word, it is not enough to read sentences out of the Bible, especially if we understand them without a twentieth century mentality and take them as direct answers to our twentieth century questions. If nothing else, the Christian biblical scholars of our time would tell us this.

And—as far as the second approach goes—to be able to discern the general purpose God has for the realities He created does not mean we can discern a fixed, specific purpose He has for a particular kind of act, a precise purpose which must be respected every time the act is performed. The Christian philosophers, thinking in the mode of the philosophy of our time, would say that we cannot.

To the ethical question concerning homosexual behavior, therefore, some Christians employ an approach that is different from the two we have been discussing. People have come to label the approach "the new morality." As should be clear from preceding chapters, the term means something general: a certain way of thinking about ethical questions, a way of thinking which is widespread among Christians trying to lead examined lives. The new morality offers an answer for at least certain forms of homosexual behavior. But before considering the answer, let it be clear what the new morality is and is not.

Suppose I face a decision to make in my life concerning homosexual behavior. Suppose I say to myself, "I don't recognize any absolute moral law of God prohibiting this behavior. Therefore I'm free to do as I please." I may have different reasons for saying that no absolute moral law, no divine prohibition, applies here. Perhaps I do not think that God has laid down any moral laws at all. Or perhaps I just do not think it is clear and certain that He prohibited all homosexual behavior. In either case, my reasoning runs the same: "I hold the new morality. I do not admit that God has absolutely prohibited homosexual behavior. Therefore I may do as I please."

Except that this is not the new morality. It does not accept the principle I am going on, namely that where no absolute prohibitions apply, one is free to do as one pleases. It would consider my way of thinking to be a childish form of legalism. All that matters is what Daddy and Mommy say. But they didn't say that *every day* I should stay away from the cookie jar. So, to the cookie jar I go. I don't have to worry about what the cookies may do to my stomach. I don't have to worry how much will be left for my brothers and sisters. I'm not old enough for that.

The Christians who live according to the new morality do not, it is true, base their moral judgments on any absolute, specific prohibitions laid down by God. But neither do they feel free to do as they please. They base all their moral judgments and their lives on something else, something positive, though general: the absolute, Divine, command to love. Facing the question of homosexual behavior, they would say: God has laid down no specific and absolute prohibitions against homosexual behavior. But He and I do want absolutely one thing: that I live a life of love.

Here again one could misunderstand the new morality. One could claim to be living according to the new morality and not be doing so at all. It depends on what I mean by "love." Suppose what I mean by "love" comes down to affectionate impulse and nothing more. By "love" I mean I have a genuine fondness and affection for another person, a deep and strong feeling for him or her. The affection makes me want to express it physically, sexually. I appeal to the new morality: love is the only absolute. This is love. I go ahead.

Except that the Christians who live according to the new morality would not call that "love." The impulse of feeling is often part of love, but love is always more than that. Here a man's experience comes in. If a man is honest with himself, his experience shows him that some of his affectionate impulses lead to actions which, in the long run, badly hurt the person he loves. For example, he may recognize that some of his impulses towards his teenage son lead him to overprotect him, run his life for him, keep him from exercising responsibility. He concludes that these are not impulses of love. He is coming to realize, as most of us human beings do, what we really mean by love. It lies deeper than feeling. It must include the free determination, commitment, of a man or woman to further the good of a certain person.

There is nothing new about such an understanding of love. The situationist, Joseph Fletcher, defines "love" this way.[3] But exegetes like Spicq and Dodd testify to the same sense of the word ($\dot{\alpha}\gamma\acute{\alpha}\pi\eta$) in the New Testament.[4] Christians of the new and old morality can agree that love, as the promotion of human good, is what makes Christian ethics. As Thomas Aquinas puts it, a man offends God only inasmuch as he acts against the human good of himself or another man.[5]

But here, I believe, the Christian of the new morality adds something new. Or at least introduces a new emphasis. To understand what is good for a person, he, a man of the twentieth century, relies exclusively on experience. For him, love knows no *a priori* laws, sees only the ones loved and what experience shows is happening or likely to happen to them. Love is, therefore, pragmatic, hard-headed, often unromantic. It is pitiless for all that experience shows will oppose the good of the person loved, whether the opposition comes from within the lover or without. Moreover, love's view, looking to experience, is long-range. It, therefore, is tough, puts up with all things, holds out, goes for distance. A man's love for the woman he marries and the children he begets, is judged authentic—to really be love—only after the test of the years and of the problems and burdens and dangers life brings down on his family one after another. There is no other test for anyone else. Love has to be as mighty as death, as strong as hell. Let the buyer beware.

Christ emboldens the Christian to buy love. The Christian sees in Jesus Christ how great a thing love is. God's forgiving love, communicated through Christ to the Christian, gives him the confidence and strength to love. But only if he understands what love is, and only if he has bought love, taken it on, and is trying to live it, only then has he the right, according to the new morality, to come to a question like that of homosexual behavior with love as his sole norm. Only then can he, with the love of a twentieth century man, turn simply to experience for an answer to his question: "Would homosexual behavior really be good or bad for myself and the other person?"

One man's experience of homosexual behavior is extremely limited. The man of the new morality must turn to the experience of the community. Most of the community have little or no experience with homosexual behavior. They must turn to those who have extensive, critical experience, preeminently the psychologists, psychiatrists and analysts. Dr. Isadore Rubin, in a "Discussion Guide" for SIECUS (Sex Information and Education Council of the U. S.), reports that though there is no unanimity among specialists, the most commonly held opinion is that all homosexuals are mentally ill or neurotic.[6] Moreover, many psychiatrists who would not judge homosexuality so negatively, if considered abstractly in itself, do believe "that homosexual behavior could not be maintained in the face of a hostile and punitive environment [i.e., present day society] unless strong neurotic fears blocked the path to heterosexual adaptation."[7] Furthermore, according to prevailing psychoanalytic opinion, says Dr. Rubin, homosexuality represents a fixation at, or regression to, an immature state of development.

The word "homosexual" has, of course, a spectrum of meanings. But what the specialists have defined as the kind of person they are discussing is, in fact, a kind of person who poses acutely ethical and pastoral problems for the Christian. By "homosexuals" are not meant here those who at one time or other have indulged in sexual behavior with members of their own sex, nor those who often feel sexual attraction toward their own sex, but, generally speaking, feel a stronger attraction toward those of the opposite sex. What is meant here is rather "those individuals who more or less chronically feel an urgent sexual desire towards, and a sexual responsiveness to, members of their own sex, and who seek gratification of this desire predominantly with members of their own sex."[8] Such persistent, preferential emotional and physical attraction to members of the same sex, a committee of the Group for the Advancement of Psychiatry declares, without qualification, to be "a severe emotional disorder."[9] "As the understanding of the various psychological causal factors of homosexuality has increased, it appears more and more evident that the homosexual is an emotionally immature individual who has not acquired a normal capacity to develop satisfying heterosexual relationships, which will eventuate in marriage and parenthood."[10]

In other words, homosexuality is not just a physical oddity like colorblindness or being left-handed. Its roots go deep and spread wide in the personality. Like all our basic sexual attitudes and patterns of sexual behavior, it is psychosexual, organically expressing an attitude and stage of growth of one's very person. What homosexuality expresses, as Dr. Philip Heersema puts it, writing in the *Journal of the American Medical Association,* is an "arrest of personality growth," "stunted devlopment and disturbed personality."[11]

These conclusions of the community's experience are not certain. There are psychologists who dissent, seeing little cause for alarm in many cases of homosexual behavior. Unquestionably, there is need for more quantity and analysis of data. New evidence suggests a nuancing or even a revision of the above conclusions. Nevertheless, the conclusions, as they stand, represent the most reliable experience in our community at the present time. Most generalizations distilled from the community's experience, including those refined by scientific analysis, are far from certain when applied to individual situations. Even relatively reliable principles, e.g., concerning safe and unsafe ways of auto-driving or courses of physical illnesses, will turn out often enough to be unverified. Less certain are the applications of the community's experience in obscure areas such as economic inflation, population growth, air pollution, adolescence, etc. As I noted in an earlier chapter, a lack of certainty can be crucial for an ethic based on law. But not for a morality of love. One who loves does not demand certainty before deciding how to help the one he loves. He uses the best evidence at hand. A man will arrange an operation medically indicated for his wife simply because it is less likely that she will die with it than without it.

A man with genuine love for himself and others will refrain, in his behavior, from expressing and deepening particular feelings when the evidence on hand indicates strongly, if not with certainty, that the feelings are profoundly immature and disordered. Thus a Christian moving in the spirit of the new morality condemns homosexual behavior more severely than one using traditional arguments. According to a traditional argument, homosexual behavior is wrong in that it frustrates a faculty of man. According to the Christian who is moved only by love and relies on the experience of the community, homosexual behavior is wrong in that it frustrates the man himself. It fixates him at a stage far short of the full emotional and sexual development of the "living man" who is "God's glory."

In other words, a Christian for whom love is the only absolute understands that love is free, strong, open. (One might think of the analyses of Erich Fromm.) If I act in a particular way basically because I am afraid to look a woman in the eye, to relate with her independently as one grown person to another, if, for example, the affection I am seeking by my homosexual actions—though I may not realize it, but as psychological analysis finds—is Mommy's love for her little boy, then I must say to myself that I am not acting out of love. I am fleeing from love. Which is the greatest sin and the greatest failure for any man and, in a special way, for any Christian.

To have impulses in this direction is neither a sin nor a failure. According to Dr. Heersema, evidence of the universality of homosexuality can be found to some degree in every individual.[12] He adds that there is a brief period, usually at the onset of puberty, that may properly be called a normal "homosexual" stage. In fact, all of us adults have strong, recurrent impulses that correspond to "an immature stage of development" or "an arrest of personality growth." In other words, we all have childish impulses. They draw us from the free, strong, open love that we want to have. The impulses may have nothing to do with sex. I may have strong impulses to self-pity. Or to vindictiveness. Or to fear and anxiety. My impulses may be more childish, more opposed to love than the feelings leading this other man to homosexual behavior.

The point for every man is: how do I react to the childish feelings? He has to ask the question over and over again. Do I go along with them, confirm and strengthen them, express them in action and live according to them? Or do I choose to love? Do I free myself, inasmuch as I can, from childish feelings and choose to do only what expresses and furthers a mature love within myself and others? In real life, it is a hard choice. If I am a Christian, Christ helps me choose.

Recently, evidence has been shown that for certain individuals the choice of homosexual behavior has been the kind just described—i.e., a choice of something contributing to, or at least fitting in with, a life of mature love.[13] There are active homosexuals whose emotional life seems to be no less mature and healthy than the average heterosexual. Insofar as I can judge, the evidence is still too fragmentary to unseat the prevailing scientific appraisal of homosexuality as the living-out of sick and stunted emotions. The odds are still high that the average individual who chooses homosexual behavior will be choosing a sick, immature way of life. The odds should determine the ethical decision, it seems to me, at least for the individual for whom professional analysis has confirmed his emotional sickness or whose personal experience has offered no grounds to believe that he is an exception to the general scientific rule.[14]

In one sense, therefore, the Christian of the new morality condemns homosexual behavior more severely than a Christian of the old. He sees its evil not in the abuse of a human faculty, but in the refusal to love, i.e., to live and let live a full human life. But this is only an ethical answer to an ethical question. It says what one ought to do. It says nothing about sin or guilt and responsibility or Church membership or civil laws. It is one thing for me to say that to be an alcoholic or a shrewish wife is wrong, in open contradiction to the life and love Christ calls us to. That is an ethical statement a Christian can make. It is another thing for me to say that alcoholics and shrews are great sinners, that all alcoholics and shrews are guilty and responsible for what they do because they are free to do otherwise, that all alcoholics and shrews should be excluded from Church membership, that alcoholism and shrewishness should be made a criminal offense, punishable by law. The four statements are, at best, unlikely. But that alcoholism and shrewishness—and homosexual behavior—are wrong and unChristian is, I submit, true.

I would like to allude to a second and older way a Christian can answer the ethical question of homosexual behavior. When he believes in Jesus Christ, he does not believe in a person who only lived on earth 2000 years ago and now is in heaven. He believes in a person still present here today in His body and in His community, the Church.

For he has given us some men as apostles, some as prophets, some as missionaries, some as pastors and teachers, in order to fit his people for the work of service, for building the body of Christ, until we attain unity in faith, and in the knowledge of the Son of God, and reach mature manhood, and that full measure of development found in Christ. We must not be babies any longer, blown about and swung around by every wind of doctrine through the trickery of men with their ingenuity in inventing error.

We must lovingly hold to the truth and grow up into perfect union with him who is the head—Christ himself.[15]

I read this, not simply as a sentence out of the Bible, but as
a word understood and lived by Christian communities from
the beginning until now, whether they be Roman Catholic
or Lutheran or Greek Orthodox or any other. In different
ways, but always in some way, the man who believes in
Christ, as he faces concrete questions of living such as that
of homosexuality, knows that the "pastors and teachers" of
Christ's Body play their part in helping him "hold lovingly
to the truth." In the closing chapters of the book, I will discuss the limits the Church has always set to the role of the
pastors and teachers. But to limit is not to deny. For many
Christians, heeding the words of their pastors and teachers
is a wiser and, therefore, more loving response to the question of homosexual behavior than reading the evidence of
the psychiatrists and psychologists of our secular city.

5 THE ABORTION DEBATE

Irrespective of the intrinsic merits or demerits of any position, the abortion debate going on in the United States is a disaster. In setting influential Americans against each other, it absorbs the energy of men who otherwise would be working together to meet the needs of society. The suspicion and rancor it engenders passes over to other areas where cooperation is called for. The witness of the Church to the world becomes for many a testimony to its inhumanity, since this is the only way they can interpret its official stand on abortion.

The debate shows no sign of waning. True, the debaters represent a spectrum of views and some intermediate positions could come to a consensus on practice. True, hospital regulations and state legislation, enforced or proposed, reflect a working compromise between the extremes: not all direct abortion is prohibited, but only under certain conditions is it permitted. Nevertheless, the men who take extreme positions see no way to modify their moral assessment of abortion, either a condemnation of all direct abortion or a ready justification of abortion for relatively minor reasons. Consequently, many feel bound not to cease their efforts until all public restrictions on abortion are removed.[1] Many feel bound to resist every proposal of liberalization as a step on the way toward permitting abortion-on-demand.[2] The prospect is of a bitter, costly tug-of-war over the years.[3]

The rhetoric of the debate illustrates the seriousness of the deadlock. Most public statements entrench and fortify positions that do not face the other side. Those favoring abortion plead for freedom of conscience, although they know that the anti-abortionists agree with them on its value and place in civil society.[4] The abortionists would not recognize the freedom of conscience of a woman who beats her child to death, and they know that their opponents regard abortion as essentially the same thing. The anti-abortionists, in turn, state the evil of infanticide and genocide, although they know their adversaries are not lacking in appreciation of these evils, especially since some of them lost family and friends in Nazi camps.[5] The rhetoric of the debate, therefore, shows a despair of communication. One seems to speak only to hearten (with the moral pathos of the cause) those who already agree but might be tempted to flag in their efforts.

Whatever the reason for most of the rhetoric bypassing the precise point of disagreement, it does make clear, by implication and occasionally by express statement, what the point is. Is abortion essentially the same thing as infanticide or genocide or whatever civilized people today recognize as murder? More centrally, is the human fetus essentially the same being as the born child or adult? This is not the only issue in the debate. Robert Drinan and André Hellegers, among others, have pointed out that important legal and medical questions can be taken up apart from this central question concerning the nature of the fetus.[6] But it is the affirmative answer to that question (which at least the philosophers would call a philosophical question) that dictates the conscience of most opponents to abortion.[7] It is the negative answer that frees the conscience of most abortionists to ignore any rights of the fetus and concentrate on the needs of the mother and society in general.[8] The public debate in its present dimensions would collapse if either side began to doubt their answer to the question.

Identifying the parting of the ways after which it becomes impossible, logically and psychologically, to rejoin paths or even to hear each other, does not yet clarify what is going on in the debate. Why does most of the rhetoric simply presuppose a negative or affirmative answer to the central question of the nature of the fetus, offering no arguments nor even discussing the question? Why do those who do address the question argue as if the opposite answer to theirs were clearly untenable and needs no discussion?[9] Why do those who oppose abortion in the name of "the essential humanity of the fetus" generally ignore the ambiguity of the term "humanity," making no effort to establish the sense in which the fetus is "human"?[10] Why do abortionists, premising that the fetus is not a human person, not face the next and crucial question: how does one determine when the former becomes the latter?[11] Why is it that those who do not fail to do any of the above and who, in a sincere, intelligent, informed manner go into the question, still disagree radically on what the fetus really is?[12] And yet the pertinent empirical data is limited and undisputed—which is not the case in most questions dividing Americans today, e.g., the Vietnam war, sexual behavior, law and order, responsibility of whites to blacks, etc. Those who affirm and those who deny that the fetus is a human person accept the same data of the sciences concerning it and use the same data to justify their affirmation or denial. A pretty puzzle, if it were not tragic.

As psychological analysis or sociological survey might better solve the puzzle and explain the abortion debate. The following pages offer an epistemological explanation. The working hypothesis carrying along the explanation is suggested by the words of Cardinal Newman:

> The fact remains that in any inquiry about things in the concrete, men differ from each other, not so much in the soundness of their reasoning as in the principles which govern its exercise, that those principles are of a personal character, that where there is no common measure of minds, there is no common measure of arguments.

> The first principles are hidden for the very reason they are so sovereign and engrossing. They have sunk into you, they spread through you; you do not so much appeal to them as act upon them.[13]

Does Newman's epistemology make sense of the abortion debate? Does it explain why there is no meeting of minds although the possessors of the minds recognize the same empirical data and are talking about the same thing? Are there hidden, personal principles determining the positions on abortion and on the nature of the human fetus?

How does one find hidden principles? In the passage from *Present Positions of Catholics in England,* Newman underscores the influence of the group in forming the principles upon which the individual judges and acts. One epistemological method of discovering the principles at work would be to see whether the moral stance of an individual on one question is part of a pattern of moral positions that he shares with a given group.[14] It would appear to be the case in the abortion debate. Debaters for each side have noted that those disagreeing with them on the morality of abortion tend to have a peculiar constellation of positions on the taking of human life—so peculiar that the one side finds the constellation of the other difficult to understand and even inconsistent.[15] It is recognized or easily recognizable, I believe, that two general mentalities are operative and opposed in the debate, whatever other trends of thought are also represented.

Mentality A prohibits unconditionally all direct abortion just as it prohibits unconditionally all other direct killing of an innocent person.[16] Mentality B does not prohibit unconditionally all direct abortion just as it does not prohibit unconditionally any kind of killing.[17] Mentality A permits, under certain conditions, the indirect killing of an innocent person, e.g., a dying patient or a wartime civilian. It permits, under certain conditions, the killing of unjust persons, e.g., attackers or convicted criminals. Mentality B permits, under certain conditions, direct and indirect killing of innocent and unjust. But in comparison with mentality A, mentality B permits much less widely certain kinds of killing, e.g., capital punishment or the killing of wartime civilians or even war itself.[18]

What are the principles determining the two ethical constellations? One principle of mentality A is not hidden: human life is sacred and inviolable. But the full meaning of the principle is hidden. Since "inviolability" means the exclusion of violations, the "inviolability" of human life can be understood only by understanding the "violations" it ex-

cludes. But not every killing of a human being is such a violation of his life. According to the principle, the sacred
"inviolability" of this patient excludes that I take his life
by mercy-killing. It does not exclude that I take it through
a bombardment of the whole military installation. The
former is a "violation" of his life; the latter is not. Moralists
of mentality A do not agree on why this is so, why the sacred
inviolability of human life does *not* exclude killing in capital
punishment, defense against unjust aggression and various
forms of indirect killing.[19] The life of the convicted criminal
or would-be thief or wartime civilian is no less human nor
is his dignity as a human person inferior. It would follow
that it is also partly hidden to possessors of mentality A why
the humanness of life *does* exclude unconditionally other
types of killing (such as abortion) no matter what good results from them. It does not follow that mentality A is inconsistent or arbitrary or that any of its positions are false. It
does, however, follow that there is a hidden principle
mentality A "does not appeal to, but acts on," and raises the
question what the principle precisely is.

The principle of the inviolability of human life does not
prohibit *per se* something that falls within the experience
of the victim and those who knew him. If I kill directly an
innocent wartime civilian, I violate his life. If I kill him indirectly, and under the conditions required by the principle
of the double effect, I do not violate his life. But his experience may be the same—a moment of terror, a second of
physical pain, the cessation of love, hate and all the interpersonal relationships he had with those about him. Their
experience, too, on losing him, would not be greatly different
if they knew he had been killed indirectly rather than directly. What results in his and their experience plays no part
in determining whether or not the killing was an offense
against the inviolability of human life.

On the other hand, in dealing with cases of killing where
the inviolability of human life does not come into play, mentality A takes into consideration the experience of the man
to be killed and of those who knew him. The moralists dispute about the title justifying killing such as war or capital

punishment or defense against aggression, but they agree that no killing can be justified unless it is a necessary means to a given good and unless the good outweighs the parallel evil. They regularly assess the evil in the light of the experiential consequences.[20]

The purpose of the present chapter is not to probe further the hidden principle of mentality A, but to try to uncover the corresponding one of mentality B. Mentality B has no principle of the inviolability of human life, at least not in the sense as does mentality A. Unlike mentality A, mentality B is always experience-oriented. In every case submitted for ethical analysis, mentality B focuses spontaneously and exclusively on what would occur, in the short or long run, in the experience of the people involved. It sees no need for another focus to come to a sound moral decision.[21] But the contrast of the two mentalities is even more striking in those cases where both consider the experiential consequences to be decisive for the moral judgment, e.g., the experiences of the dying in war and those they leave behind in comparison with the experience of those who, the war being won, will live in a non-Communistic, free country. Or the experience of the men in death row and the experience of people in a society where the death penalty deters criminals. There will, of course, be disagreement about the experiential consequences themselves. What will be, in fact, the experience of the South Vietnamese people if they win the war? What is, in fact, the effect of the fear of the death penalty on would-be killers? Significant for our epistemological inquiry, however, is that mentality B consistently registers a far greater evil in the actual dying of individuals than mentality A does, even when they both agree on the facts. The difference is impossible, I believe, to define intellectually or to verbalize or conceptualize, but it is equally impossible not to notice it in present-day discussions. It is evident that the casualties in Vietnam morally disturb and weigh down some Americans more than others—to such an extent that the charge of sentimentality is not infrequently heard. This sensitivity, or oversensitivity, to the evil of death in human experience leads many of mentality B to condemn in fact, if not in principle, all war and capital punishment. What human good can outweigh this evil? For mentality B, therefore, the killing of a human being is never the violation of the inviolable, but is usually an experiential evil to which little, if anything, compares. Correspondingly, human life is usually one of the most fundamental experiential goods.

That the operative principle of mentality B is, in part, hidden is evidenced by the difficulty of its possessors to meet the charges of inconsistency. As is the inviolability of human life for mentality A, the presuppositions of mentality B are so "obvious" that they have not come to be conceptualized in a way satisfactory to the whole group, nor does the group feel the need to do so. They cannot see the need to explain why their position does not lead to a justification for infanticide or genocide and, when driven to give an explanation, they usually find themselves incapable of doing so. The difference between fetus, on the one hand, and born child and adult, on the other, is so obvious that one cannot express it. Similarly, the evil of wartime death or criminal execution is so obviously enormous to them that they cannot, and feel no need to, articulate it for those who take the evil less seriously.[22] As Martin Heidegger, among others, has insisted, some of the most significant elements of a man's view of life he can never put into words. They are too deeply a part of his whole way of viewing things for him to dislodge them for conceptual analysis.

The epistemology of Heidegger, positing as it does, the metamorphosis of human thought in succeeding epochs, encourages a further hypothesis: the attitudes of mentality A and mentality B on the taking of human life are organic growths of two fundamentally different mentalities in Western history: the classical or Hellenistic-medieval and the modern. In the abortion debate, it is not merely two ethics facing each other, but the world-views of two epochs, two cultures—one on the way out, one on the way in. It is a time like that when the barbarian mentality was destroying, assimilating and transforming the Roman.[23] Or perhaps a more suggestive analogy would be what would be happening if the culture of the Australian aborigines were evolving into a culture similar to the Aztec. That a struggle between the Hellenic and modern world outlooks dominates our times, particularly in Christian milieus, is a familiar thesis.[24] The contention of the present chapter is that this is what is happening in the abortion debate. The abortion debate is, at the same time, a paradigmatic clash of the old and new moralities. But according to our hypothesis, the two moralities form respectively part of the two deeper, broader world views, Hellenic and modern. To understand the two views, therefore, should help us to understand not merely the impasse on abortion but also the opposition of the two moralities.

I characterized the modern mentality as experience-oriented. In a sense, the classical mentality also (and for all I know, the mentality of every culture) centers on human experience. But the experience that primarily concerned the classical mentality was not the worldly experience of the ordinary human individual. Where the mentality took Platonic, Neo-Platonic, Augustinian or any of the medieval forms, all human events were evaluated according to the degree to which man moved toward the beautifying vision after death, or perhaps, in rare ecstasy, possessed it now.[25]

The Stoic held no hope for an afterlife. Yet the experience central to his outlook was not located in the worldly life of the individual, but in the good of the species as foreseen by the all-ruling wisdom of God. Traditional Christian sexual morality arises out of this perspective.[26] Contemporary Catholic ethicists who cite Thomas Aquinas' endorsement, with Aristotle, of human experience and its relativities as the matrix for the formation of specific moral principles, can find no example of sexual morality where Thomas Aquinas practices such an empirical relativism.[27] Moral principles deduced from the conjectured wisdom of a divine legislator planning the common good have to be absolute, since all laws are, of themselves, absolute. The third corner, to complete the framework of the classical mentality for locating human life, was human nature. Like the other-worldly end and the Divine Planner, the nature of man did not fall within human experience, but was known through metaphysical analysis and reasoning. The three corners were, of course, connected. God implemented His plan for man and man's union with Him after death, by creating man's nature, keeping it in existence, and acting through and with it.

Modern man did not begin to part ways with classical ethics when he began to discard moral absolutes, but when he began to lose the view that human life was best understood in terms of an other-worldly destiny and/or the wisdom of the Divine Legislator and/or human nature. The shift of perspective in viewing man's obligations occurred within the larger shift of perspective in viewing all of man and his life. As in many movements, the essence of the modern mentality is strikingly visible in its beginnings, even though it soon shed the concrete form it first took. What is man? A new kind of answer begins to arise, "Description de l'homme. Dépendance, désir d'indépendance, besoins." "Condition de l'homme. Inconstance, ennui, inquiétude."[28] "But what then am I? A thinking thing. What is that? It is what doubts, understands, affirms, denies, wills, refuses, imagines also and feels."[29] Neither Pascal nor Descartes said anything new. What is new is that they are basing all human accounts of man on what they are saying, namely, on what they find disclosing itself within an individual's experience in this life.

Descartes' label, "clear and distinct idea," and his pervasive geometrism never spread widely, but what he meant by the label remains as the principal source of modern understanding, "I call that perception clear, which is present and open to the attending mind, just as we say those things are clearly seen by us which, present to the onlooking eye, move it sufficiently, openly and strongly."[30] Descartes' example of a very clear, but not distinct idea is "where one perceives some great pain."[31] When one reads, "And I call that perception distinct, which, when it becomes clear, is so detached and separated [praecisa] from everything else that it contains in itself absolutely nothing else except what is clear," one recognizes the beginning of a story which has not yet reached its end, but whose mid-twentieth century chapter could be entitled, "Phenomenology and Logical Analysis."[32]

A culture is shared by people of every level, but can find

clear, abstract expression in the words of philosophers whose role is to "grasp the mind of the times in concepts." Descartes and Pascal, like Sartre and Husserl and Dewey, express the mind of modern men.[33] Western man has become increasingly preoccupied, even obsessed, with his worldly experience, brooding over it, attempting to read it in order to understand what he is and who he is, suspecting any thesis about man that cannot be verified in experience. One could adduce non-philosophical evidence for this contrast of classical and modern mentality, e.g., the art and literature of the last 100 years *versus* the popular Gnostic and mystery religions of Hellenistic times and the images in medieval cathedrals. But the contrast of the two mentalities in regard to experience, and the other contrasts about to be listed, are, I believe, generally recognized. I am bringing them together to illuminate the abortion debate as well as the clash of old and new moralities today.

In the seventeenth century, too, there appeared a shortening of focus in ethics analogous to, and undoubtedly influenced by, the current of anthropology exemplified by Descartes and Pascal. Following Dietrich Bonhoeffer, many Christians of the second half of the twentieth century ring the changes with Grotius' "even if there were no God."[34] In fact, Grotius' ethics signals the emergence of an autonomous, secular ethics, unprecedented in the West, and still dominant today, namely one where specific moral principles are worked out apart from the existence of God. The ethics of Hobbes and Francis Bacon (like Grotius, professed theists) are in the same current.[35] The trend, though not so pronounced, is seen in the Scholasticism of the period which had its influence on Grotius.[36]

The concentration on man's worldly experience, studied apart from the existence of God, forged new patterns of ethical thought. But to understand the historical process and its outcome, several other agents must be noted. In the seventeenth century, too, scientists began to experiment. They started to approach nature not to record its doings and profit from them, but to see what they could do with nature and get out of it. Nature was no longer a finished vessel, whose fixed structure one must respect as well as one must respect the intent of the potter. Nature, no matter what shape it has, is clay to be broken and remolded responsibly and creatively, to your heart's desire. A perfect example of the clash between the classical and modern mentalities, precisely in their approach to nature, is the recently departed contraception debate.

Another agent in the creation of the new concrete ethics is the concern for "the common man." The classical mentality of the West is second to none in recognizing the dignity of every individual man and of every individual life. The dignity, however, was seen to surface in worldly experience only for a minority: the hero, the virtuous man, the sage, the mystic, the saint, the priest and the nun. The dignity, therefore, of the individual life of the common man lay outside worldly experience, in his metaphysical nature imaging God, the governing of his life by loving divine providence, and his destiny to reunite with God after death. Each human life is a drama, but the average man escapes tragedy and makes his life a success if he reaches the end with sufficient obedience to God to still be in His favor. For the success and greatness and dignity of an ordinary human life, terrestrial happiness, richness of experience, clarity and depth of understanding, quality of motives, maturity of decision and degree of love became relatively unimportant.

In focusing exclusively on the worldly experience of the individual and making complete abstraction from God, the modern mind would seem to be trapped in a *cul-de-sac* in its efforts to establish the dignity of the common man and the drama of his life. The absorption with clear analysis of experience and the growing appreciation of the power of the sciences should have led back to Greek rationalism, an exaltation of the intellectual and a depreciation of the terrestrial life of the common man. It did, in fact, with the Enlightenment. But opposing forces were at work, eventually obtaining the upper hand and lapidary expression by Rousseau and Kant.

Kant himself has vividly expressed his admiration for and indebtedness to Rousseau. It is to Rousseau that Kant owed his "belief in the common man." In a marginal note to the essay on the beautiful and sublime, he noted during this period: "I am myself by inclination a seeker after truth. I feel a consuming thirst for knowledge and a restless passion to advance in it, as well as satisfaction in every forward step. There was a time when I thought that this alone could constitute the honor of mankind, and I despised the common man who knows nothing. Rousseau set me right. This blind prejudice vanished; I learned to respect human nature, and I should consider myself far more useless than the ordinary working man if I did not believe that this view could give worth to all others to establish the rights of man" I *learned to respect human nature:* this central fact constituted the inspiration for that central concern with ethics which stands at the heart of Kant's fully developed system. Too frequently has Kant been considered primarily from an epistemological viewpoint, and his *Critique of Pure Reason* has been put into the center of things. The re-establishment of ethics as the central human concern is the real core of Kant's philosophy. This, in turn, explains why Kant could become the philosopher of peace *par excellence.* Rousseau stimulated Kant's thought immeasurably by directing the sharp scalpel of his analysis to the realm of the "inner experience."[37]

Kant and Rousseau discovered the nature, and therefore the dignity, of every man in a manner analogous to Newton's discovery of the whole universe. As Newton through outer experience discovered the law of the universe, Kant and Rousseau through inner experience, marked out the law ruling the interior life of man, i.e., his autonomy or "freedom," man as self-legislating and self-creating, and thus legislating and creating for all men as persons and ends in themselves. This vision still dominates the modern mind. The vision moves like those of Sartre and Nietzsche, in the opposite direction to Kant's and Rousseau's, namely, to despise the large number of men who, in bad faith and weakly huddling together, fail to exercise their freedom or even admit that they have it. Certainly, to discern the concrete form which this freedom takes in the life of the ordinary man, to see to what extent and in what way he creates himself, is extraordinarily difficult. Much of the research in contemporary behavioral sciences and much of contemporary art attempts this discernment of spirits, yielding a picture of man and his self-creation more fleshed-out and more pessimistic than that of Kant and Rousseau. Nevertheless reverence for and love of this freedom, be it ever so tiny a spark, engenders the concrete ethics of the modern mind. It is what one respects unconditionally in a man. It is what one feels responsible to create and let grow in oneself and in others.

The modern mind, therefore, sees man and his life, human good and human evil, by focusing principally upon: (1) what is revealed in his experience in this world; (2) as the experience would be even if there were no God; (3) as it is shaped, or can be shaped, by man's technological power; (4) as it occurs in the lives of ordinary men and (5) as it is created by the unique self of the man, by his ongoing self-creation or freedom that is "I," by the creative interaction with "Thou."

The five elements, artificially abstracted and crudely expressed as they are above, operate, not as premises of explicit reasoning, but as hidden principles energizing and directing the reach and grasp of the modern mind. They have brought about well-known shifts in moral sensitivity from medieval to modern times, sensitivity, for example, to torture, freedom of speech, the sexual pleasure of married couples, war (what pontiff before the twentieth century cried, "No more war!"?) They have brought about new moral concerns and achievement, which, though they fall far short of what should be, go far beyond anything in the same area in medieval times: the rehabilitation of alcoholics, drug addicts, deaf, dumb and blind, stroke victims, etc.; the easing of emotional disturbance through psychiatry, psychology and counselling; the improvement of the labor and leisure of the working class; organized care for the aged, the sick poor, the unemployed and their families; assurance for the accused of just treatment by police and courts; the combating of racial and religious prejudices; economic aid for developing nations, etc. This is not evidence that the modern mind is more moral than the classical, and the question is an idle one. But these and other examples of new moral sensitivity and action illustrate the single eye of modern man: his resolute focus upon the worldly experience of the individual, his refusal, or inability, to look elsewhere so as to belittle the importance of that experience, his sense of responsibility for making and remaking his experience and for helping the individual to do the same.

The focus makes clear why the modern mind sees vividly and reacts strongly to the experience of persons going knowingly to death in the war zone or on death row. It makes clear why for it there is no comparison between a fetus for which there is no sign of experience and a baby already in the process of experientially developing its unique personality and humanness in reaction to the persons around it.[38] There is, without doubt, a problem of "drawing the line" to define the point where the experiential self-creation begins. The modern mind neglects the problem and will have to face it some day. But to say there is a problem of drawing the exact line is not to say that there is a problem of indicating times when the reality is evidently on one side of the line or the other. The same problem is faced and responsibly met by both classical and modern mentalities in determining when a human person becomes a corpse, especially in the necessity of transplanting organs before it is too late.

The focus of a "mentality," be it classical or modern, is never intellectual insight alone, but involves will, emotions, imagination, language etc., and, therefore, multiplies the difficulty of debate or dialogue. Abstractly speaking, one can agree to define any word in any way. But a word like "humanity," for example, stands for so much concrete involvement of the whole person of one mentality, that he cannot use it meaningfully in the sense of a person having the other mentality and cannot understand what he is saying. But if one avoids loaded terminology, perhaps an anti-abortionist could come to some understanding of what the modern focus, sketched in the five elements listed above, sees when confronted with the death of the fetus, whether it be by miscarriage or abortion. The reaction will usually be at least a little sad. There might have been a unique person, but there never will be. The reaction will often be intensely sad. These parents wanted the child to be born and live with them in love; the child would have been fortunate in life and love; the common creation of the parents had progressed this far only to come to naught. Or the reaction can be one of moral anger or disgust: the child did not come to be only because a child was not wanted.

But in no case can the modern mentality react to the death of a fetus as it does to the death of a human person. To choose examples from the newspapers: the death of Dwight Eisenhower or John Kennedy, of a neighbor's son in Vietnam, of a young couple in a head-on collision, of a drug addict hanging himself in prison. The reaction can range from acceptance and grateful, admiring farewell to a numb refusal to admit that it happened. But it has little in common with one's reaction, painful though it may be, to the death of a fetus.

If the above analysis of the modern mind and its necessary view of abortion were correct, what would follow? At least two practical conclusions. The position of abortionists in our society could be seen as an inseparable component of a total outlook which is held by many people and likely to be with us for some time. There is no reason to doubt that people who have this outlook share universal human weaknesses and, like the rest of us, will show themselves at times hypocritical, superficial, inconsistent, selfish and choosing the easy way out. But their position on abortion arises organically out of their strength—a responsible, intelligent, moral synthesis that has served mankind well, whatever its limitations and drawbacks. The laws of the nation should treat these men with their views as a mature segment of a pluralistic society. The law should not prohibit their carrying out their basic moral convictions.

The second practical conclusion could be drawn by certain Christians, who find they have difficulties holding consistently to any moral position on abortion. A Catholic internist, knowledgeable in traditional Catholic morality, told me that when the treatment required for an organ involves abortion, he refers the patient to a Jewish colleague. A religious superior, who has never publicly endorsed abortion, phoned recently for information to aid a young woman in obtaining an abortion. Would either have acted this way if they believed that abortion is murder? And yet they publicly speak and act as if it were. I would suggest that many Christians of the present historical juncture are ethically schizophrenic. They have both mentalities, classical and modern, and are torn between them. They continually compromise. Abortion is far from being the only question where this occurs. They welcome much of contemporary insight, abandoning classical theses on the intrinsic evil of contraception, on the superiority of Christian celibacy to Christian marriage, on the necessity of "restoring the order of justice" by capital punishment, on the acceptability of torture, on the value of Latin in the liturgy, on restrictions to freedom of religion, etc. They often do not see that they have not changed their opinion each time on the merits of the particular question taken in isolation, but that in changing their minds they are each time acting out of and nurturing a new mentality, whose spirit moves them ever toward new stances on other questions such as abortion. Recognizing the new mentality as a whole for what it is may aid them to decide whether to peacefully accept it as a whole or to resolutely reject it as a whole. A good Christian knows it is not prudent to put new wine in old bottles.

6 SIN

The innumerable changes going on in the American Catholic Church present at first glance a scene of confusion and diversity. On closer scrutiny, however, many changes are seen to proceed from currents beneath the surface. One witnesses, for example, a decline in the reception of the Sacrament of Penance, a changing attitude toward extramarital sexuality, a move toward more general confessions, and a mounting rage in young people directed against institutions: the "Church," the military-industrial complex, the administration of a university. There is, I suggest, a deeper undercurrent that carries along the four surface developments, namely, a metamorphosis of the Catholic sense of sin. I would like to try to delineate the entire phenomenon.

The decline in the number of confessions is thought-provoking inasmuch as it is taking place among actively religious people. In parishes or on campuses where the number of communions remains steady or rises, the number of confessions is decreasing sharply. Priests and religious go less and less often to the Sacrament of Penance, some not even once a year.

A parallel change is the diminishing seriousness with which actively religious people consider sexual behavior outside of marriage. The principle, held generally by moral theologians and ably popularized in books like Gerald Kelly's *Modern Youth and Chastity*, that any sexual pleasure, directly willed or consented to outside of marriage, is a mortal sin, receives decreasing acceptance.[1] Many younger Catholics have never heard of it. When they do, they cannot believe the speaker is serious. Actual sexual practice is hard to gauge, but there are signs throughout the country that sexual enjoyment of films and books, masturbation, making out, and even intercourse are being combined with a life on the whole genuinely moral and religious.

Both changes, "good Catholics" seeing less good in frequent confessions and less evil in extramarital sex, are complex phenomena, undoubtedly due to many different causes. One cause is the current moral re-evaluation of sexuality, accelerated by public and private dissent from *Humanae Vitae*. The dissent, motivated by the practical needs of married people, was justified ethically by the principle that deliberately chosen sexual activity need not always be open to procreation. The principle is opposed to that of the classic natural law principle on the basis of which not only any use of contraception in marriage, but also any deliberate sex outside of marriage was prohibited. So far as I know, the theologians who rejected the natural law principle in order to permit contraception have found no convincing principle to replace it and prohibit all extramarital sexual behavior. Similarly, the classic principle that any sexual offense is an objectively grave matter constituting a mortal sin is losing credibility if one can judge by some of the latest theories of theologians and the practice of the faithful.

However, beneath the same two phenomena regarding confession and extramarital sex, there lies a more widespread development, a metamorphosis of the sense of mortal sin. The metamorphosis itself is, again, a complex thing. One pole of mortal sin is man; it is his decision to reject God. Catholics are finding it difficult to believe that a man can decisively reject God (or any other person, for that matter) by the ordinary type of decision, deliberate and firm though it may be, with which he makes everyday choices. Man is not so built as to be able to discard or take on so easily a real, interior commitment to a person. All the more difficult to believe is that the remainder of the person's decisions will consistently reflect loyalty to the same person. It is still more difficult, as John Glaser recalled in *Theological Studies*, when the individual is seen as decisively rejecting the other person (God) every Friday night, and turning back to Him decisively every Saturday afternoon or Sunday morning before Mass.[2] Modern theories, such as those which are found in depth pyschology or in the philosophy of the basic option, scientifically call into question this traditional interpretation of mortal sin. Robert O'Neill and Michael Donovan, in *Sexuality and Moral Responsibility*, published last year by Corpus Books, did not hesitate to affirm that it is "psychologically impossible" for there to be "any single action that a person could perform which would be sufficient to warrant condemnation."[3] The reason is the nature of human freedom: "man cannot totally commit himself in any one personal act."[4] "Only throughout a more or less lengthy course of action (conceivably only in a lifetime) can a man freely express what is his ultimate and innermost self in a truly definitive way."[5]

Rather than discussing this subjective side of mortal sin, human freedom, I would like to consider the objective side: what a man does that merits eternal death and separation from God. Here, too, a change is in process. In the traditional interpretation of this aspect of mortal sin, it is the grave evil of certain external acts which, if they are willed with sufficient reflection and full consent, merits the catastrophic punishment. In his *Law of Christ*, Bernard Häring discusses the problem of the distinction between mortal and venial sin, the speculative problem that "persistently plagues all theologians."[6] Häring holds, and interprets much of the tradition as holding, that the distinction lies fundamentally in what I have called the subjective side: a mortal sin is any fully free and basic decision chosen against God's law, no matter what the content of the law may be. But Häring also insists, with one of his characteristic attempts to maintain both conflicting positions, that "we surely may not conclude" that acts are not distinguished as mortal or venial sins, i.e., according to the objective "greatness" or "smallness" of the matter.[7]

At least since the Irish penitentials of the seventh century, the faithful have been told that there is a list of actions which are such that, if done even once with normal deliberation and free choice, the agent merits and receives separation from God and, unless he repents and turns to His mercy, eternal separation and misery. I would like to suggest in the remainder of this chapter how this traditional understanding of the objective determination of serious sin is being replaced by another in the current experience and reflection of the American Church.

Traditional understanding has colored the lives of sincere Catholics as much, if not more than the lives of apathetic ones. The generous adolescent found a major test of his generosity to Christ in refraining from self-abuse. It was often the supreme test: mortal sin was such a grave affront to Christ that other forms of generosity were suspect as long as one continued to commit that sin. Here he concentrated his religious aspirations, emotional forces and volitive energy. On failing the test he experienced the greatest guilt and shame.

Many religious and priests asked themselves over and over again—some tormentedly, some peacefully—to what extent they had yielded to temptations to impurity. They did not underestimate the responsibilities of charity and justice, but their humility and contrition before God was often dominated by the memory of sexual weaknesses. This was not due to an obsession with sex, but to a sense of mortal sin. For one trying to love God, what could be more humiliating and regrettable than to have deliberately risked mortal sin or even committed it!

Traditional understanding marked the life of laymen. Married people stayed away from Communion for years because they practiced contraception or lived in an invalid marriage. On the other hand, reconciliation with God in the Sacrament of Penance took the form for many of an accusation of missing Mass or eating meat on Friday since these automatically constituted grave matters.

Essential to the sense of mortal sin which had such an effect on the lives of sincere Catholics was the understanding of mortal sin as the deliberate choice of a single, specified action. For better or worse—probably for both—Catholics are losing this understanding of mortal sin. The change is better understood when seen as part of the more widespread evolution of moral sensibility going on among Americans of the latter half of the twentieth century, whether or not they be religious people. One could illustrate the new sensibility with the horror many Americans felt on reading a newspaper story some time ago. A girl of college age in a far Western state had gone to a dance and did not return at 1 A.M., the hour her parents had set as a curfew. When she came home four hours later, she told her parents that she had been intimate with an Air Force officer, and she retired to sleep. When she got up, her father handed her a pistol and took her and her pet dog into the backyard. He ordered her, as a punishment, to shoot her "Beauty." She hesitated, then put the revolver to her head and killed herself.

Hopefully, few readers presumed to judge the motives and guilt, if any, of the father. But what he did assuredly sickened most Americans who read the story. It would not, I believe, have done so to most Americans of the nineteenth century or the early part of this century. Because American Catholics are undergoing the same change of sensibility as their countrymen, the old understanding of sin can shock and sicken them, if they are still aware of it. After all, they had accepted, probably from religion class or a sermon or a retreat talk, that if the girl had done what she did with knowledge of its grave sinfulness and with full consent of the will, and if she had died shortly after in an auto accident without having repented, God would have sent her straight to hell for eternity. God's punishment would be far worse than that of her human father's. God *Himself* would blow *her* brains out. Whether or not any draw such a macabre analogy, more and more Catholics find it impossible to believe that in God's eyes a single act of this sort merits the death penalty.

To make sweeping statements about shifts of national sensibility and Catholic religious attitudes may well be foolhardy. But to try to understand our whirling times, we have no other choice. Flannery O'Connor described the present age as an age of tenderness. The description is accurate, I believe. We are passing from a climate of prevailing justice to one of prevailing tenderness. Nor is the tenderness as soft and sentimental as Miss O'Connor seemed to think. The tender mind recoils at a father whose response to the single offense of his child was a harsh, heart-rending punishment. But the same tender mind would follow up with tough questions of love: could not the father have reacted in a dozen ways far more conducive to helping the girl and, among other things, which might have prevented her from making the same mistake again?

"Vindictive justice," the restoring of justice by punishment commensurate with the crime, is not a bad word, but it does not characterize our moral sensibility the way it did that of the men of the Middle Ages.

Man at that time is convinced that right is absolutely fixed and certain. Justice should prosecute the unjust everywhere and to the end. Reparation and retribution have to be extreme, and assume the character of revenge.

. . . .

Torture and executions are enjoyed by the spectators like an entertainment at a fair. The citizens of Mons bought a brigand, at far too high a price, for the pleasure of seeing him quartered, "at which the people rejoiced more than if a new holy body had risen from the dead." The people of Bruges in 1488, during the captivity of Maximilian, king of the Romans, cannot get their fill of seeing the tortures inflicted, on a high platform in the middle of the market-place, on the magistrates suspected of treason. The unfortunates are refused the deathblow which they implore, that the people may feast again upon their torments.[8]

The sense of vindictive justice and the fitness of extreme punishments did not wane with the Middle Ages. When Maryland's 246-year-old blasphemy law was judged unconstitutional, Circuit Judge Edward O. Weant, Jr. traced the history of blasphemy laws back to 1656 in England, when the penalty for a first offense was that "a hole be bored in the tongue." Someone committed a second offense was liable to be "stigmatized by burning the single letter B on the forehead," while someone committing a third offense was "sentenced to death without benefit of clergy."[9]

A desire for vindictive justice and extreme punishment is

not totally absent from our time. Popular reaction to the assassins of national leaders or disrupters of public order, for example, often takes the form of insistence on the judicial sentences "they deserve." But we react this way, it would seem, only when carried away with anger or fear. When we try to discuss the matter more calmly and objectively, we justify penalties by what the common good and the good of the individual demand. It is rare today that a public proponent of capital punishment will argue that a murderer *deserves* death.

What determines tender moral sensibility in giving out penalties could aptly receive the classical term of "distributive justice," the right and duty of authority to act for the good of the community. It could also receive the term of "love" in its classical and contemporary sense of willing the good of another. Having such a moral sensibility, one has doubts about whether the death penalty should be exacted for even the most heinous crimes. One does not even think of it for acts such as fornication. How then could one envisage God as acting in that way?

The difficulty, however, goes deeper. The only God contemporary man can believe in is one who loves him, one-to-one, I-to-Thou. Trying to understand God, he has to use analogies. He cannot imagine God as a judge or king loving His people effectively, but at a distance. He can only envisage a divine father, a divine husband, a divine lover. The analogy itself is not new, but rather that it dominates his representation of God.

That is why Catholics who take their faith seriously, more so than the indifferent Catholics, are resisting the traditional concept of mortal sin. It is true that in this concept the evil and just deserts of mortal sin do not come from the gravity of the action itself, but from its being a transgression of the divine law and, therefore, an offense against the Divine Majesty. But if one regards God purely as a loving father or husband, there is no place for so juridical a concept. Juridical relationships are good and necessary, but do not belong between father and son. Could a modern father and daughter have the understanding that any serious act of disobedience

constituted her rejection of her home and family and, therefore, would merit her immediate eviction? The application
of the analogy to the obligation of Sunday Mass illustrates
how ludicrous the old notion seems today. Would a husband
make it clear that if his wife refused to show up for Sunday
dinner, it would constitute a mortal offense against him and
she should leave the house immediately unless she apolo-
gized? The traditional concept itself is far from ludicrous,
but, transposed and inserted into today's tender view of God
and man, it is out of place.

Incidentally, the view of God principally as one-to-one
lover, on the analogy of the best kind of father or husband,
explains also the shift of understanding of mortal sin to its
subjective side. The normal freedom involved in deciding an
important action (like buying a house) can, in the juridical
order, suffice to constitute responsibility for treason or per-
jury or other crimes. It would never suffice, in the eyes of
the lover or in its psychological reality, to constitute a decisive rejection of the lover by the beloved. The "basic option"
theory, offering a metaphysical support for the above psychological truth, may perhaps have rendered a disservice by ob-
scuring the fact that no metaphysical support is needed in
order to recognize this commonplace of interpersonal relationships.

On the other hand, those of us who are happily shedding
the old sense of sin cannot get away with it that easily. We
must have a new sense of sin. An excellent spiritual counselor
I know reminds people discouraged by their faults that being
a sinner does not prevent one from being a Christian. On
the contrary, one cannot be a Christian unless one is a sinner.
From exegetes and theologians to sign-painters of roads and
store-fronts, all Christians believe the same Good News:
Jesus saves. He saves us from our sins. "If we say we have
no sin, we deceive ourselves, and the truth is not in us. If
we confess our sins, He is faithful and just, and will forgive
our sins and cleanse us from all unrighteousness. If we say
we have not sinned, we make Him a liar, and His Word is
not in us."[10] Some of the oldest and newest phrases of the

Eucharistic liturgy express the Christian's abiding sense of sin.

Faith in Jesus Christ is, therefore, faith in the possibility and actuality of one's own sins. A sense of sin permeates any authentically Christian experience. Central to Christian life is the fear of the Lord, fear of sinning gravely against Him and of receiving one's deserts. Central, too, is guilt and sorrow at having sinned seriously. Central is grateful, peaceful belief in His forgiveness of one's sins.

Another abiding fact of Christian experience is that the Christian does not always feel to the same degree fear or contrition or trust in forgiveness, for he finds that not all his sins are equally grave. Some are petty, humbling and unpretty, but do not require serious concern. Some are so bad as to constitute the greatest evil a Christian's faith meets in human life. Between the two extremes lies a spectrum of sins of varying gravity. The contemporary Christian does not share the concern of the Irish monks and subsequent moralist to grade kinds of sin so that appropriate penances may be given. But in facing evil unflinchingly, his human experience and Christian faith disclose that there are things he should fear doing more than others and for which, if he has done them, he should grieve more. The guilt he knows he has for certain actions make God's forgiveness more urgent and more surprising. Any new sense of sin, therefore, must include a way of measuring the gravity of sin.

We have discussed above the norm of positive obligation in contemporary moral thinking: to what extent is the action loving? That is, to what extent does it bring about good consequences in human experience? It is evident, though perhaps not often reflected upon, that the positive norm for obligation generates a corresponding negative norm for evaluating sin. A sin will be grave to the extent that it is a failure to love, i.e., a responsibility for the presence of bad consequences, or the absence of good consequences, in human experience. In brief, a sin will be grave to the extent that it hurts, or fails to help, someone, myself or another.

Even those who know the positive norm for obligation, love, may perhaps not appreciate how the negative norm operates. Let me briefly offer two concrete illustrations before discussing some implications the norm has for the sense of sin. A businessman once told me that several years ago he had discovered that his wife was having an affair. After talking it over with his repentant wife, he came to the conclusion that, as he put it, he had sinned more than she. It was because he had neglected her, left her in loneliness, not shared her feelings and met her needs, that she turned to another man, much to her pain and shame. He did not excuse her; he blamed himself more. Being no intellectual, he would have been surprised to know that his reaction typified the new moral thinking on sin.

A certain woman had been refusing to have intercourse with her husband. He consulted priests and, on their authority, informed his wife that she was sinning gravely in refusing him his rights. Reluctantly she agreed, but gradually came to see that the main cause of harm to her marriage was her negative attitude toward sex, her own frigidity and that she was sinning more gravely as a wife in not trying to do anything about these psychological blocks.

The two examples illustrate how the Christian who uses the new norm to evaluate the gravity of his sins comes to a different kind of grave sin than formerly. Most evidently, they are rarely individual acts. Adultery and the refusal to grant marital rights are single actions taking place at certain times. Neglect of a wife's personal needs and the refusal to do anything about one's psychological problems cannot be pinned down to single acts. Yet, characteristically, the latter worked greater harm, blocked greater good, and thus constituted a greater failure to love. For one having the new sense of sin they call for greater remorse and contrition.

The new kind of grave sin has other properties. Just as it rarely can be pinned down to a single act, it usually occurs only over a period of time. To harm one's wife seriously by neglect is not a matter of a day. One is not responsible for psychological hangups simply because one did not try to get professional counsel last Friday evening. Grave sins usually take place only over a period of time because in everyday life it generally takes time to seriously hurt a person. What is perhaps the gravest sin of the white American, that we have branded black souls with shame and alienation, took us decades. The loneliness and despair of the aged can result only from long apathy on the part of their children. There are exceptions. A single betrayal of a confidence or telling of a lie can ruin another's career and mar the remaining years of a life. But generally speaking—perhaps because we prefer our viciousness to remain hidden from ourselves and others —the way we choose to hurt people seriously, or to refuse them badly-needed help, takes the form of numerous small decisions over a period of time.

Finally, grave sins of the new kind are usually sins of omission. All the examples given above do not consist of doing something, but in a *failure* to do something, e.g., to spend time with one's wife, to consult a marriage counsellor, to sell a house to a black or to offer him a job, to visit a senile mother. Ogden Nash favored sins of commission: "No, you never get any fun/ out of the things you haven't done." Most men, however, favor sins of omission—again, perhaps, because we like to keep our sins inconspicuous, or perhaps because we incline to a less strenuous and less dangerous type of sinning. It is not because we wish to do less harm. By our sins of omission, we easily outdistance the active sinner. The human damage resulting in our cities because we could have helped, but chose not to help, for example, the misery in the lives of addicts, those stricken with certain diseases, slumdwellers, the mentally retarded, long term prisoners, etc., far eclipse in evil the work of the murderer or pervert, thief or embezzler.

Our Lord seems to have the new as well as the old sense of sin. The sin whose gravity He underscores is often not a single act, but failure to act over a period of time. The description of the last judgment in Matthew 25 and the parable of the Good Samaritan are good examples.

The growing trend toward general confession is due, in part, to the new sense of grave sin. As he is about to take part in the Eucharistic sacrifice and meal, the Christian has always felt his sinfulness and still does. In recent centuries the Christian conscious of grievous sins would receive the

Sacrament of Penance after detailing to the confessor the number and species of the actions by which he had sinned grievously in order to receive God's forgiveness and approach the Eucharistic table. But, as has been seen, the contemporary Christian is ceasing to see his grievous sins in the individual actions he has performed. Perhaps, even more than earlier Christians, he is weighed down by his sins. But he sees them in his continuing failure to act lovingly in innumerable situations over a period of time. He can best express sins like this by general statements. "I did not concern myself with the troubles of a friend." "I have not tried to listen to my teenage children." "I have not concerned myself with those dying in Vietnam."

The new sense of sin is responsible, too, for the white anger, bordering on desperation, of younger Christians who resort to sit-ins, the destruction of files and disruption of lectures, etc. If my contacts are typical, it is more the evil they incredulously see going on which rouses them to action rather than any good they hope for by their efforts. The evil that angers them most is the corruption of the self-righteous establishment, i.e., its failure over the years to help the blacks out of the ghettos, to stop the deaths in Vietnam, to make theology courses relevant, to stop the development of biological and chemical instruments of war, and so on. I suspect that the use of obscenities is a maddened way of telling the establishment that they see through the whitewash to the inner filth. That these young Christians take extreme, apparently self-defeating steps, e.g., bringing on themselves years in prison, comes, I believe, from a fear of sharing the sin of the establishment, the worst sin there is: to continue to stand by and permit what one way or another brings needless suffering to human beings. A young Jesuit explained his looting of a Dow Chemical office: "I'd been knowing for a long time what was going on. I just couldn't stand it any more. I had passed the point of tolerance." One can question to what extent the judgments of these young Christians are factually justified. There is no question that they share, authentically and profoundly, the contemporary sense of sin.

Christian faith, hope and charity are positive things and

motor a positive life of achievement and service, peace, fellowship and joy. But they engender, too, a sensitivity to evil and a cold eye for detecting the truly grave evils permitted in the drama of human life. The new understanding of sin does not determine by categories the gravity of sin. Who is worse? The homosexual, the nagging wife, the rebellious adolescent, the lazy priest, the gossip, the puritanical nun? There is no answer. Each Christian must evaluate for himself the harm he does or permits to occur. If he does so honestly and perceptively, the new sense of sin will bring him to his knees with the sight of his sinfulness and make him cry out as loud as any Christian of any time, "Lord, be merciful to me a sinner!"

7 BECOMING FREE

There is a theological question that students often raise today. The question is not an easy one; it unsettles many Christian educators. The students raise the question not only by talking theology, but by doing things. Let me give some examples from my experiences a short while ago as professor and prefect at Fordham University.

The freshmen on my corridor did not bother to conceal the evidence that they drank in their rooms. This was forbidden by the regulations and punishable by expulsion. On several evenings one freshman had come back to the dorm noisily drunk. Several sodalists to whom I was giving a closed retreat told me they had picketed my Provincial and my Archbishop. A freshman boarder had fired off a personally abusive letter to the dean of men. A student told me he had decided not to believe in God.

Another student got nothing out of Holy Communion and couldn't see what he was supposed to get out of it. He had stopped going to Communion. When his parents noted this, he said simply: "I've discussed it with a priest." He meant me. I asked a junior why he did not come to philosophy class. He said he was reading Kant and Hegel by himself and got more out of it that way. A senior and his girl had an apartment of their own in New Jersey. He worked forty hours a week to pay for the apartment and to send the girl through college. With work and commuting, he didn't get to many classes. A former seminarian felt that the sexual prohibitions he once was taught could not apply to him since he truly loved. A bright freshman in the dormitory did no studying, but read the complete works of Carl Jung. A few questions revealed that he understood little of what he read. Many of the boarders were agitating for the right to invite girls to their rooms.

Fordham has since lifted the ban on alcohol and girls in the boarders' rooms, but now faces drugs and demonstrations, occupation of the President's office, harassment of military recruitment, etc. One of the coeds registered for courses this year wearing above the waist only a transparent blouse.

Such incidents are, of course, typical of the modern campus. They have one thing in common: the student moves toward freedom. In ever-new ways, he wants to be free from the directives of those whose role is to direct him. He wants to do what he wants. How should I, a Christian educator, react?

One sense of the question is not theological, but practical. What should I do? Should I tolerate marihuana in the music room? Should I let my students determine how they learn philosophy? Should I encourage sodalists to picket Church authorities? Should I ignore topless dresses?

But behind the practical question, "What should I do?" is another question, one that surprises and perplexes me: "How should I feel?" Should I be glad? Should I be sad but resigned? Should I be tolerant and hopeful? How should I react interiorly, affectively?

The men and women who are involved with the contemporary college student vary greatly in their affective value response to the tidal movement toward liberties on campus. One prefect at Fordham was disturbed at the trend. As a matter of fact, he accorded his charges many new liberties, but he did so simply because he had to: he saw no alternative. The things which depressed him most were not the new liberties, but the attitudes of the students seeking them. As the prefect saw it, the students had turned their backs on authority, tradition and established principles of conduct, and feverishly craved freedom for freedom's sake. The attitude was immature, irresponsible, anarchic. The best the prefect could hope for was that if he went along with the trend they would grow out of it.

Another prefect felt nothing but uncontained joy at the

new movement. He exulted every time a new restraint fell. All restraints were bad, fit only for children.

The two moods illustrate the extremes of a wide spectrum of reactions that educators experience in the face of the drive of students for liberties. Though the reactions are interior, their force is felt; they cannot fail to influence the educator's actions. Moreover the interior reactions themselves cannot stay hidden. They become evident to the student and affect him negatively or positively. Whether I rejoice at the prospect of a new freedom or am fearful of it can make a greater impact on the student than whether I permit or refuse to permit it. The impact the interior reactions of the educator make on the students plays no small part in the educative force exercised by the college.

It is therefore worth asking: How should I, the educator, react interiorly to the movement toward new liberties? The question goes deeper than the level of feelings. It probes an even more interior reaction, a basic value judgment. The basic value judgment concerns the new liberties, of course, but, more fundamentally, man himself and what a man should be. The question looks for a basic vision of man and where his greatness lies. Our colleges are, above all, places where a boy or girl grows toward being a man or woman. A fundamental reason why the interior reactions of college educators to the new liberties differ widely is that they have different basic judgments, different visions of their goal, of what a man or woman should be, of where their greatness lies.

This is the theological question the Christian educator faces. What is the true and relevant vision of man today? The vision must not just be true; it must be native to the *Zeitgeist*, to the mind and experience of men of our times. The educator himself cannot share authentically a Hellenic or medieval vision. He is not an Athenian of the fourth century B.C., or a Parisian of the thirteenth century. More importantly, his vision of men cannot fail to be evident to his students. It must be one that they can share.

What is a man, as we of the last third of the twentieth century see him? First of all, there are certain things he is not. Man, in his greatness, in what makes being a man worth-while, is not a rebel. We do not rejoice in seeing a man whose most fundamental posture is gazing upward and shaking his fist. First, if he is a man, there is no one to gaze upward at, not even God. God and His Kingdom are within him. Secondly, if he is truly a man, he does not take authority seriously enough to bother rebelling against it, when he can possibly avoid the effort. He encounters authority fairly far down the road. With Aristotle and Thomas and Luther, he finds it has a use, *usus politicus legis.* He uses it when useful. Otherwise he drops it and turns to more interesting matters. Which means that he usually obeys better and more often than those who make an issue of authority.

On the other hand, man in his greatness, in what makes man worthwhile, is not a conformer. A man who puts the final meaning of his life into obedience to the law is a sad sight. A man who puts the final meaning of his life in any external way of life may well not be a sad sight, but he is living on the surface. The same may be said of a man who puts the final, central meaning of his life into meeting obligations and respecting the rights of others, or in serving some cause, or in living according to human nature. If his gaze goes no deeper than that he, too, is living on the surface. The basic attitude of all these men is conformity to something outside their person. They have not yet reached the level where a man is finally a man. Their vision of man may well be true as far as it goes, but it is superficial.

It is also not relevant to our times. It is amusing to hear educators summon students to be "responsible" and "committed." The educators have taken strong language from the contemporary jargon, but the ones I am thinking of use it in an old-fashioned sense. By "responsible" they mean meeting one's obligations. By "committed" they mean being dedicated to some cause. And so what they mean by these words is the opposite of what the words mean today. They mean some kind of conformity of the man to something outside him. The vision they have of man is not contemporary, relevant, nor, I submit, does it get to the heart of the matter.

In an analogous manner, some educators summon contem-

porary youth to meet this or that challenge. The implication
is that part of man's greatness lies in meeting challenges.
But our young men do not see this vision. They reply: "So
I'm challenged. What else is new?" One meets a challenge
because one wants to prove something. But to whom do I
want to prove anything? I am not denying that contemporary
youth, like all youth, does want to prove itself. But they
would see it, I think, as their weakness, not their strength.
Or rather, what they want to prove most of all is that they
don't want to prove anything to anybody.

What, then, is man as we of the last third of the twentieth
century see him? Where lies his greatness? Not in rebellion
against some authority that threatens or weighs upon him.
Not in conformity to anything outside him, whether it be
laws or patterns of behavior or duties or natures or causes
or challenges. At times he must rebel, and at times he must
conform. But his greatness lies in something deeper, which
dictates *when* he should rebel and *when* he should conform.
Since 1785, philosophers have known that man's greatness
lies in himself, in the conscious core of himself.[1] It lies in
the center of the core, in his freedom. Here he is subject
to no authority, and there is no place for conformity to anything outside him. Except for the empirical positivists,
every serious philosopher who wrote after 1785 knew this
and underlined it. And the philosophers were, as usual, simply
articulating the experience and the insight of the people of
their time—what William James calls philosophy, "our more
or less dumb sense of what life honestly and deeply means."
And so, whether we like it or not, we see today man's greatness in his freedom. Only the Don Quixotes and the Miniver
Cheevys hope to wind back history.

What is the freedom in which man's greatness lies? It is
not civil freedom, academic freedom, freedom of conscience.
These and other freedoms flow from a more radical freedom
that is man when he is truly a man. A man who is truly a
man is one who—and the one and only one on earth who—
can completely be himself, take possession of himself, determine himself. On this earth, only man wants something
simply because he wants it. He wants it simply because he

wants to be, and wants to be wanting this object. The wanting is the man. Another way of saying it is: a man is one whose reality is his making of himself from the core outward. He is the making. A hand cannot close on itself. It meets itself and must stop. Man closes on himself, is the closing on himself, is the self-possession, the self-creation, the freedom.

The vision may sound abstract and speculative. It is. But it is the vision, I submit, that drives our contemporaries, whether they be students or not, to protest Harlem or Vietnam or St. John's. We may disagree with their conclusions, but we must share the driving vision. Harlem life is unpardonable because the life can soak slowly through a man and rot his core of freedom. Torture of a war prisoner is unpardonable, because it can do the same thing in a few hours. A university scandalizes us if it appears to neglect the most important thing on campus. The most important thing on campus is not that people be kept from saying bad things or doing bad things—not even that people be helped to say good things and do good things. The most important thing on campus is that people be helped to grow in freedom, inner freedom, to get the confidence and zest and strength to determine themselves and their lives, to make themselves at the core and, working organically outward, make their lives.

By the fact that the educator is a Christian, the philosophical vision receives new light. There is the "freedom of the Christian man," a freedom God's Word proclaims and gives. One might listen to Paul, for example.

What our unbelieving contemporaries worship as unknown, this we proclaim to them. The God who made the world and everything in it, will set creation itself free from its bondage of decay and give it the glorious freedom of the children of God. This is the freedom for which Christ has freed us. So stand firm in it and do not get under a yoke of slavery again. For you, brothers, have been called to freedom. Where is this freedom? Wherever the Spirit of the Lord is, there is freedom. From the Spirit of the Lord comes to us the freedom to remove the veil, to re-

flect the glory of the Lord on our unveiled faces, to be
changed into His likeness, from one degree of glory to
another.[2]

What is the growing glory the Spirit gives us, the growing
likeness to the Lord? Today's faith seeking today's understanding would think that it is our growing freedom at the
core of our being. This is how we grow in glorious likeness
to God.

For God is the unbound, the lawless One. What could
bind Him, arch and original breath? What law could He
obey? He knows no rules. He simply is what He is: one,
sovereign, untrampled act of love. This is His very reality,
His whole reality. He is freedom. Nothing can compel or
awe or swerve Him in His love. By His one supremely free
act of love He makes Himself and all that is. Perhaps that
is why the Bible refers to God as a lion or a bull, Christ, the
tiger!

He makes man in His image, and gives him dominion over
every living thing that moves upon the earth. When man
falls enslaved to sin and law and death, God speaks to him
by His Son. He says to man: "You, I love you. Live with
Me. Be like Me. Be free."

For the Christian student, as a result, the Good News of
Christ accelerates his movement to freedom. The truth that
God wanted nothing for Himself but His own freedom, His
own free love, can encourage the student to want nothing
but that. The truth that God's glory is His freedom can in-
flame the student's desires. The truth that God with His
finger touched the young man afresh, with love called him
by name, gives him courage and confidence to try to grow
in the freedom for which Jesus Christ has freed him and
called him. The Christian educator, by the very fact that he
manifestly shares the vision, will aid the student to grow in
his Christian freedom.

In closing, let me recount three incidents of my year at
Fordham. They are not meant to illustrate techniques of education. But they can illustrate, I think, what I've been trying

to say of the vision of man's freedom, to be shared by the Christian educator and the Christian student.

I let the student mentioned above read his Kant and Hegel at home and not attend classes. I encouraged and rejoiced in his activity on his own. I only insisted that he show up regularly for oral quizzes. At the end of the semester I passed him, but gave him a low mark on the basis of the quizzes. Later he admitted this was fair; he was chagrined at his incomplete success in carrying out his project.

Only one freshman on my corridor had shown himself cocky and disrespectful. One evening, we organized a beer party. The freshman sat across from me and defiantly consumed vast quantities of the liquid. I made no objections until toward the end of the party (which went for six hours), when he began to get loud and repetitious. I said: "You'd better stop drinking. You're boring us." He filled up his glass again, but said: "If that's the case, I won't say anything more." Which he didn't until, on the way to bed, he said to me: "I'm sorry, Father." We've been on the best of terms ever since.

Would that the two incidents were typical of my pedagogical success at Fordham. Anyway, I feel that in both cases an exceptionally alive and mature student was trying to be a man and had a keen sense of man as free, as one who wants what he wants. Since I shared that sense, they were enabled and encouraged to express this freedom and get a taste of living it, and thus picked up momentum for more of the same in the future. On the other hand, being given free rein, both failed precisely in freedom; they failed, in part, to do what they wanted—in one case, to learn philosophy unaided; in the other, to drink and be entertaining. As I see it, they learned to love freedom more, but they also learned that freedom is not easy to grasp; that as a matter of fact they weren't so very free. They didn't fully want what they wanted; they were posing somewhat in their own eyes. The incidents are trivial but illustrate, I think, a significant point.

One final illustration. At the closing Mass of the sodality retreat, the sodalists expressed their intentions. One said:

"I'll probably be drafted this summer. I'm coming to think that the war in Vietnam is immoral. Please pray that I get the light and courage to decide whether I should refuse conscription." Another said: "I'll probably be drafted this summer. Please pray that I get the courage to fight well in Vietnam."

There was no polemic in this, no attempt to contradict or refute. The sodality had an atmosphere where freedom of speech and the difference of views were serenely accepted. Living with the sodalists I felt that the atmosphere arose from the theological vision I've been trying to describe. The most important thing for a man is not *what* he decides, but *that* he decides, not *what* he wants, but *that* he wants something—from the core of him outward. This is the freedom for which Christ has freed us and called us.

After the preceding pages appeared in *America*, the editors received a large number of letters, some of which they printed in their May 27th issue. My reply, appearing in the same issue, was as follows.[3]

A year ago, I wrote an article for *America* entitled "The Loyal Opposition in the Church."[4] Most of the negative criticism it drew was to the effect that I had given an absolute value to law, authority and the Christian's obligation to obey, and that I had thus downgraded the integrity and dignity of the individual.[5] My latest article has drawn the criticism that I have given an absolute value to the integrity and dignity of the individual and thus downgraded law, authority and the Christian's obligation to obey. It might help if some of my critics read both my articles.

Then again, I am not so sure it would. Even in reading my more recent article, the majority of my critics (both those whose letters were printed by *America* and others who have written or spoken to me) have attributed to me something I neither said nor meant. By the freedom I extolled, they understood a freedom of a practical sort: that the student be allowed, and even encouraged, to act "as he pleases," "without restraint," "without direction," "irresponsibly." Now, first of all, both at the beginning and at the end of the article, I state that I am not discussing the practical question facing the educator: "What should I do? Should I tolerate drinking in the corridor, etc.?" The answer I give to the *theological* question I do discuss is a vision of freedom that, I say, is no practical strategy or technique, but "abstract and speculative." Thus one can share the vision and still disagree with the protest it inspires about Harlem or Vietnam or St. John's. Similarly, the interior reaction determined by the vision is distinct from the fact that the educator is, in fact, permitting or refusing the student some new freedom.

What I tried to sketch out for college educators was a vision "of their goal, of what man or woman should be, of where their greatness lies." Moreover, this greatness of man, at which he and the educator aim, lies "in himself, in the conscious core of himself." It is not, therefore, external freedoms, such as civil or academic, or freedom of conscience, but something interior: the very "wanting . . . self possession . . . self creation."

Being a goal to be realized progressively in man's interior life, the freedom I speak of cannot be identified with some kind of freedom in external conduct, much less with anything like license or irresponsibility in action. So far from excluding restraint is this freedom treasured by twentieth century man that Sartre could say, "Never were we so free as under the Nazis!"

Of course, whatever vision one has of man's final greatness, speculative and abstract though the vision be, it exercises enormous practical influence. The words of Chesterton, applauded by William James, apply here: the most practical question to put to a man is "What is your philosophy?" In my article (originally a talk given at Woodstock to an institute of college educators) I emphasize that it is the educator's basic vision of man that will determine his interior reactions to the prospect of new liberties on the practical level—witness the violence with which educators can take a position on matters as trivial as long hair or jeans. In this way, the vision of man as free would, I say, influence the action of educators and, becoming evident to the students, affect them. But I do not say that the vision of man as free should lead the educator to remove all restraints and cease all direction of the student.

On the contrary! I do not deal with the question at length, but I do indicate in passing that practical restraints are necessary for the man possessing or moving toward freedom. Thus I state that the man with the greatness I speak of is not a rebel, but recognizes the use of law and authority as expounded by Aristotle and Thomas and Luther and usually obeys better and more often than those who make an issue of authority.

Similarly when, in concluding, I try to illustrate the vision of man's freedom, in two of my three examples I reject the abuse of liberty by a student and criticize it—in one case by telling him to be silent, in the other by giving him low grades. The negative action of the educator was called for because "they failed in freedom," "they weren't so very free." From the standpoint of freedom, I come to the same practical conclusion as Fr. Shea and others: students often do what is not good and need supervision and direction. In the third example, also, the theological vision of freedom leads to restraint. The point of this example of a sodality retreat is that in an atmosphere dominated by the vision of freedom, the sodalists refrain from polemics, contradiction and argument; they limit their freedom of opinion among themselves.

In brief, the freedom I extol is not to be identified with a freedom in practice from all restraint and direction. As a matter of historical fact, the modern vision of freedom as the sole absolute has been abused rather to justify totalitarianism (e.g., the first governments of the French Revolution, Nazism, Marxism) than to justify anarchism.

Why then the misunderstanding? Why have some of my readers found in my article something I neither said nor meant? I am sure that the misunderstanding arose neither from hasty reading on their part nor from lack of intelligence or good will. I don't believe it arose from my own lack of clarity, though I have the uncomfortable feeling here of echoing the words of a Woodstock professor of yore. To all criticism and questions he replied: "It's objectively clear in my book."

In any case, the misunderstanding some of my critics have of what I said reflects rather a genuine difference of view on a deeper level. I have taken the trouble to document the misunderstanding precisely to draw attention to the site of real disagreement. The question is the theological one "of what a man or woman should be, of where their greatness lies." But it is not merely that my critics and I answer the question differently. The difference begins a step farther back. To this question they believe there are only two alternatives, two possible answers. Naturally, they have reasons for holding which alternative is true and which false. But the point is that they reduce all the answers to the question to one of the two alternatives they know, and on this basis judge whether it is true or false. I, on the contrary, with modern thought from Rousseau and Kant on, believe there is a third alternative.

What it comes to is this: to the question "What, in the last analysis, should a man be?" one answer is "free for freedom's sake," and it means that whatever impulse or whim or decision we follow is fine as we act it out. No philosopher or theologian has ever proposed this answer seriously. Even a hedonist knows one must choose carefully in order to avoid pain and gain maximum pleasure. But this sense of freedom is rightly considered one of the alternative answers because we all are tempted to live by it and at times do. Modern thinkers, however, as well as more traditional ones, agree in rejecting this answer as false.

There is a second alternative answer to the question "What should a man be?" It presents a heteronomous ideal for man. According to this answer, what a man should be, his greatness, lies in relating to something outside his conscious core, e.g., his nature, his purpose, God. Most pre-modern thinkers adopt this answer as true. Modern thinkers recognize it as an alternative answer. Some (like Nietzsche and Sartre) deem it false. Others (like Kant or Bonhoeffer) believe it to be true so long as it leaves place as well for the third alternative answer: man's moral autonomy, man come of age, man's absolute worth in freedom.

I tried to present one form of the third alternative: man's

sole absolute value and greatness lies in freedom for freedom's sake. One has to use the same formula as the first alternative and mean something different. To explain what I do mean and why it is true and important would be simply to repeat my article. What I want to point out now is that my critics seem never to suspect the possibility of a third answer. It is not that they examine the third alternative I offer and find it false. They simply cannot focus on any third alternative. The harsher critics reduce my answer to the first alternative of irresponsibility, etc. The kinder critics reduce it to an unclear form of the second.

It is indicative, it seems to me, that none of the critics deal directly with the issue that would decide whether the third alternative is true or false, namely, the issue "What *is* the absolute value and greatness of man?" Even in what strikes me as one of the more thoughtful letters, this fact stands out. For Fr. Rohan, it is enough that freedom must be directed to goodness. He does not discuss *what* is good. Might it not be freedom in a deeper sense? Fr. Roth rightly introduces the value of love. But *why* do I love the other? Might it not be that it is his striving for and growing in freedom that I find worthy of reverence and love in him as well as in myself? It is no historical accident that contemporary personalists use the words of Kant's categorical imperative: "Treat every person as an end in himself, never as a means." For Kant, the imperative flowed from the sole unconditioned value man knows (*unbedingten Wert, absoluten Wert*), man's *Freiheit*, his determining of himself unconditionally, his command over himself absolutely.

What Fr. Avery Dulles wrote recently, in a different context, illustrates how difficult and even impossible a person may find it to focus on "third alternatives."[6] For most informed Catholics, man is justified either by faith alone or by faith and good works. The former alternative is false, the latter true. Fr. Dulles suggests that there is a sense of the phrase "justification by faith alone" that a Catholic could accept as true. I presume that Fr. Dulles does not mean that this would merely be different words for what the Catholic has understood by "justification through faith and good works," or that it means what the Church has always condemned under the formula "justification by faith alone," but that it is a third alternative, and true as well.

One of the greatest joys the Council has brought by encouraging an openness to other faiths and to modern thought is the discovery of third alternatives. By dialogue we discover, on question after question, something we did not believe was there. Only with time and discussion can we focus on it at all, much less see its truth. We realize that it is neither what we already held (and still hold) to be true, not what we held (and still hold) to be false, but something that, perhaps under a formula we rejected, turns out as a new and true vision enriching our lives and bringing us closer to God and men. I suggest to my critics that this might be the case with what modern man means by "freedom for freedom's sake."

The letters of my critics reflect grave concern for the harm my words might do to the Church, to the people of God. The concern is understandable and creditable, and it will move me once more to re-examine and reappraise my position.

Let me close by expressing my own concern. I fear that a vacuum is building up among the people of God. More and more, old views and old ways fail to find acceptance. Yet satisfactory new views and new ways do not arise to replace them. We begin to encounter Catholics who are suffocating in the vacuum. To fill the vacuum in our communal life of faith is no easy task. But the greatest obstacle, I believe, is the conduct of those who see no need for radical change, who refuse to permit anything newer than token concessions or refurbishing of the old, who take anything truly new that comes along and reduce it in their minds to something that they have always known all about—whether it be true or false. My concern is that not enough of us American Catholics will be willing and able to look for third alternatives.

8 THE BEHAVIORAL SCIENCES

As we noted in earlier chapters, the theological foundation that contemporary ethicists lay supports an ethical methodology that is pragmatic and empirical. Characteristic is its use of the collation and analysis of human experience by the sciences. Moral decision itself is now understood in the light of contemporary social and behavioral sciences. If man is seen as a multi-levelled being, the same decision has a different reality at different depths. Christian ethics is thus starting to assimilate an understanding of man that won acceptance in intellectual circles some time ago, and has become a popular way of thinking.

Americans automatically assess decisions on different levels. A man decides to buy a new car. Superficially, he seems to himself and to his neighbors only to be choosing something of practical and aesthetic value. Yet almost anyone today, including the man himself and his neighbor, knows that the stronger and more decisive motive for the man might be one arising out of an inferiority complex or from an outer-directed orientation that needs the approval of the group. He may really be choosing the support of his ego through display. Psychology, sociology and anthropology have established that, at deeper levels, a man is often choosing something different from what he chooses on the explicit, conscious level. The multi-levelled view has become one of the clichés and truisms of our time, but only now is moral theology grasping its implications. One example might be the conduct of two students in the face of a projected sit-in. One chooses to participate, the other refuses. On the conscious level, the former has chosen to protest some injustice, the latter to

make studies and the pursuit of his career his primary concern. Yet on a deeper level, the first student may be motivated far more by hostility to all authority. The actions of
authority regularly infuriate him, and he regularly chooses to
oppose them. The fact of social injustice is irrelevant to
his decision at the deeper level. If the university authorities
had chosen on their own initiative to call on the students to
work for the elimination of the injustice, this student would
have had no interest and would probably have found reasons
for criticizing the initiative of those in authority.

The second student might have chosen, on the deeper
level and for the thousandth time, to conform to authority
rather than to think for himself. In other words, it is not his
career as a primary concern that he has chosen, but the security that comes from being on the side of authority. What
both students choose at the deeper level is to express their
basic attitude toward authority. In one case it is blind hostility, in the other, blind submission.

Any educated person today could suggest the above example. A psychiatrist could probe deeper. For him it would be
possible to see that both attitudes regarding authority, opposite though they are, arise from the same fundamental
stance—fear. Because one is profoundly terrified of authority,
he continually chooses in panic to attack. Because the other
is profoundly terrified of authority, he continually chooses
unconditional surrender. The above analysis leads to a different moral judgment than the data of explicit consciousness.
The key moral question for the two students (and for those
counselling them) becomes not to what extent should a person be involved in social issues and to what extent should
a person prepare his career, not when to resist authority and
when to obey, but how to find and take at the deepest level
an inner stance in regard to authority—a stance not based on
fear but on a sense of one's own personal dignity and of the
true function and value of authority. The key moral question
for the students is, therefore, what is this stance and how
can they achieve it. This question is central because the
deeper psychological attitudes are what *consistently* determine the life of the person. To speak of deeper attitudes is

simply to use a spatial metaphor that expresses the greater influence these psychological attitudes have on the decisions of a person and on his actions and life. Since the central question of morality is what a man ought to do, its central concern must be to form the attitudes through which what he does will be a good action.[1]

The determining attitudes in the students could be different from the attitudes suggested. The student protesting injustice might also, at the deepest level, be choosing to do precisely that. But if so, it probably arises from some basic attitude like sympathy for the oppressed. The student's present decision to protest is not as morally crucial as the process over the years which led to his now abiding sensitivity to injustice. This makes him the kind of person he now is, someone who acts the way he now does. The major battleground of life, therefore, is the "depths" where the attitudes are found which determine most decisions. For example, in those cases where the promiscuous sexual behavior is often an expression of personal discontent with one's own sex, the discontent is a more important moral problem than the promiscuity and more urgently demands understanding and help.

A multi-level view of man's decision-making relocates the consequences toward which the Christian strives. In an ethic advocating a solely pragmatic responsibility for consequences, the implication is far-reaching. The consequences now identified as prime ethical goals are those within the person himself, i.e., the attitudes making him the kind of person who acts consistently in a good way. Correspondingly there is now a serious moral obligation to work for similar consequences in other persons. The moral injustice of racism, for example, arises ultimately not from some absolute right to be treated as a man regardless of race, but ultimately from the fact that current racist practices engender or preserve in men of the demeaned race profound attitudes of shame, alienation and hostility, and so thwart them from fully becoming men. Their right to develop in the core of their person is what determines their right to just and human treatment. When social scientists note that in the United States forms of "black power" are among the more effective means of creating the sense of personal dignity lacking in many black Americans, then white and black Christians have a paramount obligation to encourage forms of black power. The authorities of a university do not meet the ethical demands of racial justice simply by accepting black students without discrimination.

Besides their determinative influence on most of man's decisions and actions, there is a second reason for sound basic attitudes in oneself and in others becoming significant consequences for which the Christian should strive. The attitudes themselves do not constitute intrinsically the highest value for the new ethics. The supreme value, the absolute value that is the source of all other human values, is what the ethicist borrowing from contemporary philosophy describes as the unique "I." It is core freedom, the self as self-creating. But the basic attitudes of a person are key forces in restricting or favoring the inner freedom. A compulsive personality will be far less able to exercise his unique self-creativity than will a person possessing an attitude of self-confidence. Furthermore, although the self created is primarily the self of the moment (the act of self-creation and the self created are one), still it is also the self which perdures, both the self that is me and the self that I may be molding in others. An important part of me, the perduring self, is the constellation of current attitudes that make me the kind of person I am. That the attitudes make up the self is also evoked by the spatial metaphors of "depth" and "core."

The profound shame, alienation and hostility of a black American is, therefore, a moral outrage for two reasons. Such emotional attitudes restrict his inner life of freedom, of personal self-possession and self-making. Secondly, along with the inner freedom, they make up the current self of the man. Regularly to do hating actions is bad enough, but it does not come near the moral tragedy of becoming a hating person. One could ask how new this multi-levelled view of man and its integration into the science of ethics is. Analogies with the scholastic theory of habits, virtues and vices come readily to mind. The ancient and medieval thinkers occasionally anticipate the methodology and findings of the modern behavioral sciences. The uniqueness of the sciences in their present state lies in their awareness of their own methodology, their purifying it of foreign elements, their carrying it out with the concentrated efficiency and, as a result, their gleaning of a vast and wide-ranging knowledge of human behavior. It is not surprising, then, that whatever might be or not be the novelty *in principle* of the methodology of the behavioral sciences and their multi-levelled view of man, moral theology is *in fact* changing and will continue to change as it integrates them into its inquiry.[2]

We saw that one change was the relocation of the results toward which the Christian ought to strive, namely, at the deeper levels within the person. New goals, however, also introduce changes in ethics concerning the means to be followed. Obviously, one necessary means is the discernment of a person's basic attitudes. But they are not easy to discern. They are not conscious in the ordinary sense of the word. They can become clearly conscious as a counsellor, for example, will often try to effect. And in a sense the person has always known of them. Freud said that the sign of a successful completion of therapy would be the cry of the patient, "I always knew it." Even popular reading of psychology or sociology can bring us to realize emotional patterns that have gone on for years in a dimly conscious state, although we have never admitted to them. I now can experience clearly, let us say, the pang of anxiety I have always felt in speaking with persons of authority. More often, however, a man is not clearly conscious of the attitudes he has that make him act in a given way.

The lack of clear consciousness is not the only difficulty in discerning operative personal attitudes. Neither can they be inferred from behavior in a simple, obvious way. The old moralist presupposed that the man who regularly performed unchaste or unjust or gluttonous acts did so because of the habit, or vice, of unchastity or injustice or gluttony. The direct correspondence presupposed between behavior and habit made it easy to conclude from patterns of action the virtues or vices behind them. Incidentally, the same presupposition freed him to focus his inquiry on the morality of individual acts and not on the virtues and vices, although he might admit that in a certain sense virtues and vices were more important in a man's moral life than the isolated acts.

Accepting the contemporary scientific understanding of man, the new ethicist knows he cannot interpret patterns of behavior such as promiscuity or theft or overeating so simply. An unmarried girl may be promiscuous mainly because of hostility toward her mother. A thief from a slum area may be stealing mainly out of a need to prove his manhood. A man may overeat and overdrink mainly out of anxiety. In brief, the attitudes which determine human behavior are difficult to discern, not merely because they are not clearly conscious, but also because they cannot be easily inferred from the resultant behavior. The behavior does not correspond to them in a direct and obvious way, at least not to the eyes of the layman. The old moral questions (How often did I miss Mass? How often did I commit adultery?) could be easily answered. But not the new questions now deemed important. Am I going to Mass out of my abiding faith in Christ and the community? Or do I go out of a need to conform socially and be respectable?

The radical character of the new problem is illustrated by Karl Rahner's "unbelieving believer." The man thinks he is a good Christian, possessing faith, hope and charity. In fact, in his depths, he has never turned to God. His fundamental posture is concerned only with self, not with anyone else and, least of all, God. He is an atheist. Another example, perhaps more easily recognizable, could be the young man undergoing temptations to doubt his faith. He yields to temptations and doubts. He continues to lead a Catholic life, but wonders whether he believes at all. What should he do? Perhaps behind the doubting are drives toward promiscuous sexual behavior. He doubts his faith, not because he has reasons to question its truth, but because it condemns what he wants to do. By encouraging doubts about his faith, he is working at sapping the position that has hitherto prevented him from satisfying sexual desire. On this hypothesis, his doubting deserves blame because he is facing squarely neither the moral question of sexual behavior nor the moral question of believing. However, what could be behind his doubts is that he is adopting, for the first time in his life, an attitude of taking Christ and his faith seriously. He is trying, therefore, to adopt an honest, responsible position in this regard. He finds he can do it only if he admits his doubts, accepts them, and lives with them for a while. With this hypothesis, his doubting is praiseworthy at least as a necessary concomitant of something fine he is doing.

The difficulty of discerning the attitudes responsible for external behavior affects ethical methodology in several ways. It makes unsound much moral generalization, e.g., declaring from the pulpit or the podium that all doubts against one's faith should be put away or resisted. It requires the counsellor (and the person being counselled, too) to get to know the person and his life as a whole before giving moral advice on a problem such as doubting one's faith. It often calls for the use of knowledge gleaned by the behavioral sciences or, analogously, by professional experience such as that of the trained, full-time counsellor or social worker. Even the layman can come to understand and apply certain principles of psychology or the social sciences, although it is particularly true in this area that a little knowledge can be a dangerous thing. A knowledge of some of the hidden forces at work in the average adolescent can be communicated without great difficulty to teachers and parents and even to the adolescent. All this is recognized today, of course, but the point is that the use of such knowledge is seen by the new ethics as a matter of moral obligation.

Since the Christian ethic recognizes as a primary obligation the strengthening or modification or re-channeling of the attitudes determining behavior, the behavioral sciences have not only the role of identifying them, but the role of indicating how to deal with them once they are discovered. Once again the pragmatic, empirical bias of the new ethic turns to scientific experience, this time to learn how to bring about the desired experienced consequences, i.e., to learn, given the psychic, social, cultural forces at work in an individual's personality, how to lead him to be a happier, more mature and more loving person. The Christian ethic learns its practical principles from Carl Rogers and Hans Morgenthau, Lester Kirkendall and Margaret Mead, Rollo May and Theodore Roszak. It starts with the recognition that it must do *something* about the drug addict, the alcoholic, the alienated married couple, the soldiers returning from Vietnam, the homosexual, the aged. But to know the something to do the Christian must often turn to professional experience. Once again, the behavioral scientists are not the only source. The social worker, the marriage counsellor, the high school principal, members of Alcoholics Anonymous, Saul Alinsky and Dean Acheson can give practical advice out of their experience of doing things for people as well as from sharing the experience of others engaged in the same professional activity. What is new is that this kind of advice is seen as able to determine moral obligations. What *ought* a homosexual do? The answer could well be: what his psychiatrist tells him to do. Since the new Christian ethic holds no absolute principles, even in the sexual domain, but aims solely at that fullness of personal living concretely possible for the given individual, the ethical goal for the individual need not differ from the goal a good psychiatrist would have for him. And the psychiatrist is much likelier to know what the homosexual can do to draw nearer to his goal. In given situations, there will be an obligation to avail oneself not merely of professional experience in the form of advice, but also of techniques or treatments elaborated out of the experience with a view to modify and redirect forces of behavior. Psychotherapy, psychoanalysis, professional counselling, rehabilitation centers for drug addicts and alcoholics—all are already in common use among American Christians. They are beginning to appreciate applications of group dynamics as in T- groups, sensitivity sessions and encounters.

As we noted in chapter two, the ethical importance of professional and scientific experience severely limits the contribution of the general "moral theologian" or "Christian ethicist." There can no longer be one man who can proclaim principles on a wide spectrum of moral problems, in the manner of John Ford or Francis Connell. There can only be ethical specialists for given areas, such as environment, population, race relations, urban planning, business ethics, faculty-student relationships, child rearing. The ethical specialists will need extensive formation in the pertinent behavioral sciences or in corresponding professional training and internship. The strictly theological elements of Christian ethics are the most important, but—if one can speak of intellectual understanding in a quantified way—are the fewest in number. In order to be able to indicate usefully ethical obligations in dealing with the high school dropout or the divorce legislation before the assembly, the ethical specialist needs to have spent much more time studying secular sciences and gaining secular experience than in studying theology. This is why those who are professional ethicists and nothing else generally restrict themselves today to foundational questions or to the description and recommendation of general goals such as racial equality, peace or conjugal love. They do not presume to spell out, for example, the concrete ethical responsibilities of a husband and wife. They have neither the experience themselves nor the time to glean from the reports of sociologists, psychologists, doctors, marriage counsellors and married people what effective forms conjugal "love" can take in the light of the differing physiological and psychological makeup of male and female, the social pressures of our time, the influence of our culture, etc.

Given the limitations of everyday life, the average Christian will not often find it practicable to obtain the professional treatment or advice given specifically for his situation. But through communication media he can acquaint himself with some of the fruit of professional experience and make his own applications. One truth that he can learn applies to all situations: deeper, more influential attitudes can be changed only slowly. They form, like glaciers, little by little over the years. They can be changed only in the same way. A good deal of the formation and change is independent of the free choice of the person. Opinions range widely about the extent of human freedom and the degree to which a person can mold the attitudes determining the kind of life he leads. Moral theologians who are influenced by existentialism tend to accord a large place for man's freedom to create himself, to *make* himself over the years into the kind of person he is. Some proponents of the "basic option" theory appear to share this optimistic view of human freedom. American moral theology will, I believe, be more influenced by the behavioral sciences and see human freedom rather as a spark, affecting only in small part the onrush of human life—although it will see this spark of self-creating as the most precious and most human part of the life.[3] In any case, whatever the extent of human freedom might be, the data of the behavioral sciences indicates that its effectiveness in changing basic attitudes will be at best gradual. The sciences thus increase the need the Christian has to find in his faith a light and strength that help him to accept himself peacefully, despite his abiding weaknesses and continuing failures. Protestant ethicists, influenced by the original Reformation experience, have contributed more towards meeting the need than their Catholic colleagues.

That basic attitudes change only gradually applies also to cases where the attitudes are at an immature stage of development. In the past, the masturbating adolescent was told of his immediate obligation to break the habit by strong acts of will and by strengthening his will through prayer, manifold Christian and human motivation, avoidance of the occasion of sin, frequenting of the Sacraments, good habits and frequent self-denial. The new approach, on the contrary, would put little stress on stopping immediately the acts of masturbation. They are a natural expression of a sexuality that is maturing, but still at an immature stage. One reason the boy is masturbating may be that he is attracted to girls, but does not yet have the confidence to make friends with them. Nor will he acquire the confidence overnight. The maturing of the attitudes, drives and powers that make up a person's sexuality cannot be sped-up at will. Increasing the guilt feelings of the adolescent is certainly not going to help and may well hamper the maturing process. What often will help and move things forward is the counsellor's making little of the masturbation question and encouraging a more active social life.

An understanding of the slow maturing of personal attitudes offers a crosscut view of the problem of doubts about one's faith discussed above. A boy, a young man, or even an older man, struggles day by day . . . to be a man. He is struggling to be responsible, to have the courage and confidence to think for himself, to make his own decisions, to answer for the consequences. Obviously, this will not relieve him of the inevitable human necessity to obey and believe and conform. But now he could do these things and everything else as a man. The trouble is—and here our psychological truth is confirmed by ordinary experience—that becoming a man, becoming responsible, is a slow, difficult enterprise of years or perhaps a lifetime. It often ends in failure or quite limited success.

These are clichés of our time, but out of the struggle for a responsible life, some Catholics become atheists or agnostics. It starts with something of which they may not be clearly aware: their practical inability or unwillingness to take on a life of faith responsibly. Why won't they or can't they? Perhaps the life of faith that has been taught to them and that they have seen about them has not been one worthy of a mature person and seems, therefore, irreconcilable with their present efforts to grow. Or perhaps the fault is more their own: their present efforts toward maturity are too weak and sporadic to assimilate the demands of a responsible life of faith.

In any case, they take a second step and become atheists. One may officially announce to himself that he is now an atheist. Another, without telling even himself, gives up the fight and simply reserves a corner of his life where a small boy will always be worshiping God and hopefully disturbing the rest of his life as little as possible. The man will be a professed Catholic and a practical atheist. Recently, an alumnus said to a priest teaching at a Catholic university, "Father, don't worry about the lack of religious practice among your students. Those fellows will meet a good girl some day; she'll tell them to go to church and they'll go." But is it likely that a man who goes to his God because a woman tells him to, goes as a man? If not, is it likely that his belief in God, sincere as it may be, will affect his life? One can go to church, pay bills for the Catholic schooling of one's children, and still let one's faith in Christ determine few of one's actions.

Christians are more and more willing these days to let God judge such practical atheists as well as the professed ones. But Christians question: how can we prevent such atheism (or agnosticism), such loss of faith in thought or action? If the cause of atheism is practical, the action of the Christian must be practical and directed at the cause. Pedro Arrupe, General of the Jesuits, speaking at the Second Vatican Council, argued that the best way to overcome atheism, whether speculative or practical, was not intellectual argument, but action and living. He may have been thinking of cases where one maintains faith by filling empty stomachs. In the case we have considered, the Christian would try to help psychologically, to support the man or boy in his struggles toward a responsible life. Imagine, for example, the college freshman reading seriously on his own for the first time, the couples coming to the C.F.M. meeting, the seminarian facing growing difficulties in prayer. How to help them? The Christian for whom the question arises will often be some sort of authority figure: teacher, parent, spiritual director, moderator, etc. But often—perhaps more today than in the past—he will be simply another Christian whom the person going through the crisis of faith trusts and to whom he confides.

Nowadays there is no need to emphasize that to help such a person one must leave him considerable freedom. But it might be worth adding that the freedom cannot be mere permissiveness or indulgence. To be of help in the slow formation of responsible attitudes the Christian must show his genuine respect and interest in the person's struggling efforts. He must prove that he takes them seriously. It normally means a continuing contact, much listening and watching, consequent response and reaction, which will range from enthusiastic to severely critical according to what the person has done. The combination of granting great freedom and yet following closely and reacting at each step is obviously demanding and exhausting, when it is possible at all. The image that comes to mind is the cornerback backpedalling and covering the receiver in a football game. It is perhaps the most effective means to speed slowly the interpenetrated psychological growth of faith and manhood in the individual.

There is resistance in the American churches to the way the behavioral sciences are transforming and, in good part, constituting the methodology of Christian ethics. Some of the resistance is a justified reaction to the sciences' being applied to ethical problems without regard to their limits. They are far from infallible. By nature, they are always tentative and subject to revision. On many important questions, the schools do not reach a consensus and even contradict each other flatly. Nor can the generalizations universally agreed upon be applied to individual cases with anything like the rigor of the old moral principles. Finally, the generalizations of the behavioral sciences are never of themselves statements about morality or objective values.

But much of the current resistance to the use of the behavioral sciences in ethics does not arise from their misuse. It arises rather from a dissatisfaction, often vague and undefined, with the ethical nature of the use. "We assuredly can and should use the behavioral sciences in making decisions, but is this morality?" Hopefully, preceding pages have made clear that for contemporary ethics the use of the behavioral sciences *is* morality. But part of the dissatisfaction with new approach is the objection that in any case the question is academic. Modern Christians avail themselves of the behavioral sciences and professional know-how in general. They need no urging to do so. There is nothing to be gained by making the use obligatory.

The reply of the new morality to the objection epitomizes its whole thrust. There is much to be gained by recognizing an obligation to use contemporary empirical sciences and methods. Moral obligation comes to the Christian from Christ himself and through Christ's community. If the Christian is open to Christ and to the community, he is energized and impelled in this way to do the necessary actions. We do need energy and the impulse, not to use professional and scientific experience in general, but to use it to fulfill responsibilities we do not like to face: toward the old, the problem child, the neighbor we do not talk to, the Communist, the rebel, ourselves in certain weaknesses. By persistently bringing the sciences to bear on the full range of human problems, Christian ethics can make a difference in American life—perhaps revolutionize it.

9 CRITICISM
OF TRADITIONAL MORALITY

If preceding pages have succeeded in their intent, it should be clear that the new morality is not a negative reaction in the life history of Christian ethics. Its dynamics are not essentially polemic or escapist; they arise from its own native insights. At the same time the new morality has, from the start, been also reacting critically to the traditional morality it is replacing. Some of the questions the new morality has been urging on the old help us to understand its own positive thrust. As with other facets of the new morality, this aggressive side shows itself as much in popular reactions as in professional literature and discussion.

Traditional ethicists and moral theologians rely on certain axioms when they deal with the questions of the day. One axiom, above all, fails to be understood outside the ranks of the tradition and, surprisingly enough, is rarely explicated and discussed in its general bearing. The neglect in explaining the principle, coupled with the frequency in applying it, is the cause of much present-day bewilderment concerning what is presented as natural law—for example, in sexual matters. As I will try to show in the present chapter, the new morality forces light on the principle by focusing questions on it and suggests what it finds to be a more solid alternative. The criticism made here by the new morality is another phase of the same confrontation concerning moral absolutes discussed in Chapter One. One of the conclusions of the present chapter coincides with a conclusion in Chapter One: the new morality is not as foreign to the old as it might appear.

The ethical principle in question is the axiom that the

specific purpose of a particular act suffices to determine its moral and immoral uses. The tradition bases the axiom in reason and not in divine revelation. As it stands, the principle is unexceptionable. Clearly, everything created should be used for the purpose God has marked for it. And God's purpose is its purpose. But when the principle is applied, e.g., to marriage, to the physical life of deformed babies, to sexual activity or to man's speech, its meaning loses clarity, even becomes ambiguous. The application of the principle is the main argument for the prohibition of contraception by the encyclical *Humanae Vitae*, and is one of the main reasons for dissent from the encyclical within the Catholic Church. It leaves uncomprehending many educated Catholics today, many a husband and wife facing their large family and their love and need for each other and many a priest trying to counsel them. As to professional moralists, Richard McCormick writes in conclusion to his brief roundup of reactions to *Humanae Vitae*:

> . . . anyone who reads the current literature on *Humanae Vitae* cannot help but notice that articles favoring the papal teaching manifest a heavy, almost exclusive concern with tradition and authority. Those which dissent are concerned largely with the analysis of evidence and reasoning.[1]

Even the defenders of the traditional ban on contraception are abandoning natural law argumentation and therefore the traditional application, repeated in the encyclical, of the principle under discussion in the present chapter. Significantly, the target of the dissenting criticism is not the particular application of the principle made by the encyclical, but the principle itself. It must, consequently, affect all applications of the principle to moral questions. As the Church, the Catholic people, are gradually endorsing the criticism as valid, widening waves are moving out from the now dead controversy about the encyclical into much of Catholic moral theology.

The source of the division of views lies in two different ethico-intellectual syndromes. Many ordinary educated American Catholics of the last third of the twentieth century, unlike their fathers and unlike the traditional ethicists, do not form moral judgments by instinctively looking first to God's *particular* purpose for the thing to be used. It is not so much that they contest in principle such a point of reference, but their minds implicitly move another way. They look first to God's *general* purpose for man and they measure the questioned action against it. One might articulate their understanding of God's general purpose as *gloria Dei vivens homo:* "The glory God would have of a man is simply that he truly live." One day the life will be the vision and intimate love of God; today it is an imperfect anticipation of that goal through the understanding and love a man ekes out in the world for God and for his fellow man and for himself. When the question of how to act in a certain situation arises, our ordinary man does not inspect the total complexity of the object to be used in order to deduce what God must have envisioned in all these details. Rather, he finds out what he can do. From what he can do he chooses as morally right those actions by which human life, i.e., the life of understanding and love, his own and his neighbor's, can be further realized. For example, speech which misrepresents one's views is wrong, and wrong before God, because it thwarts a life of understanding and love among men. Ordinarily, a man feels no need to inspect the complex details of tongue, larynx, lungs, etc., and discern God's specific purpose for the faculty in order to make his moral decision.

There are then two approaches to moral evaluation. Both base their judgment on the "purpose" of the prospective action,[2] but they do not envisage the same thing as this morally decisive purpose. One traces out first the specific purpose and does not doubt that the ultimate purpose and good of the whole man will be attained thereby.[3] The other measures the action directly in the light of man's general purpose, a full life of understanding and love, and does not doubt that the relation to the general purpose coincides with any specific end. It may be that often the dichotomy lies only on the surface. Nevertheless, it is a dichotomy which many a man today does find: the way the traditional moralists think and the way he thinks.[4] From the dichotomy, profound or superficial, arise conflict and confusion of conscience.

The confusion permeates discussion of significant issues and raises questions in the modern mind. The prolonged existence of a baby extensively deformed in body and soul may be demanded by the specific purpose of man's physical existence in this world, but does it constitute the *vivens homo*, the living man, who alone is God's glory? Should not conjugal morality for given families in a given society be governed by the fact that the general good of this society and this family can be most practically furthered by generous childbearing to a certain extent and then by continuing expression of conjugal love with the use of contraceptives? Are the mental gymnastics of a *reservatio mentalis* necessary or even worthy of a grown man in circumstances where mutual love and understanding clearly demand that a certain other person entertain a false opinion? Questions of this type, met today at every turn, may often betray the subjective confusion of the modern mind rather than obscurities in the presentation of the tradition. But they betray also a vague, implicit insight that is articulated by the new morality in more precise questions.

One attempt at a more precise question aims at a foundation for further questions. When a process (e.g., the total physiological process that brings about ocular vision) regularly terminates in the same result, in what sense is the result necessarily the "purpose" of the process? The regular result is, of course, the purpose of the process in the sense that anything that happens can be called the purpose of the action immediately producing it, and therefore of the divine concurrence. Furthermore, one need not contest the principle (whose meaning and basis, however, the scholastic philosophers dispute) that whatever acts regularly in the same way is necessarily ordered to its term by an intelligent director. So watered a sense of purpose neither requires nor invites the kind of moral judgment at stake. The mere fact that my hair regularly tends to grow long has, as such, no decisive influence on any moral judgment. Clearly, the constant term of a process is not necessarily the kind of purpose under present discussion—one intended, in a stricter sense of the word, by nature and God, i.e., one absolutely incorporating intrinsic value, orienting means, demanding unconditionally moral respect and prohibiting any violation or frustration.

Similarly, even when the process produces its regular result only through a complex convergence of numerous factors, does it follow necessarily that the result is the kind of absolute purpose under present discussion? One could take once more the example of the process that makes vision possible. Does the degree of complexity argue the degree of importance the term has? Even the most anthropomorphically conceived divine watchmaker must labor effortlessly. He has no need to proportion the complexity of His created processes to the value of their terms. Yet there are moralists for whom the relatively small proportion of a total bodily system that participates in a given activity proves the relatively small importance intended by God for that activity within the system.[5] One wonders how they would discern the primary importance God envisioned for man in the universe.

The point of these two tendentious questions is not that the purpose which the tradition finds in human processes are irrelevant to moral decision. On the contrary! But how does one know the proportionate value of each one? Neither mere regularity nor mere degree of complex convergence reveals the proportionate value of the term or "purpose" of a process. To prolong a *simpliste* image often invoked: if a man's father gives him a watch, the son recognizes its purpose in the regular term of its complex processes, namely, that it tells time for him. But would this suffice to situate the proportionate value of the term or purpose, i.e., the importance the father gave to it in his mind? Might there not be other purposes indeterminately envisaged by the father? How would the obvious proximate purpose be measured with a given remote one? Would the father be excluding the sale of the watch if this were the only way of paying for an operation for the son's wife? Or the use of the watch as a hammer (and thus its destruction) if this alone on a given occasion could save the son's life?

How then can a man know the absolute and inviolable

purpose of anything? How can one know . . . ? The epistemological question is a central one the new morality urges.
To clarify the question, one should note that there is one
way of knowing absolute values that both new and old morality recognize. That certain things are inviolable values is
known immediately upon learning what they are. If one discerns what can be the authentic love between a man and a
woman, one recognizes its absolute worth. One sees that no
man may seek to frustrate or destroy it. The discerning required is clearly no indirect, superficial conceptualization. To
reveal the worth of human love, genuine understanding and
therefore some experience of it are needed. One could use
the overused word "insight." But once human love is understood, the insight realized, man sees immediately its absolute
worth. It is a question, obviously, of immediacy of evidence,
not necessarily of time. No further evidence is required. One
need not consult the further consequences of the act. To
know what it is, i.e., to know its direct, specifying object, is
to stand before an intrinsic, absolute value. It is, therefore,
one way of coming to an absolute, inviolable purpose of God.
Both new and old morality take this way.

Can the same immediate evidence be found for all acts
where a moral decision is called for? Evidently not. A man
may well understand what marriage is and what dissolubility
would be, but does that immediately reveal to him that marriage should always be contracted as indissoluble? Clearly
not. Traditional ethicists adduce ulterior evidence for their
position. A man may well understand what a lie is, *locutio
contra mentem*, speaking contrary to one's mind, and not
yet have enough evidence to discern its immorality. On this
point, too, traditional ethicists feel constrained to adduce
further evidence.[6]

This, then, is the sharper focus of the epistemological
question: what is the nature of the "further evidence?" In
the eyes of the new morality, the importance of the question
is underscored by the inconsistency of the tradition in using
or identifying such evidence. In the present controversy concerning abortion, some Catholic moralists confront humani-
tarian outcries *simply* with the assertion of the inviolability

of human life.[7] But the inviolability of human life is not an immediately evident principle. It is not evident simply on understanding what human life is (i.e., physical existence in this world) and what its physical suppression would be.[8] It can only be a conclusion of further premises. The contention of the new morality is that thematizing epistemologically the nature of such further premises or evidence, not merely for the case of abortion, but insofar as it is relevant throughout the science of morals, is essential to the progress of the science.

Here is one final example of the neglect of this epistemological question. Several traditional moralists have conceded that the universal condemnation of contraception cannot be based on the invalid principle that *no* faculty or act may be used against its purpose. On the contrary, they say, the force of the traditional argument proceeds from a principle peculiar to the procreative faculty and act: "Just as innocent human life itself is inviolable, so those things which immediately pertain to the beginning of human life are also inviolable."[9] This may represent a valuable clarification of the traditional approach, but the moralists have characteristically left one question unanswered which many of their contemporaries would ask them: What is the evidence for this principle? How do we know it is true? Even granted the inviolability of human life, why does it follow that the life-giving processes are equally inviolable? Recall that the principle, as used in traditional morality, does not mean simply that one may not violate the processes in such a way as to harm life. It means that one may not violate the processes even when life would suffer no harm as a result, e.g., in the cases where the only reasonable alternative to contraception would be continence. Taken in this sense, the principle is not immediately evident. What is the evidence for it? Once more one finds unanswered the question concerning the nature of the further evidence that would ground a prohibition of a certain action.[10]

The new morality, in its turn, offers an answer. I am not sure that all proponents of the new morality would agree, but as I understand the dynamics of the trend, its answer is that such further evidence in the last analysis is always empirical. It is the evidence of the probable or certain consequences which result from the act in question. Will its eventual result be to contribute to, or to oppose, the concrete realization of those absolute values already recognized through the immediate evidence discussed above (e.g., the absolute value of human love)? And the evidence of what is going to result can only be, as David Hume showed more lucidly than anyone else, the observation of the past sequence of individual events; it indicates "what generally happens." One suggests, therefore, that it is not immediate insight into what something is, but empirical evidence—the observation, correlation, and weighing out of numerous facts—which reveals the value of most human acts; for it shows what effects the acts are likely to have in the concrete, existing world on those absolute values a man discerns by direct insight.[11]

Traditional moralists do not ignore such empirical evidence. They do not condemn divorce simply by describing what marriage is and what dissolubility means. They describe these, but then appeal to what is going to result, namely, what is going to result in marriage if its dissolution be allowed: the hindrance to the fitting education of the child, the damage to married love, etc.[12] To show what is going to result, they are appealing implicitly to empirical evidence (at least to what a man has by way of analogy or vicariously through observation), e.g., empirical evidence of what generally happens to a child whose parents are separated, of what generally happens when one has committed oneself totally to another and knows one can be abandoned, etc. That the fitting education of the child and the love between husband and wife are absolute values and purposes is clear to anyone who understands what they are. But it is only empirical evidence which can reveal that the allowance of divorce would oppose these absolute values and therefore that divorce itself is wrong. Only in the empirical context can it make sense to say that divorce is wrong because it violates the purpose of marriage. Could not this relatively simple case constitute a paradigm for more complex moral evidence?

Nor do traditional ethicists condemn lying simply by describing what it is. Here, however, they disagree on the nature of the decisive evidence.[13] Some hold that the very nature and purpose of speech, the manifestation of one's thought, suffices to prove the intrinsic evil of lying, since the lie by definition violates this nature and purpose.[14] Of these moralists, some advance also an empirical argument, based on its consequences for social life. But they proffer it as a parallel proof, not as the foundation for the argument from nature or purpose.[15] They find no need to offer evidence that this nature or purpose is of such a kind as to be respected absolutely. They neglect completely the epistemological question which I have tried to bring into sharp focus and which the new morality presses on the old.

Other ethicists of the tradition, however, after describing what lying is, appeal ultimately not to the nature and immediate purpose of speech but to what is going to result in society if lying is permitted: the damaging of social life itself.[16] To show what is going to result, they appeal implicitly to man's empirical evidence of what generally happens when one cannot rely on his neighbor's speaking the truth. That man's social life is an absolute value and purpose is clear to anyone who understands what it is. But it is only empirical evidence that can reveal that the allowance of lying would oppose the absolute value of social life and therefore that lying itself is wrong. Only in the empirical context can it make sense to say that lying is wrong because it violates the purpose of speech. Could not the presentation of these moralists provide a paradigm for most moral evidence?

The discussion might seem to have come full turn. The problem set up at the beginning of the chapter, the dichotomy between the intellectual syndromes of the traditional ethicists and the contemporary mind, might now appear to have been neither a dichotomy nor a problem. At least in the cases we have just seen, both new and old moralists ultimately invoke empirical evidence. To evaluate certain actions, they assess what is likely to result from the actions for certain absolute values, those intrinsic values that constitute a "living man." But, the new morality submits, the examples of divorce and lying are not paradigmatic, in practice, of much of traditional moral reasoning. The ethicians often do not keep in mind the empirical nature of the evidence. They do not apply consistently any epistemology of ethics, much less the apt empirical one.

The epistemology suggested by the new morality could be recapitulated from a negative point of view. An act is known to be wrong in one of two ways. Either (e.g., cowardice) it is by definition the absence of a quality (courage) whose absolute value is seen immediately upon understanding what it is, or empirical observation of a number of cases indicates that the act is likely to result in some absolute evil, itself recognized in the former, immediate way (e.g., damage to the fitting education of the child). The new morality suggests that any talk of frustration of purposes must rest on one or both of the above kinds of evidence.

Such an epistemology makes a large place for the empirical. Few are the acts whose value direct insight suffices to establish. They would be restricted to acts such as "love and honor and pity and pride and compassion and sacrifice." Moreover, although moral qualities are needed to appreciate these and to live them fully, they pose no intellectual problems for the educated Christian. On the other hand, for the numerous acts whose value direct insight does not suffice to establish, e.g., sexual actions, the ethical question is frequently open or being reopened. If the epistemology of the new morality is justified, such questions could be more fruitfully explored and any answers more convincingly communicated, if it were kept in mind that the decisive evidence is empirical.

Not that empirical evidence would make all conclusions completely contingent and uncertain. An empirically established necessity is a true necessity.[17] Just as arsenic, placed in the diet, would necessarily destroy the physical life of men, so the allowance of adultery would necessarily damage their social life. The necessity is not absolute; exceptions occur. But most men who have a sense of responsibility, reality and humor, will never find a need to raise the question whether they are in the exceptional situation. According to the suggested epistemology of ethics, it is precisely such an empirically discovered necessity that determines most moral judgments. To uncover the necessities, the exacting complexity of empirical techniques, evolved to a point of fine perfection by the sciences in the last few centuries, must be brought to bear. Should Christian ethics neglect the techniques or apply them merely as a gratuitous reinforcement? Should it not rather see in them the main source of light for the involute obscurity of many moral problems? Can, for example, the evil of homosexuality be clear unless the methods of contemporary social science attests to its probable disastrous consequences: for example, as we discussed in Chapter Four, that the homosexual relation generally results in an unstable, stunted caricature of love? And might not the scientific attestation merely render more clearly and convincingly the empirical insight behind the old formula that homosexuality violates the nature of the faculty?

On the other hand, many empirical conclusions are contingent enough that the time may come for their denial. Any relative necessity they had is gone. The traditional ethician readily admits this in the "nature" of money or in occasions of sin in the matter of chastity. He rightly disclaims a reversal of position when he declares to be allowed what was formerly condemned. Empirical evidence has revealed that something different than what has happened before is going to result from the loan of money or the wearing of a certain costume. Consequently and consistently the traditional morality changes. The new morality asks only whether the ethician should not recognize more thematically his empirical evidence and show himself more widely sensitive to contingency in conclusions and change in evidence.

Similarly, the contemporary ethician maintains that some arguments of the tradition are based, not on the pretended absolute conclusion that evil is going to result from a given action, but on a relative conclusion, a likelihood of the result within the area observed thus far. The Church then comes along and, going beyond the evidence, wisely imposes an unqualified obligation, furthering the general good and moving the Christian people toward a higher ideal of life. In scholarly literature, traditional moral theologians are often modest with the force of their purely rational arguments. It is suggested only that a more public and more universal methodological modesty would be fruitful.

A case in point might be that of euthanasia and suicide. The decisive argument against them is not the value of physical life, although this is a link in the reasoning. Ultimately, the traditional ethician faces the question of why a man cannot in a given case and because of the enormous good at stake, presume God's permission to take a life. He often answers with the empirical argument of what is going to result if men be permitted, even if only in exceptional cases, directly to end lives according to their own good judgment.[18] The empirically evident likelihood of abusive extension of the privilege would come into play here. This traditional type of empirical argument (called *ex semel licito*, "from granting the permission once") has force, but not enough to apply indubitably in all cases. One would touch here, not so much the native limits of human intelligence, but the particular limits of the empirical evidence in question. Yet both the force and the limits of the evidence could justify and render credible unqualified condemnation by the Church.

One advantage of a more extensive recognition of the empirical nature of much moral evidence would be, independently of any refinement or revision of conclusions, a gain in force and clarity in communicating principles to the Christian layman of the present age. Educated, committed Christians are turning from traditional moralists with one word, "Casuistry!" One often hears, "I simply follow my conscience." This progressive alienation from an indispensable tradition is tragic. But what are the causes? One cause, intimated throughout the chapter, is the empirical tenor of contemporary thinking, at a loss before the rationalistic garb of much professional moralizing. In the last four hundred years Western thought has grown more and more consciously empirical. In some Christian circles one is wont to condemn the creeping empiricism for its excesses. But has it not also been progressive? Has it not clarified and uncovered resources of man's knowledge? Is not the critical sense of the empirically-oriented contemporary, insofar as it goes, something good and sound, a gain over the contemporary of

Thomas Aquinas? Might not the ethician profit from it more consistently than he has heretofore? Might he not thereby be more faithful to the best in his tradition and more relevant to the problems of his contemporaries?

10 THOMAS AQUINAS AND EXCEPTIONS TO THE MORAL LAW

In the preceding chapter, the new morality was seen to confront the old as far as the way to understand God's purposes as they determine the morality of human acts is concerned. New and old morality were seen to agree that, at least for some acts, God's purposes and the act's morality are often concluded from empirical necessities. But whatever the evidence for the conclusion may be, the old morality maintains that some of the purposes concluded are absolutely inseparable from the given act, and that therefore the morality, or immorality, of the act is absolutely the same in all circumstances. No exceptions are possible. The new morality differs. In the present chapter, I shall try to illumine the difference further by a historical probe into the old morality.

We can recapitulate the difference by recalling the traditional principle that the end never justifies the means. The principle is understood by the tradition in two different ways. It can mean that a good end can never justify the use of immoral means. Or it can mean that certain acts, specified by their effect, are always immoral when used as means, no matter how good the end. In the second meaning of the principle, the effect is defined from a purely physical, i.e., nonmoral, point of view (e.g., a definition of adultery acceptable to all, no matter what their moral judgment on the act may be). According to the tradition, one can conclude from the physical nature of the effect that the act is always immoral when done as a means to an end.[1]

One can exemplify the two senses of the traditional principle by its application to murder and abortion. Murder

is, by definition, immoral, i.e., unjust killing. It can, consequently, never be used as a means. Abortion, on the other
hand, is defined in physical, nonmoral terms: the expulsion
from the mother's womb of a living fetus which is incapable
of surviving outside the womb.[2] Precisely on the basis of such
a nonmoral definition, natural-law reasoning concludes that
the act is always immoral if used as a means and, therefore,
never justified.

The contemporary opposition to the absolutely universal
prohibitions of the tradition arises from its opposition to
both prongs of the general principle of the tradition concerning the use of means. In opposition to the first sense of the
principle, not a few contemporary Christian ethicians, particularly those of Lutheran background, maintain that in certain
situations the only moral course is to use immoral means to
achieve a good end. They envisage situations in which all
practical alternatives, especially that of the refusal to act,
have a bad side. Instead of inquiring whether any of the alternatives are absolutely unjustifiable or whether the principle of double effect could be applied, they say, "One
must do what one must do—and say one's prayers." One must
choose. And even if it be the lesser evil and the greater good
that one chooses, one still must turn to God for His forgiveness.[3] On the other hand, it is not easy to say how many of
the ethicians of this type would come out for the direct
opposite of the traditional principle in its first meaning and
hold that any proportionately good end can justify any
means.[4] In any case, the present essay is not going to deal
with this first sense of the natural law principle being de-
bated.

The more widespread opposition to the traditional principle meets it on the second meaning. Whether or not they
grant, as some of them do, that *immoral* means are never to
be used, a large and growing number of Christians fail to see
how a specific external action, defined in physical, *nonmoral*
terms (as abortion or adultery), can be condemned absolutely, i.e., never be used as a means no matter what the
circumstances or the end in view. In other words—to use the
terminology that we will employ to express precisely this

type of moral principle—they fail to see how there can be any "negative moral absolutes." They see how a specific kind of action could be condemned generally, i.e., for the most cases, because the action generally does serious harm and relatively little good. Joseph Fletcher grants that sex relations outside marriage can be wrong for many individuals because it hurts them, their partners or others. This gives them reason to abstain altogether except within the full mutual commitment of marriage.[5] But it is the possibility of an *absolute* condemnation of any physical action, i.e., a condemnation applying in advance to all possible cases without exception, that leaves the contemporary Christian ethicist uncomprehending.

The only thing that absolutely matters to them is to respond in love to God's loving presence in the world of men. How can one tell in advance that the physical action in question, such as abortion or adultery, might not in some cases be the best or only means of serving love. Among the most decisive in the rejection of negative moral absolutes (in the sense in which we are using the term) are Paul Lehmann and Joseph Fletcher.[6] But in the current debate among American Protestants, no prominent theologian, not even of those closest to the natural law tradition in their way of thinking, accepts any negative moral absolutes. None agree with any condemnation of a given physical means that excludes the possibility of exceptions to that condemnation.[7]

The controversy among Christians has grown far out of proportion to its importance. In practice, the disagreement often centers about exceptional cases such as those of *Untergrundmoral*. As we noted in the first chapter, the kind of physical actions that the natural law tradition condemns absolutely are, though important, few in number. The average Christian may well be tempted at times to fornication or abortion, but it occurs rarely in comparison with the daily and hourly temptation to irresponsibility, selfishness, lethargy, narrow-mindedness, moodiness, etc. It has become a scandal that the controversy over negative absolutes has absorbed emotional energy and ethical reflection badly needed elsewhere, for example, in the problems of the inner city or of mental health or of environment. As a result of the con-

troversy, many on one side have come to look at the thinking
of the other side with such bewilderment and even bitterness
that dialogue and cooperation in noncontroversial areas are
also hampered. In the present chapter, not for the first time
in the book, I will suggest that one could ease the tensions of
the controversy by locating more accurately the point of division.

The burden of the present chapter is historical. Most of
the present day champions of negative moral absolutes are
maintaining a natural law ethics. They trace their origins,
however, far less to Grotius or Pufendorf or Locke than to
Thomas Aquinas. Thomas did not merely play a major part
in the development and transmission of their natural law
tradition, which he had inherited from the Greeks and Romans, but his positions and arguments are frequently advanced by natural law proponents today exactly as they stand
in his text.[8] It is a truism that one can often see more clearly
and deeply into an intellectual movement at its source than
in its tributaries—in Hegel or Augustine rather than in
Hegelians or Augustinians. It might not, therefore, be merely
of historical interest to examine the mentality of Thomas
Aquinas. What are the dynamics laying down negative moral
absolutes? What is the precise point of difference from those
who refuse them? Is there any common ground on which
each side could meet and learn from each other?

Thomas does agree with present day natural lawyers that
there are negative moral absolutes: certain actions, identifiable by their physical effect, are never to be used as a means.[9]
Many of Thomas' examples coincide with those given by
traditional moralists today: direct killing of an innocent person, extramarital sexual relations, stealing, etc. But Thomas,
like the new moralists, also brings into the picture the God
of Abraham, Isaac and Jacob: His command to Abraham to
kill the innocent Isaac,[10] to Hosea to have sexual intercourse
with a prostitute,[11] to the Israelites to despoil the Egyptians.[12] In a similarly traditional fashion, Thomas condemns
as naturally wrong a man's taking of his own life and a private
person's execution of a criminal.[13] He maintains that both
divorce and polygamy are against the natural law.[14] Yet

precisely in connection with these four negative absolutes he ponders how the God of the Bible has, on occasion, commanded or permitted these condemned actions.

The exceptions to moral principles recorded in the Bible reinforce for Thomas the same thing that, in general, Abraham's faith symbolizes for the twentieth century theologian: God's sovereign freedom in dealing with man and human life and action.[15] As Thomas sees it, at least some of the negative moral absolutes do not bind God. If this is the solution of one problem, it is the datum of another. How is it possible for God to authorize what is otherwise absolutely wrong for a man to do? Like twentieth century theologians, Thomas recognizes that the revelation of God's sovereign freedom must tell us something about man and the morality that binds him. That God could command Abraham to kill Isaac cannot fail to put into new perspective the reason why Abraham could not do it on his own. From the point of view of our historical study: why certain negative moral absolutes are understood by Thomas not to bind God should cast light on why they bind men.

Like Barth, Brunner, Bultmann and Tillich, Thomas knew that he stood at a historic confluence of thought. He welcomed the new and the old. In moral theology he welcomed the newly translated ethics of Aristotle. The self-contained humanism of Aristotle's ethics he fitted into the theistic metaphysics long a part of the medieval mind, originating in Stoicism and Platonism. The gradual accrual of Stoic elements in the medieval world view, the Stoic theory of natural law, for example, had been mediated particularly by texts of Cicero and the continuing tradition of Roman law. The Platonic vision of man's nature as a radical orientation to the Absolute had been conveyed especially by the omnipresent Augustinianism of the early Middle Ages. Thomas pondered these immutable necessities of the philosophers in the light of something about which they knew nothing, the sovereign freedom of the God of Abraham, Isaac, Jacob and Jesus. Thomas shows little sign of doubting that, on the whole, converging currents of thought can move on in a single direction.[16]

At the present stage of medieval research, it is impossible to say how original Thomas' personal synthesis was. For one thing, there are the great number of medieval manuscripts that have not yet been edited. Moreover, what comparisons have been made by scholars such as Dom Lottin on the basis of manuscripts, edited and unedited, show numerous antecedents to many of Thomas' statements on moral theology.[17] Almost as difficult and more important is the question of what Thomas' own thought was behind the formulae he borrowed to synthesize the Greek and Christian traditions as they had come down to his time.[18] In medieval literature, as in Hellenistic, the extreme respect, or at least courtesy, shown the wisdom of the past makes it dangerous to interpret the thought of a man by his isolated statements. The medieval use of sources or "authorities" was to save, whenever possible, the formulae of earlier figures even when the medieval thinker himself meant something different or conflicting. Thomas Aquinas was no exception.[19]

To penetrate behind borrowed formulae to the genuine dynamics of Thomas' synthesis on a given question requires a survey of Thomas' voluminous works, an understanding of the historical development of the question up to his time, and a concentrated theological analysis and reflection on the pertinent texts. I have been unable to find such a study of Thomas' thought on our question: God's freedom in regard to man and to the necessity of the moral principles binding men. The limits of the present investigation, restricted to Thomas' treatment of certain biblical accounts of divine intervention, keep any conclusions from being more than hypotheses. The hypothetical nature of the conclusions is increased by the fact that Thomas does not accord a central place to the biblical stories, but deals with them as possible objections to some other truth he is expounding. I will show evidence of a unified pattern of thought in Thomas' treatment of the cases. But until further investigation, it will remain hypothetical how seriously Thomas took his own views. Do they reflect his basic moral theology or are they merely *ad hoc* solutions to passing problems that do not fit into the structure of his ethical thought?

Nevertheless the formation of an hypothesis on the basis of some evidence is a useful beginning. I have been unable to find in the literature an extensive study of this sort by gathering the evidence of Thomas' view of negative moral absolutes in the light of biblical exceptions.[20] Moreover, the view which emerges from the following sifting of the evidence is a promising one for dialogue today. Thomas is no situationist and he does hold the unpopular theory maintaining negative moral absolutes. But the evidence suggests a way of thinking less foreign to contemporary ethical reflection than one might gather from today's Thomists. The contemporary situationist and one who would share Thomas' way of thinking would not, in dealing with the question of negative moral absolutes, disagree as do those who cannot comprehend each other's position and can only trade charges of "legalism" and "moral anarchy." They would have a remarkably similar vision of man before God, and only because they have different experiences of man would they disagree on the concrete realization of the vision. By acknowledging their common ground, they might well end up quietly talking to and learning from each other.

In regard to one problem, Thomas consistently presupposes that divine intervention in human morality is possible and justified, but offers no explanation of how this might be. To kill oneself is completely wrong.[21] Yet Samson is excused for having killed himself while destroying his enemies. And the holy women are excused for having thrown themselves into the flames in a time of persecution. How were they permitted to take such means? Thomas merely appeals to a command or "instinct" given by God or the Holy Spirit.[22] He does not concern himself with an explanation of how this can be.

In other contexts, Thomas does attack the question of why a particular means that is always evil for man ceases to be so when God commands the man to take it. In one place, however, his answer comes merely to affirm that whatever God wills must be good, simply because He wills it.

. . . fornication is said to be a sin inasmuch as it is contrary to right reason. But man's reason is right inasmuch as it is ruled by the divine will, which is the first and highest rule. Consequently, that which a man does at God's will, obeying His command, is not contrary to right reason, although it may seem to be against the common order of right reason—just as what occurs miraculously by divine power is not contrary to nature, even though it is contrary to the common course of nature. Therefore, Abraham did not sin in being willing to kill his innocent son because he obeyed God, even though this, looked at in itself, is commonly contrary to right human reason. Thus, too, Hosea did not sin by fornicating on divine command. Nor should such intercourse be properly called fornication, although it is termed fornication in reference to the common course of events.[23]

Thomas appears to be as nominalistic as Joseph Fletcher could desire.[24] To be sins the acts of Abraham and Hosea would have to be contrary to right reason. But human reason is right if it follows the divine will. The acts of Abraham and Hosea, performed in obedience to God's will are, therefore, not sins, although, taken by themselves, they normally would be.

But elsewhere Thomas distinguishes his position from any thoroughgoing nominalism. There are things the divine will cannot do, actions it cannot command. As Thomas expounds this on various occasions over the years, his language varies. In two closely parallel passages, he says that God can dispense man from precepts of the second tablet of the decalogue, but not from precepts of the first tablet.[25]

In both passages, the limit on God's action is grounded exclusively on the impossibility of His turning men away from Himself. Since the precepts of the first tablet simply order men to God, a dispensation in this matter would turn men away from God, e.g., a special precept to despair of God or to hate him.[26] The two passages diverge in explaining why it is that God cannot do this. Obviously the reason cannot be any imperfection in God, but must be some transcendent perfection such as His identity with Himself or the unconditioned dependence of creatures on Him. The *De*

Malo passage, invoking a text of the Second Letter to Timothy, says simply that God cannot deny Himself. The *I Sent.* passage argues that God's power cannot render good, even by way of special dispensation, that which would not be ordered to Himself, its final end, just as God's power cannot make a thing exist without the efficient causality of Himself, the first cause.

However, both passages justify the dispensations God can give from the precepts of the second tablet by holding simply that the order to be observed between men need not be observed by God. In the *De Malo* passage, dealing with God's command to Hosea, God can dispense from precepts of the second tablet, by which man is ordered directly to his neighbor, because the good of the neighbor, unlike God's goodness, is only a particular good. The *I Sent.* passage, mentioning the case of Hosea, but making its application to the case of Abraham, complements the explanation. All goodness in created things has to come from their last end, God. The natural order of one creature to another has its goodness simply because through it the creatures are duly ordered to their last end. The order to the last end is thus the cause of the order between creatures. Just as God, and God alone, can work a miracle and make something exist without using the secondary causality of creatures which normally is required, so He, and He alone, can make something good without that order to a certain creature which normally would give the thing its goodness. Where the order to the creature was the natural way by which the thing in question was ordered to its last end and received its goodness, now God gives it goodness directly by giving it, through His command, a direct ordering to its last end.

Both passages come to the same principle. God can do what He wants with men and human relations as long as He is still relating them positively to Himself as their final end. The two passages imply by their argumentation that there is no further qualification. Precisely because an order is directed only to a "particular good," precisely because an order is first to something that is not the final end, God can dispense from it.

Although he employs a different image, Thomas makes a similar implication in the *De Potentia Dei* as he takes up again the case of Abraham and Hosea.[27] A ruler can, in the interests of the justice which is the end or purpose of his rule, render virtuous what in itself would be sinful, e.g., killing a man. Similarly, God has all things in His disposition to direct to the purpose of His rule, which is His goodness. He can thus, by the purpose He foresees and orders, render meritorious what would itself be sinful, e.g., killing an innocent child. The same can be said of God's command to Hosea, since God is the orderer of all human generation.

Thomas' principle, if carried out logically, excludes that there could be some means which, because of its physical nature, God could not authorize. All things are at His disposition. The sole absolute for Him is that the means He authorizes bring His subjects to His Goodness. On the other hand, it would go beyond the evidence to claim that Thomas would have been ready to apply to all particular cases the principle he employs in the three passages just considered. Could God authorize a man to practice contraception or commit sodomy? In the passages seen thus far there is no evidence that Thomas has been concerned with thinking out all the practical implications of that view of the sovereignty of God which he sketches in order to explain the Bible stories.

The fact remains that his view emerges as uncomplicated and, in several respects, close to that of contemporary Christian ethicians. Both they and Thomas find in the God of revelation a free Lord who can bypass any moral order among men and any human good and can authorize any means for man to take to make his way to God. The difference is that for Thomas God gives the authorization only by way of exception and miracle. Consequently, it is, practically speaking, not a real possibility for a man to take into account and the certain negative moral prohibitions concerning human relations hold for man as absolutes. For twentieth century theologians like Brunner and Thielicke, on the other hand, God has worked the miracle for all men through Jesus Christ and the authorization Thomas speaks of is, for them, just one aspect of the freedom every Christian has. True, the Christian must respect the orders of creation, but it is always up to him to discern whether God's individual command to Him in the concrete situation requires that he bypass natural order, as Abraham once did. A dialogue proceeding out of such agreement and disagreement could be stimulating and profitable.

More often, however, Thomas takes a different tack to explain how God can command a man to adopt certain means which would always be sinful for the man by himself. Thomas' language is closer here to that of present day natural law proponents and it appears to contradict what he has said in the three passages just considered. It does not pertain to our purpose to discuss whether the contradiction is more than verbal. In any case, the following analysis should show that there is no profound contradiction and that, as a matter of fact, Thomas' new approach fills in and shades the one already seen.

Thomas sets forth the second approach squarely in two articles in which he is asking, "Do the precepts of the decalogue admit of dispensation?"[28] The answer, surprisingly enough, in the light of the passages previously considered, is a universal negative: none of the precepts of the decalogue allow for dispensation. It is possible that in the formal question of the articles Thomas is inquiring only about the possibility of dispensation by a human being. In any case, dealing with objections he has to face the question of God's apparent dispensing from the precepts of the decalogue. The occasion once more is God's command to Abraham and Hosea and the Israelites in Egypt.[29]

In the *III Sent.* article, Thomas merely asserts that "God never commanded anything contrary to the precepts of the decalogue inasmuch as they belong to the decalogue."[30] This suffices to neutralize the objection. He does not assert that God *could not* command such a thing and he does not use the word "dispensation" for what God has never done. I think that by textual analysis one could mount a case that Thomas means to exclude even the possibility of God's "dispensing." But for the purpose of the present essay, a minimal interpretation seems advisable.

In the article of the *Summa*, however, Thomas flatly denies the possibility of God's giving a dispensation in regard to the precepts of the decalogue, though at the same time he is careful to make clear what he means and what it is God could not permit a man to do. "And therefore God cannot give a dispensation in the sense that a man be permitted not to be ordered to God or not to conform to the order of God's justice, even where it is [merely] a case of men being ordered to each other.

It is, of course, in denying God the possibility of the second type of dispensation (". . . not to conform to the order of God's justice, etc.") that Thomas advances beyond, if he does not abandon, the position taken in the *I Sent.* and *De Malo* passages. In the present passage, as in those two, the precepts of the second tablet "contain the order itself of justice to be observed among men."[31] But in apparent contradiction to the other two passages, the present one denies that God can dispense in this regard.

What grounds does Thomas offer for his new position? The objection to which he is replying argued that God, like any legislator, can dispense from the precepts of the law which He himself has established. Thomas gives the classic metaphysical reply to any such nominalism: God cannot go against Himself. He invokes the same text of the Second Letter to Timothy that he did in the *De Malo* passage. But he draws a different conclusion: ". . . as the Apostle says . . . 'God remains faithful, He cannot deny Himself.' And He would deny Himself, if He removed the order itself of justice; for He is justice itself."[32]

Since even God must always observe the order of justice, the precepts that express it should obviously be termed immutable. "Thus, therefore, the precepts themselves of the decalogue, inasmuch as they contain the quality of justice, are immutable."[33] Is Thomas contradicting not only statements made by himself in other passages, but also the basic position of the twentieth century Christian ethicians who oppose negative moral absolutes? Is he not saying that there is an immutable order of justice, grounded in the Divine Essence, and that the negative, moral absolutes constituting the order bind God and man? Have we not come to the primal point of separation between Thomistic ethics and that characteristic of the twentieth century? To answer, one must scrutinize more clearly what Thomas means by "the order of justice." Does he include in the immutable precepts of justice anything corresponding to "negative moral absolutes" as we defined the term for our problem?

In the two articles presently being considered, Thomas explicates the immutable order of justice in connection with a famous text of Aristotle: *Nicomachean Ethics*, Book V, 1134^b–1135^a.[34] Thomas equates Aristotle's "natural justice" (*iustum naturale*) with his own "natural law" and the "justice" embodied in the precepts of the decalogue. Aristotle's words, therefore, give rise to an objection. "The precepts of the decalogue belong to the natural law. But natural justice fails to hold in certain cases and is changeable, just as human nature is, as the Philosopher says in the Fifth Book of the Ethics." Therefore, there is place for dispensation.[35]

Thomas meets the objection by an exegesis of Aristotle's meaning of justice in the words quoted. "The Philosopher is not speaking of that natural justice which contains the order itself of justice; for this never fails to hold, that justice should be observed." The corresponding reply in the *III Sent.* passage is fuller: ". . . there are two kinds of natural justice . . . : one which is always and everywhere just, as that in which the essence of justice and virtue in general consists, as keeping the mean, observing what is right, etc." But it is the other kind of justice that the philosopher is talking about, the kind that holds only in the majority of cases, being an application of the first and universal norm.[36]

In another passage in which the dispensations accorded Abraham, Hosea and the Jews in Egypt are discussed, Thomas raises again the problem of Aristotle's assertion "that nothing is so just among all men that it does not take different forms among some." The solution is similar to that of the other two passages: Aristotle is not talking of the common principles of natural justice, but of certain conclusions derived from them and holding only in the majority of cases.[37]

In all three passages, Thomas merely says that Aristotle

is not talking about one and the same justice that holds everywhere, but is speaking of the relative, mutable kind. But
when discussing the Aristotelian text in his commentary on
the Nicomachean Ethics, he seems to say that Aristotle himself affirms also the universal, unfailing kind of justice earlier
in the passage.

> And first of all Aristotle presents natural justice in two
> ways. One, according to its effect or virtue, when he says:
> natural justice is that which has everywhere the same power
> and virtue to lead to good and restrain from evil. It hap-
> pens, indeed, because nature, the cause of this kind of
> justice, is the same everywhere among all men . . . In
> the second way Aristotle explains this justice according to
> its cause, when he says that natural justice does not con-
> sist in seeming or not seeming, i.e., it does not arise from
> some human opinion, but from nature. For just as in specu-
> lative matters . . . , so also in practical matters there are
> certain naturally known principles, as it were indemon-
> strable, and some close to these, as "evil should be
> avoided," "no one should be unjustly harmed," "one should
> not steal," etc.[38]

Thomas recognizes that Aristotle goes on to assert equally
that *all* human justice is changeable, because everything in
a man, even what is natural, is changeable either *per se* or
per accidens.[39] Thomas does not contest Aristotle's assertion
and, as we have seen, accepts Aristotle's presentation of the
mutable kind of natural justice. But he adds his own gloss
by reaffirming and further explaining the immutable kind of
justice he had found a few lines earlier in Aristotle's text:

> One should note that the essences of changeable things
> are immutable and therefore nothing that is natural to us,
> belonging as it were to the very essence of man, is changed
> in any way, for example, the fact that man is an animal.
> On the other hand, the things that follow on nature, for
> example, dispositions, actions and movements, do undergo
> change in less common cases [in the preceding paragraph
> Thomas referred to Aristotle's example of men being right-

handed]. Similarly, also, those things which belong to the very essence of justice cannot undergo change in any way, for example that one should not steal, which is to do something unjust. But those things which follow on the essence of justice undergo change in the less common cases.[40]

By basing natural law and justice on immutable principles, Thomas is certainly adding to, if not contradicting, what Aristotle himself said about *justum naturale* and ethical knowledge in general. But in so doing he makes clearer what he, Thomas, means by the immutable order of justice that even God must observe. To return to our question, then, does Thomas include among the immutable principles any principles that fulfill our definition of "negative moral absolutes"?

By the use of the term in our problem, it will be recalled, we mean principles according to which a specific external action, defined in physical, nonmoral terms, may never be used as a means, no matter what the circumstances or end in view. There is no question whether or not Thomas holds negative moral absolutes. He does. But does he identify them with the immutable order of justice, grounded in the Divine Essence? Or does he see another basis for them? The answer will affect any attempt to make his ethics comprehensible to contemporary ethicians.

In our four passages, there are certain immutable principles that Thomas enunciates explicitly. Others he implies by justifying God's commands to Abraham, Hosea and the Jews in Egypt. The immutable principles he affirms explicitly come to ten. For most of them, the fuller context has been quoted above.

1. Evil should be avoided.[41]
2. What is undue should be done to no one; what is due should be rendered to all.[42]
3. One should not act unjustly.[43]
4. No man should be harmed unjustly.[44]
5. No man should be killed unduly.[45]
6. Justice should be observed.[46]
7. It is always just and virtuous to keep the mean.[47]

8. It is always just and virtuous to observe what is right.[48]
9. It is right and true that one act according to reason.[49]
   (In the context, it is fairly clear that Thomas would be willing to formulate this and the preceding two principles, "One should . . .")
10. One should not steal.[50]

None of the above principles constitute the "negative moral absolute" of our problematic. In the first five, the act which is absolutely condemned is itself expressed in moral terms: evil, what is undue, unjust acting, unjust harming, undue killing. Moreover, the first three are too general to be negative moral absolutes in the sense being discussed, since such absolutes condemn specific actions, such as abortion. The following four principles are affirmative, but could be taken as implying a negative one, i.e., as condemning acts in which injustice is done, the mean is not kept, what is right is not observed, or in which one does not act according to reason. However, they are still too general to be one of the controverted "negative moral absolutes." One could argue, too, that even in the last three of the four the act which is absolutely condemned is already expressed in moral terms. The prohibition of stealing, the final principle given above, comes closest to being a negative moral absolute. It is negative, takes a specific action, and condemns it absolutely. The question is whether Thomas means by "stealing" something already defined in moral terms. At least in this context he seems to do so: his point seems to be that stealing should not be done because it is, by definition, unjust.[50a] The principle would not, therefore, be a negative moral absolute. The issue, however, need not be urged, since Thomas' understanding of the absolute condemnation of stealing will become clearer in certain passages which will be discussed shortly.

Consequently, none of the immutable principles of morality that Thomas sets down as binding God and man can be said to be negative moral absolutes. We turn now to Thomas' direct justification of God's commands to Abraham, Hosea and the Israelites in Egypt. How does he justify them? He will be seen to presuppose that God always acts according to justice and virtue. Does he imply any negative moral absolutes binding on God? Does his justification of God's commands cast any light on the grounds upon which the negative moral absolutes do bind men?

In the matter of taking human life, Thomas sees no negative moral absolutes binding God. True, God is not free to act unjustly, but He can authorize a man to take an innocent life, although it would be unjust and a violation of the natural law for the man to do so on his own.

> . . . the command given Abraham to kill his innocent son was not unjust, because God is the author of death and life.[51]
>
> One question arises [concerning the command given to Abraham] because the slaying of an innocent person is against the law of nature and thus a sin . . . I reply that he who kills on the command of his superior, if the superior licitly gives the order, he obeys licitly and can carry out his service. But God has authority over life and death . . .
>
> . . .
>
> Moreover, when God takes the life of someone, even if He is innocent, He is doing injustice to no one. For this reason, many men, guilty and innocent, die every day by divine disposition. Thus Abraham could licitly carry out God's command.[52]

In two passages in the *Prima Secundae*, Thomas proffers essentially the same explanation of why God's command did not authorize injustice or homicide. He adds, as part of the argument, that any divine command to kill merely imposes the penalty due all men because of original sin.[53] In the text of the *De Potentia Dei* seen above, Thomas is envisaging the case of Abraham's decision to slay his son when he says that God has all in His disposition to direct to the end of His rule, i.e., His goodness.[54]

Thus in the six passages where Thomas justifies God's command to slay Isaac, he comes from three different points of view to the same effect. The authority and dominion of God over life and death, the guilt of all men because of Adam's sin, the authority of God's rule leading men to His goodness —all prove that God can dispose of man's life without restriction as a means to carry out His good purposes.[55] There are no negative moral absolutes limiting God's activity in this domain. God is not free to act unjustly or to authorize homicide even for a good end. But His authority over life and death means that any physical disposition He makes in this regard for His good end will be a just means.

When Thomas comes to justify the taking of Egyptian spoils he notes that the argument is the same as the one he used in the case of Abraham and Hosea.

> Similarly, it was not contrary to justice to command the Jews to take the property of the Egyptians, because all things are God's and He gives them to whom He wills.[56] And the same argument applies to stealing, which is taking something that belongs to another. For whatever one takes on the command of God, who is Lord of all [*Dominus*], one does not take without the will of the owner [*domini*], which is what stealing is.[57]

God's disposing of property parallels His disposing of human life. There are no negative moral absolutes limiting Him in this domain. He is not free to act unjustly, not to steal any more than to kill unjustly. But since all things belong to Him, He can dispose of them as He wills. There are no property rights He need respect. Any disposition of property that He makes for His good purposes will be a good and just means.

Even in the question of sexual morality raised by the case of Hosea, Thomas notes that God's action is justified by a reason similar to that which justifies His taking of life and property.

> Similarly, also, the command to Hosea to take an adulterous woman was not opposed to chastity, for God Himself is the one who orders human generation and that manner of having intercourse with a woman is due which God establishes.[58]

Thomas also develops the theme in a juridical fashion, i.e., not in terms of God's general dominion over human generation, but in terms of His authority over the institution of marriage, which He Himself established.

> And similarly, Hosea, too, going to a wife of fornication or an adulterous woman, did not commit adultery or fornication, because he went to a woman who was his by virtue of the command of God who is the author of the institution of marriage.[59] . . . thus also because of the authority of God Himself, who is over [supra] the law of marriage, that intercourse was not fornication which otherwise would have been fornication . . ."[60]

In two other passages, Thomas apparently understands God's authority in a similar way, though his language differs.

> Similarly, too, adultery is intercourse with a wife not one's own; but this one was given to Hosea by a law promulgated by God. Wherefore to whatever woman a man might go on divine command, it is neither adultery nor fornication.[61] God can remove from an unmarried woman the condition "not His" although she will not become fully His wife. As a result to go to her would not be against the decalogue.[62]

In *Distinctio* 33 of his commentary on the Fourth Book of the *Sentences*, Thomas describes God's command to Hosea as a dispensation from a primary precept of the natural law.[63] God's capacity to grant dispensations from primary precepts is possibly illustrated also by His granting of divorce. Thomas does not hesitate in affirming God's capacity to grant it, but is not sure whether the indissolubility of marriage is a primary or secondary precept of the natural law, nor whether God, in fact, ever authorized divorce.[64] He affirms without qualification God's power to grant dispensation even from primary precepts of the natural law, though they are, as it were, always in force (*quasi semper existentia*). But he makes no attempt here to explain how the unusual, miraculous intervention can be reconciled to the moral force of the precepts. He does render some explanation how dispensation from secondary precepts is possible, but since he presents it as essentially different from the dispensation granted Abraham and Hosea, the explanation does not fit into the present stage of our analysis.

It is, therefore, only in the first six passages considered that Thomas explains how the dispensation accorded Hosea can be morally justified.[65] In all six, God's disposing of human generation parallels His disposing of human life and property. In this domain, too, there are no negative moral absolutes limiting His activity.[66] He is not free to authorize fornication or adultery any more than He could allow homicide or stealing. But since human generation and the institution of marriage are completely subject to Him, He can dispose of them as He wills. There is no woman, no matter what her state or situation, with whom God cannot authorize a man to have intercourse, by making her, simply by His fiat, in some sense His wife.

The theological vision of Thomas, within which he places the stories concerning Abraham, Hosea and the Israelites in Egypt, emerges as remarkably unified in text after text. God is free from any negative moral absolutes that would restrict His disposing of human life, property and generation. In these matters, God has authority to take whatever means may contribute to His good purposes. More significant for our problematic is the conclusion Thomas implies for human morality. What is right and wrong for a man in killing, disposing of property, exercising human generation, depends on the extent to which God has shared His authority with man. Any negative moral absolutes that bind man in this area are grounded simply on God's free refusal to grant authorization for using the particular act as a means. He could grant the authorization, but in His wisdom and love chooses not to do so in the normal course of events.

Thomas does not merely imply the general principle that all human morality concerning the disposing of life, property and generation depends on the authority God chooses to grant or not to grant. He explicitly points out that this same principle, which justifies the conduct of Abraham, Hosea and the Israelites, applies analogously to the morality governing the ordinary human situation where no divine intervention has occurred.

The most obvious application is to the disposition of things external to man, which could come into his possession and become his property. The nature of external things is not subject to human power, but to the divine, which all things obey. But, as to their use, man has by God's ordination a natural dominion over all external things to use them for his own benefit. Precisely in sharing His dominion, God has made man to His own image.[67] Similarly, as he explains how God ordered the despoiling of the Egyptians, Thomas twice recalls that this sort of transfer of ownership can be done by human authority, although to a greater extent by divine.

> Not only God, the Lord of all, can do this, but also men with authority can at times transfer property from one person to another for a particular reason.[68]

In the matter of taking a life, too, it is in normal human morality as well as in extraordinary cases such as Abraham's, a question of God's sharing His authority with men. Secular judges who condemn to death according to law are not guilty of homicide, for they do it at God's command and with His authority. "For every law is a command of God."[69] On the other hand, in the next paragraph, Thomas uses exactly the same principle to prove that killing oneself is wrong except in cases like that of Samson and the martyrs.[70] The decisive factor, once more, is that God has not shared His authority over life with most men as He has with Samson and the martyrs.

On the basis of the same reasoning, the killing of a criminal for the sake of the common good is never permitted a private person, but "him alone to whom the care of preserving the community is entrusted . . . ," i.e., the rulers possessing public authority. As to those private persons whom God commanded through Moses to slay their neighbors, brothers and friends (*Exodus*, XXXII, 27), they ". . . do not seem to have done this themselves, but rather He, by whose authority they did it, just as the soldier kills the enemy on the authority of the ruler and the executioner kills the thief on the authority of the judge."[71]

In two of the passages considered earlier, Thomas refers to the authority of the judge and ruler to kill criminals and enemies in order to explain the conduct of Abraham and Hosea and the Jews in Egypt. The same principle applies in both cases. Thomas sums up in one general principle the two cases of natural morality and the three cases of divine intervention:

> Consequently, the precepts themselves of the decalogue are immutable inasmuch as they contain the quality of justice. But inasmuch as they are determined by application to individual acts, namely, that this or that be homicide, stealing or adultery or not, this indeed is mutable. Sometimes the change can take place only on divine authority, namely in those things which have been established by God alone, as marriage, etc. Sometimes it can take place also on human authority, as in those things which have been entrusted to human jurisdiction. For here men take God's place [gerunt vicem Dei], but not in all things.[72]

We may be belaboring the obvious, but how often in the current controversy over abortion do the natural law defenders speak of the inviolability of human life as if it were an absolute. In the moral theology of Thomas Aquinas, the inviolability of human life is not absolute, but relative to the authority of the one who could take the life. Thomas would condemn all direct abortion performed by men, but only because he believed that it did not fall within the authority God had granted men in the taking of life, such as He had in capital punishment. He denies the state the authority to kill innocent persons (which could be interpreted as the case of abortion), not because of the inviolability of all human life, but because such an authority cannot be justified by the common good.[73]

In the passage just quoted, Thomas included sexual morality under the same principle as he had the morality of disposing of life and property. Whether an act be adultery or not depends on the decision of the competent authority to authorize it or not. In regard to human generation and marriage, men do not normally share God's authority in as essential a way as they do in regard to property and human life.[74] One can say, it is true, that human generation should be directed to its ends not merely by nature and ecclesiastical authority, but also by civil laws.[75] But whereas God has shared with men some of His authority to take life and transfer property rights, no human authority, but God alone, institutor of marriage, can determine who is whose wife and therefore with whom a man may have sexual intercourse.[76] Still it remains true that the same principle applies to normal morality of human generation as to the case of Hosea: it depends, not on what eternally has to be, but on what authority has freely determined.

As we said in the introduction, the present study deals with Thomas' views on normal human morality only where he is considering it in the light of the miraculous interventions of God recorded in the Bible. The conclusions we have drawn, however, receive support from the observation of Joseph Fuchs, based on his more extensive survey of all of Thomas' sexual ethics:

> . . . it appears that the boundary between sexual norms of natural law and sexual norms of divine positive law is not precisely observed. In fact, one might ask whether the sexual norms of natural law are not simply placed here on the same level as positive law and treated as such: they are the law that serves the common good and therefore knows no exception.[77]

That certain moral absolutes of sexual morality might be grounded by Thomas rather on principles of positive law than on some intrinsic finality of nature is illustrated by Thomas' refusal to condemn marital intercourse where no child is possible and to permit fornication when the child can be properly reared. In these exceptional cases, Thomas recognizes that the reasons he has given for the natural morality of marital intercourse and the natural immorality of fornication do not apply. Yet he remarks:

> . . . the act of generation [unlike the act of nourishing oneself] is ordered to the good of the species, which is the common good. But the common good is subject to ordering by law . . .
>
> . . .
>
> [therefore] to determine of what sort the act of generation should be does not pertain to anyone, but to the legislator, to whom it belongs to order the propagation of children, as the Philosopher also says in the Second Book of the *Politics*. But law does not consider what can occur in a particular case, but what has usually happened suitably. Therefore, although in a particular case, the intention of nature can be saved in an act of fornication in regard to the generation and rearing of the child, still the act is disordered in itself and a mortal sin.[78]

In the passages just considered, the interpretation of natural law morality along lines proper to positive law appears in two contexts. On the one hand, God can grant Hosea an exceptional dispensation from the prescribed form of marriage because He has supreme authority over human generation and marriage. Thomas does not feel it necessary to discuss whether or how the "end" of generation is preserved in Hosea's action. On the other hand, even in exceptional cases where the end of nature and of the legislator would be preserved although the law were not observed, the individual does not have the right to act contrary to the law. Generation concerns the common good and therefore man's use of it is subject to law. But law makes no allowance for exceptional cases; only the legislator can dispense from it.

In the historic thirty-third distinction of his *Commentary* on the *Fourth Book of the Sentences*, Thomas introduces a third context in which he interprets the natural law morality concerning generation along lines proper to positive law. At one point in this "first treatise of moral theology to have been developed,"[79] the young Thomas Acquinas took up the classic question of the polygamy of the patriarchs and discussed it in the light of Aristotelian ethics. As he saw it, the patriarchs did not have the sort of dispensation accorded Hosea, but neither were they guilty of violating the natural law precept prohibiting polygamy.

> . . . as is clear from what has been said before, a plurality of wives is said to be contrary to the natural law not in regard to the primary precepts, but in regard to the secondary, which are derived as [*quasi*] conclusions from the primary precepts. But because human acts necessarily vary according to different conditions of persons and times and other circumstances, the aforesaid conclusions do not follow from the primary precepts of the natural law as having force in all cases, but only for the greater part. Such is all the matter of morality, as the philosopher makes clear in his *Ethics*. Consequently, where the secondary precepts do not have force, they may be licitly set aside. But because it is not easy to determine variations of the sort, it is reserved to him by whose authority the law does have force to grant permission to set aside the law in those cases where the force of the law should not apply. Now the law of having only one wife was instituted by God, not man. It was never communicated by spoken or written word, but impressed on the heart, as was also the rest that pertains in any way to the natural law. Consequently, here God alone can grant the dispensation by internal inspiration. It was done principally to the holy Patriarchs and by their example was passed on to others at that time when the said precept of nature needed to be set aside, so that there would be a greater increase of children to be brought up for the worship of God.[80]

Thomas finds a similar dispensation from secondary precepts in the concubinage of the same Patriarchs (which he considers a modified form of polygamy) and "probably" in the divorce that Moses permitted.[81]

It has rightly been pointed out that Thomas does not present the distinction between primary and secondary precepts with all desirable clarity and coherence in this first attempt

of his to deal with apparent dispensations from the natural
law. Nor does he use the distinction again in the way he
understands it here.[82] What he does do here and what he
will still do years later is not merely to explain the dispensation for polygamy and divorce as the wise and legitimate
freedom of the divine legislator, but to justify God's action
on more natural grounds than he had the commands to Hosea
and Abraham.

> . . . as natural inclination is to those things that are for
> the most part, so law is laid down according to what oc-
> curs for the most part. It is not contrary to the reasons
> given above if in some case it could occur otherwise. For
> the good of the many should not be passed over for the
> good of one, since "the good of the many is always more
> divine than the good of one" [Aristotle, First Book of the
> Nicomachean Ethics, 1094 b]. But lest the defect which
> could occur in some one case should remain completely
> without remedy, legislators and similar persons have
> authority to dispense from common statute inasmuch as it
> is necessary in a particular case. And if indeed it is a hu-
> man law, men having similar power can grant the dispensa-
> tion. If the law has been divinely laid down, divine
> authority can grant the dispensation, as in the Old Law
> there seems to have been, by way of dispensation, an in-
> dult to have more than one wife and concubines and
> divorce.[83]

In both the thirty-third distinction and the passage from
the Summa Contra Gentiles, therefore, Thomas outlines a
form of dispensation that is neither proper to human authority nor totally supernatural like the commands to Abraham
and Hosea, which were justified only by God's supreme
authority, choosing to symbolize a divine mystery. The dispensation from the unity and indissolubility of marriage lies
in between, proper to God alone, but justified by the fact
that the natural law in less frequent cases may fail to achieve
its own purpose and interfere with a greater good. Thomas
compares this kind of dispensation (opposing it to the higher

kind accorded Abraham and Hosea) to natural change brought about by chance in the physical world:

> . . . dispensation from precepts, especially those which belong in some way to the natural law, is like change in the course of something in nature. The course can be changed in two ways. One way is by one natural cause preventing another natural cause from its course; this is what occurs occasionally and by chance in nature. But the course that is varied by this way is not that of natural things which are always, but of those which are frequently . . .
>
> . . . .
>
> [Analogously] Now the grounds for dispensation from precepts of the natural law can at times be found in lower causes and thus a dispensation can be granted from secondary precepts of the natural law . . . as was said about polygamy and that kind of thing.[84]

It must be left for another inquiry to explore the implications for natural law morality of the natural grounds for dispensation from the natural law. For the purpose of the present essay, the thirty-third distinction and *Summa Contra Gentiles*, III, 125, merely illustrate once more how Thomas interprets natural law and exceptions to it not by some absolute qualities of a given act taken by itself, but on an analogy with human law, i.e., as the wise judgment of the legislator who has authority to lead men to their final end as he sees fit—whether by laying down a law or dispensing from it. The final end is God Himself and this is what determines both the law and the dispensation, whether the dispensation be to symbolize some divine mystery of the supernatural economy or whether it be to adjust a natural law to an exceptional, but natural situation.

Moreover, the natural basis that Thomas adduces as grounds for the more natural kind of divine dispensation throws into relief, by contrast, the sovereign freedom and authority of God in granting a purely supernatural kind of dispensation as He did to Hosea. Whether or not he continued to understand the latter kind of dispensation in the same way as he did in the thirty-third distinction, the fact remains that Thomas' continuing justification of the dispensation granted Hosea and Abraham never invokes the natural kind of basis he does for the dispensation for polygamy. He never reconciles the dispensation accorded Hosea and Abraham with natural ends and goods, but merely invokes the supreme dominion and authority of God over all human generation and life.

Let us recapitulate. The starting point was the current controversy over the possibility of "negative moral absolutes," principles according to which certain means, because of their physical effect, are never justified for a man. To understand the position of the natural law tradition, we turn to the writings of Thomas Aquinas. In order to form an hypothesis on what was his synthesis of divine freedom and negative moral absolutes, we undertook to analyze in detail his treatment of the incidents in the Bible where God seemed to authorize a violation of the negative moral absolutes Thomas held.

What emerged progressively from the analysis was that the moral center of gravity for Thomas did not lie in the act itself and its physical effect, though these were relevant factors. As long as the acts contributed to some good purpose, the crucial question to decide the legitimacy of a given means was the authority of the person acting—not what was to be done, but who would do it. Abortion and extramarital sexual intercourse would be absolutely wrong if the agent had only normal human authority. But God could, by a special initiative, authorize a man to perform the same acts.

Thus in the texts we first considered, Thomas merely said that whatever God willed was good. In other passages God was seen to necessarily will to bring men to Himself, but could dispose freely of any created good or order in so doing. Certain other passages, using different terminology, seemed to limit God further. He had to act according to justice and virtue. But Thomas' consistent application to practice showed that justice and virtue never excluded absolutely any particular physical kind of means for divine authorization.

On the contrary, God's universal dominion over external

things and life and generation made whatever He chose to do with them for His good purpose to be just and virtuous means. It became progressively clear that a general framework enunciated several times by Thomas dominated his methodology throughout. The framework consisted of levels of authority communicable from God to man: the authority naturally belonging to the private individual, that naturally belonging to public officials, that supernaturally granted for what could become good for man by exceptions occuring naturally (like polygamy), that supernaturally granted for *any* use of property or human life or human generation that would serve the divine purpose. Whether Thomas, in fact, had the framework in mind throughout his entire ethics and whether, in particular, he would have maintained that God could even authorize acts such as usury or contraception, remains an hypothesis, requiring further verification. That in a good number of passages he did present the framework and its principles and that they directly imply God's power to authorize any physical means for a good end is unquestionable.

In the context we have been considering, therefore, the point of division between Thomas and the more relativistic ethics of the twentieth century lies in a location that is often ignored today. The point of division is not the question of whether it is possible for certain means, because of their physical effect, to be always wrong. The point of division is the question of whether or not God has shared with man the authority and dominion to take certain means when, perhaps by way of exception, they serve the greater good. The question for dialogue, therefore, is how far God has shared His dominion with man.

John de Lugo, writing in the seventeenth century and discussing the question of suicide, pinpointed the question well:

> For some say, first of all, that [suicide] is contrary to justice because man is something belonging to God and therefore cannot be destroyed without the authority of the owner [*absque domini facultate*]. And God is said never

to have accorded the authority. But the argument seems weak unless you prove on other grounds that man is not the master [*dominum*] of his life, as he is master of his actions, his reputation, his material resources . . .

. . .

one must explain why there is no injustice done to God by dissipating one's reputation or destroying one's house or another's, all of which are things belonging to God, and yet there is injustice in killing oneself. Or one must explain how one concludes in the light of nature that man is not master of his own life as he is of other things.[85]

Few today would accept the cardinal's own solution to the objection: "master" is a relative term, involving the superiority of the master over the person or thing that belongs to the master. Therefore, one cannot be master of oneself, just as one cannot be one's own father or teacher.[86] However, John de Lugo, standing at the entry of the modern era and himself beginning already to think in modern terms, put his finger on a precise area for dialogue today between contemporary thinkers and medieval ones. To what extent has God granted each man dominion and authority?

In the dialogue, one would come quickly to a theological question which is perhaps the most central as well as the most agonizing for Christians today: how can the moral autonomy of the person, which modern man sees so clearly, be one with the theonomy demanded by Christian faith?[87] In this regard, a final remark on the dialogue may also be drawn from words of de Lugo. In the lines immediately preceding the above quotation, he writes of suicide:

The whole difficulty lies in assigning a reason for this truth [that one may not take one's own life]. For though the evil in question be immediately clear, it is still not easy to find its basis. Consequently, it happens here, as in many other questions, that the conclusion is more certain than the reasons, which, being of various kinds, are adduced from different sources to prove the point.[88]

In a dialogue between a Thomas *redivivus* and a contemporary ethician, it might help to recognize that the conclusions on both sides may be more certain than their reasons. To Thomas, living in his particular milieu and sharing its mind, it was "immediately clear" that, let us say, abortion and divorce are always wrong. To many of our contemporaries, having the mind of their milieu, it is "immediately clear" that this is not the case. And both Thomas and our contemporaries are less sure when it comes to elucidating the reasons for their position.

The same may be said of the more profound point of division which the present chapter has tried to bring out. It was immediately clear to Thomas and his contemporaries that the hierarchy of authority and law and obedience was the principal factor for good as it brought civilization and morality and religion progressively into the life of the Middle Ages. Exploiting the Greek philosophical tradition, Thomas naturally conceived moral principles in a framework of authority and law and obedience. The intervening centuries have brought man new perspective and light, centering on his inviolable liberty and personal rights as well as on his incredible power over nature and human life. For twentieth century man, the place of law and authority is not so clear, but he sees himself and his companions in the center of the stage, individual persons having "come of age," "condemned to freedom," to the unique solitude of their own moral responsibility and autonomy, as they hold in their hands undreamed-of power over nature and other men. He naturally conceives moral principles in a framework of freedom and the responsibility of power.[89]

On the deeper level, where the extent of man's dominion and authority under God is in question, the two visions, medieval and contemporary, assuredly differ: man as citizen and man as responsible. But unlike the surface conflicts concerning particular acts such as abortion, the profound difference of vision may not, on the whole, be a black and white contradiction, but rather a shift in perspective where something has been gained and something lost. It is a place for genuine dialogue as Max Müller described it:

> Dialogue and discussion with a great thinker means to work out what his total interpretation of the basic meaning of everything conceals while it is explaining, and to work out what hitherto unseen and unexplained the interpretation brings out new, while at the same time it forgets other things; for it is, indeed, finite.[90]

Might it not be that one thing new which Thomas Aquinas brought out was the Greek insight into the role of order and authority in the human community and in the cosmos? Might it not be that what he "forgot" was something he never knew because Western man had yet to learn it: the extent of man's fantastic power over nature and human life and the extent of his inescapable moral autonomy? And might not the modern vision of the greater dominion and authority that God has shared with men have led Thomas by his own principles to rethink his conclusions on negative moral absolutes? On the other hand, might not his own vision of God as Lord and of the value of law and authority be a valuable reminder to contemporary man of something he tends to forget?

11 LOYAL OPPOSITION
IN THE CHURCH

In the preceding chapters, we scrutinized the new Christian morality as it deals with ethical questions common to believer and nonbeliever, concerning student freedom, homosexuality, abortion, etc. For the remainder of the book, I will try to present the new morality as it deals with ethical questions peculiar to Christians, concerning aspects of Church life.

We are in one of the periods in the history of the Church when the rhythm of its development gathers speed like a galloping horse. At such a time, a Christian is exhilarated by the new prospects to which the Spirit is leading the Church. But the rapid pace of change also exacerbates tensions. One form of aggravated tension arises in the matter of the Christian's obedience. The direction of changes already made seem to an individual Christian to indicate where a further change should take place. Or perhaps a change may appear hasty and misdirected and call for a change back to the old way. In either case, however, those who hold authority in the Church may see things differently. The authorities may not only oppose the desired change for the moment; they may explicitly reject it once and for all. Tension mounts. And thus in a time like our own, when changes multiply around us, so do the tensions.

An obvious example is the birth control question. As everyone knows, a growing number of Catholics today—including theologians, philosophers, psychologists and doctors—cannot, despite honest effort on their part, understand the position taken by the ecclesiastical authorities on birth control. They have grown increasingly convinced that the official stand is neither infallible nor irrevocable, but badly in need of revision.

In the present chapter, I am not inquiring whether this and similar dissident opinions are well-grounded or not. I am simply taking as given the case, widespread today, of the Catholic who has arrived at convictions contrary to those of authority. Whatever worth his convictions may possess, he now holds them and finds he cannot change them. He asks himself: "What can I do? What should I do?"

Some respond by simply disobeying. If the point in question is birth control, they buy contraceptives and employ them. They encourage others to do the same. They justify themselves simply with their belief that the official Church position is wrong, inhuman and unChristian. Conscientious disobedience, they say, is the only responsible practice. Such a response by the individual Christian not only is actual disobedience but reveals as well a remarkable ignorance of what Christian obedience is.

On the other hand, one can find the opposite extreme among Christians who, like those just mentioned, cannot alter their interior conviction that the official stand could and should be revised. Such persons completely collapse. In the question of birth control, they do not merely refrain from any use of contraception and any encouragement to its use. True to their concept of obedience, they also abandon all effort to see that the Church—the whole Church "teaching" and "taught"—might come to the view they hold to be more true, human and Christian. In particular, they do not feel free to work toward changing the mind of the ecclesiastical authorities. Such a response by the individual Christian not only is not true obedience; it also reveals a remarkable ignorance of what Christian obedience is.

In brief, both reactions are too simplistic and childlike to be the mature, sophisticated, demanding thing that Christian obedience really is. More precisely, neither of these reactions recognizes that, for a Christian, obedience and responsibility go hand in hand. The first reaction proceeds as if responsibility dispensed a man from obedience. The second as if obedience dispensed him from responsibility. Of Christians choosing to react in these ways, one might well repeat the exasperated cry Robert Bolt put on the lips of Thomas More: "O sweet Jesus, these plain, simple men!" The Christian dedicated enough to be sophisticated sees as possible choices rather obedient responsibility and responsible disobedience. In the present chapter, I will discuss the former; in the following chapter, the latter. Both are traditionally Christian possibilities, and in endorsing them, the new morality is not doing anything new.

In the case we are considering, where the Christian cannot help favoring changes that the authorities oppose, obedient responsibility can mean loyal opposition. There is a long tradition of loyal opposition in the Church. Few of the changes that eventually took place in the Church during its nineteen centuries sprang full-grown from some bishop's head. Many of the changes, when first proposed, met official disapproval and rejection. But often, at these times, leaders arose in the Church, men and women of tenacity and purpose who, while obeying carefully and completely, still maintained their conviction that the authorities were wrong. They labored persistently and ingeniously—but not disobediently—to bring about the changes. One thinks of Catherine of Siena or Ignatius Loyola or John Henry Newman.

We need not look so far back into the past. In our own time we have been privileged to know those whom *America* recently called the "giants of *aggiornamento*." Now that their work is bearing fruit, we should not forget their spirit and conduct as they endured decades of waiting. No authoritative declaration of policy could weaken their convictions that certain things must be brought up to date—e.g., the liturgy and biblical studies. They complied with each order, whether it was by general decree or by direct restriction of their personal activity. But to the extent to which obedience still left them free to discuss and write and experiment, these men of the Church worked to prepare the way for an eventual change in the mind both of those in authority and of the whole Church. Fortunate were those who came to know these "giants," to converse with them at table or consult them in private. One could see in them the marks of interior suffering and self discipline. But much more, one admired and rejoiced in their loyalty to the Church, their integrity, their serene confidence in the Spirit leading the Church.

Having known these men, a Catholic could be proud of the Church. What they were doing in loyal opposition, the Church was doing. For what the Church does is by no means restricted to what the authorities do. The Church is the people of God—all of them. It is the Lord's whole congregation. The human beings in authority are no more and no less the Church than are their subjects. If it is correct to say that the Church sent Fr. Daniel Berrigan to Mexico, it is equally correct to say that the Church bought an ad in *The New York Times* to protest the sending. This is quite independent of whether or not the religious superior who sent Fr. Berrigan was right in so doing, or if those who signed the ad were right—or both, or neither. It in no way denies the fact that the Christians in authority have the right to receive obedience just as the Christians who are subject have the right to receive respect and concern from their superiors. The point is that neither superiors nor subjects are the Church in the sense of either being alone the whole Church. And both are the Church in the sense that together they make up the Church and each have their individual responsibility.

There is thus no reason to deny the perennial tension in the Church between those who on a given point would replace the old with the new and those who would retain the old. Nor to deny that authority may for a time take the side that eventually shows itself to be wrong or less preferable. It is a tension, and therefore neither comfortable nor relaxing, but it is a healthy tension, a tension that goes with life.

Incidentally, there is no reason, either, to insinuate that one pole of the tension is *a priori* better than the other. Is it more genuinely Christian to be bringing forth the new? Or upholding the old? Jansenism was something new, advanced by sincere Christians. The best biblical scholarship looks for something old, the original meaning of the sacred text. The point is rather that the tension between new and old is simply part of the continuing life of the whole Church.

And it gives rise to an equally organic tension between obedience and responsibility, where obedient responsibility can at times mean only loyal and obedient opposition. This, too, is a vital role within the Church.

It may be of use to list some key aspects of that role:

1. Take our Christian at the present time who claims to be obedient, yet interiorly disagrees with a position taken by authority. He can be called obedient only if he has tried hard to agree. Only if sincere effort to see the point of the official position has failed and the opposing evidence stands up under critical examination, can the loyalty to truth of the obedient man command interior disagreement. This is not as difficult as it may sound. Three or four years ago, the ordinary experience of an educator, reinforced by the growing censensus of other Catholic educators, could easily convince him that the Church law on prohibited books (the "Index") needed revision. Few would criticize as disobedient or intellectually presumptuous the interior opposition before the rescinding of the law.

2. The Christian of the loyal opposition recognizes his obligation to obey. He recognizes those of the people of God whose role is to command, and he respects their role. Even when he disagrees, he can obey, and obey with the peaceful interior recognition that it is good for him to do so.

3. May the Christian who obeys, but disagrees with the policy and views of authority, express his disagreement publicly in the Church? May he try to win other Christians to his dissident views? Here there seems to be no single, simple answer. In certain circumstances he unquestionably may. One cannot blame for disobedience those who ten years ago began to criticize publicly the existent liturgy and in the face of various pro-Latin declarations of authority still urged the vernacular. Nor those today who protest that the new liturgical changes are doing more harm than good. One may disagree strongly with one or the other group and still recognize that both are exercising their Christian responsibility in a way completely consonant with obedience. If such public criticism of Church law and official pronouncements is expressed appropriately (perhaps, for example, not from the pulpit, but

in a journal of opinion), it is a form of Church life that can be of great use to those in authority and to the Church as a whole.

But on certain questions, Church authorities may directly forbid any public expression of dissident views. It seems clear that the Holy Father has, at least for a time, forbidden a Catholic to defend publicly the opposite of the official position on birth control. An American bishop might forbid his priests to protest the war in Vietnam. A European bishop might forbid them to defend it. One bishop may silence any espousal of racial integration; another, of segregation.

Once more, the loyal opposition recognizes the obligation to obey, though obedience is more costly here. It is silent to the extent—though no further—that authority has commanded it to be silent. In the following chapter we will ask whether, in a given case, a Christian might be free, even obligated, to say publicly what authority has forbidden? Church lawyers traditionally hold that the force of positive law can be outweighed by other values, such as justice and charity. We are fond of reminding German Catholics who lived under the Nazis that no prescription of human authority, whether ecclesiastical or civil, dispenses a man from intrinsic moral obligations. Nevertheless, the case where a Christian would be justified in directly violating a command of silence seems so rare and exceptional, a last resort of desperation, that it need not be considered in studying that activity of the loyal opposition which is essential to the life of the Church. The loyal opposition is ready, when commanded, to be silent.

To set oneself up as misunderstood seems ridiculous and conceited. And yet, in truth (without, I think, the least touch of conceit), I do believe that I can see something, and I would like that something to be seen. You can't imagine what intensity of desire I sometimes feel in this connection, and what impotence. What keeps me calm is my complete confidence that if there is a ray of light in "my gospel", somehow or other that ray will shine forth. At the worst—of this I'm sure—it will reappear in another heart—all the richer, I hope, for having been faithfully guarded in me.—The only wise and Christian attitude is obviously to wait in all loyalty for God's own hour—if it is to come. I am counting more than ever on the influence of your prayers that I may never fail the light.

Thus Teilhard de Chardin wrote in a letter from the front, at the close of World War I.[1] Did he dimly suspect the forty years of virtually uninterrupted silence that would be imposed upon him? In any case, he was ready.

4. But the loyal opposition—obedient even, if need be, to the point of silence—can still do great things for its cause in the Church. It can, for example, turn to history. It can write a historical study of the Church's position on birth control or on the relationship between Church and State, of the liturgical practices in the early Church or of the theological views of certain Fathers of the Church, of the political evolution of Vietnam. History often inspires a requestioning of contemporary attitudes. "If these are the arguments that originally motivated the prohibition of contraceptives, are there any better ones today?" Whether the requestioning leads to a revision of the present official position or to its confirmation, the loyal opposition serves by bringing new light and perspective.

Similarly, a journalist might conduct and publish a survey indicating some negative effects of the new liturgical changes. A psychiatrist might criticize the argument of certain theologians that the marital act loses force as an expression of love when contraceptives are used. A sociologist could advance statistics on the harmful consequences of integrated schools.

Such studies are invaluable. At times, they eventually win authority over to their view. More often they do not. In any case, they are likely to stimulate the whole Church to a more critical, balanced, nuanced attitude. They should not be resented or feared. They play a part in the growth in truth of the people of God.

The above examples illustrate rather what a specialist of the loyal opposition can do. But the ordinary layman also wields power. For instance, without generalizing he can report facts. Without commentary, he can tell his pastor how individual Negroes have reacted to their reception, or rather, nonreception, in the parish. He can tell his old professor how meaningless his philosophy course now seems to this alumnus. Especially in the day of the thoughtful, articulate layman, such testimony has been having great influence on specialists. The growing number of theologians and philosophers who oppose the official position on birth control is due less to speculative objections than to the simple testimony of men and women to the harm wrought in their married life by the practice of rhythm or complete continence. The present revision of religious education in the Catholic schools was inspired in part by the comments of discontented students. The students were right in their criticisms, and their children will profit from the obedient opposition their parents once gave to authority.

Down the nineteen centuries of its history, the Church has been a wonderful thing. It has been built of nothing but living stones—the people of God, both superiors and subjects. History shows their life to have been tumultuous, confused, sinful and generally fallible. History also shows it to have been a life of faith in Christ, docile to the Spirit, always moving forward to grow in the truth and charity of God. The forward movement has grown naturally and fruitfully out of the interaction of position and opposition. Let those take heart whom responsibility compels on a given question to stand obedient, but in the opposition. They are serving the Church. They are the Church.

12 RESPONSIBLE DISOBEDIENCE IN THE CHURCH

One does not have to look far for a possible paradigm of the responsible disobedience that we have been discussing. The public expression of opposition within the Church to the encyclical *Humanae Vitae* was as short-lived as it was violent. Aside from a salvo here and there, it has died away. The opposition to the encyclical has not. Instead of being preached, it is being quietly practiced by millions of Catholics. They do not form an opposition that disagrees, but obeys. They form an opposition that disobeys and claims to do so responsibly. What merits has their claim?

Opposition to the encyclical began as soon as it was published. On July 30, 1968, the day after the Vatican made the text public, Norris Clarke, speaking in a symposium at Fordham University, could already assure representatives of the press, television and radio that the large number of theologians openly disagreeing with the encyclical made it a unique, historic moment for the Church. Despite pleas and remonstrances of the Holy Father and other authorities of the Church, public opposition continued during the rest of 1968.

The encyclical incurred criticism on various counts, but the central thrust of the opposition was a simple, practical one: Catholics were justified in disobeying the encyclical and in practicing contraception. This is undoubtedly why the opponents of the encyclical have become silent in 1969. Their chief point was practical, they made it vocally to their own satisfaction, and those convinced of it are now putting it into practice. As a subject for debate, opposition to the encyclical is a dead issue.

But in passing from theory to practice, the opposition became a current part of life in the Catholic Church and is having widening and deepening repercussions in Catholic faith and life. It scandalizes Catholics who see obedience as the only possible response to the encyclical. They ask how one can be a Catholic and disobey the highest authority. They wonder what the Catholic Church really is, when open disobedience is tolerated. Catholics living in contradiction to the encyclical ask themselves similar questions. They wonder whether they are, in effect, still Catholics. And what should the Catholic Church mean for them if they are free to ignore its teaching?

The reactions reveal a need to clarify the grounds of the disobedience, or, if one prefers, its conditions of responsibility. This is the purpose of the present chapter. It is not an attempt to prove that the disobedience is in fact justified, nor to present completely any proof that has been offered. It is an attempt to outline the rationale of the disobedience and to show how it is, in principle, consonant with what the Church is and with what it means to be a Catholic, and how it therefore illustrates the true relationship of the individual Catholic to the whole Church. One could therefore agree with the chapter that all this is true *in principle* of the disobedience to the encyclical, and still doubt or deny that it is so *in fact*.

No one contests, of course, that every Catholic ultimately has to follow his own conscience. The bishops of the United States affirmed:

> Responsible parenthood, as the Church understands it, places on the properly formed conscience of spouses *all* the judgments, options and choices which add up to the awesome decision to give, postpone or decline life.[1]

The bishops of England and Wales insist: "Neither this encyclical nor any other document takes away from us our right and duty to follow our conscience."[2] The reason is a simple, traditional one. Conscience, as the American bishops point out by invoking Thomas Aquinas, is "the practical judgment or dictate of reason by which we judge what here and now is to be done as being good, or to be avoided as evil."[3] Only the individual can make the judgment. Even God cannot do it for him. Consequently, whether his judgment be true or false, he has nothing else to follow. Traditional moral theology recognizes that when a man comes in good faith to have an erroneous conscience, he incurs no subjective guilt in following it, indeed would be subjectively at fault not to do so. This is why the American bishops underline that "*Humanae Vitae* does not discuss the question of the good faith of those who make practical decisions against what the Church considers a divine law and the will of God. The encyclical does not undertake to judge the consciences of individuals . . ."[4]

Thus the possibility of a *subjectively* good conscience is not disputed. But many in the Church, including a good number in authority, maintain that it is the most one can say for disobedience to the encyclical, just as one could say it for the misguided assassination of a great, national leader, or for other objectively immoral behavior. Those disobeying naturally deny this and claim valid, *objective* grounds for their action. This is the issue in general.

One unusual element of the present situation is that not only do a large number of competent theologians agree with the claim of the opposition, but certain national hierarchies have given it encouragement. The French and Dutch hierarchies go the furthest; their statements clearly recognize that disobedience to the encyclical can, in fact, be objectively justified. In the early, provisional statement of the Dutch bishops, the authority of the encyclical is seen as only one of ". . . many factors that determine the individual conscience in regard to the conjugal act . . . for example, mutual love, relations in the family and social circumstances."[5] Implied is that the other factors can objectively outweigh the authority. The same implication is in the motion submitted by the nine Dutch bishops to the national Pastoral Council, cited below.

Although the reasoning offered by the French bishops is, in my experience, not typical of the opposition to the encyclical, they conclude to an unequivocal justification of disobedience. They concede: "Contraception can never be a good. It is always a disorder, but this disorder is not always guilty. It occurs in fact that spouses consider themselves to be confronted by a true conflict of duty." Because they "believe themselves in conscience bound to avoid a new birth or postpone it to a little later, and are deprived of resorting to biological rhythm," the couples have to choose between two evils, to practice contraception or "to renounce for the present a physical expression of their love" and thus see "the stability of their home being threatened." The bishops "simply recall the constant teaching of morality: When one faces a choice of duties, where one cannot avoid an evil whatever be the decision taken, traditional wisdom requires that one seek before God to find which is the greater duty. The spouses will decide after a joint reflection, with all the care that it calls for by the grandeur of their conjugal vocation."[6]

Although only the Dutch and French hierarchies clearly recognize objective justification for opposition, a good number of other hierarchies have notably refrained from adopting the contrary position, that disobedience *cannot* be objectively justified.[7] Four have gone so far as to state that loyal, well-informed, thoughtful Catholics could find reasons to dissent and disobey. This would imply that here is not merely the usual possibility of an erroneous, but subjectively good conscience, but that in the objective order there are grounds for opposition that, whether or not they are truly adequate, at least are serious enough to compel the minds of sincere and competent Catholics.

Most explicit are the Canadian bishops:

It is a fact that a certain number of Catholics, although admittedly subject to the teaching of the encyclical, find it either extremely difficult or even impossible to make their own all elements of this doctrine. . . .

. . . .

Since they are not denying any point of divine and Catholic faith nor rejecting the teaching authority of the Church, these Catholics should not be considered, or consider themselves, shut off from the body of the faithful. But they should remember that their good faith will be dependent on a sincere self-examination to determine the true motives and grounds for such suspension of assent and on continued effort to understand and deepen their knowledge of the teaching of the Church.

. . . .

In the situation we described earlier in this statement [the one just cited in this excerpt] the confessor or counsellor must show sympathetic understanding and reverence for the sincere good faith of those who fail in their effort to accept some point of the encyclical.

Counsellors may meet others who, accepting the teaching of the Holy Father, find that because of particular circumstances they are involved in what seems to them a clear conflict of duties, e.g., the reconciling of conjugal love and responsible parenthood with the education of children already born or with the health of the mother. In accord with the accepted principles of moral theology, if these persons have tried sincerely but without success to pursue a line of conduct in keeping with the given directives, they may be safely assured that whoever honestly chooses that course which seems right to him does so in good conscience.[8]

The Scandinavian bishops imply the same possibility of honest, thoughtful, informed Catholics coming to disobey the encyclical:

. . . it is self-evident that no one should doubt the content of the encyclical without entering into its way of thinking and intention thoroughly, honestly and with consciousness of his responsibility before God.

However, if someone, from weighty and well-considered reasons, cannot become convinced by the argumentation of the encyclical, it has always been conceded that he is allowed to have a different view from that presented in a non-infallible statement of the Church. No one should be considered a bad Catholic because he is of such a dissenting opinion.

Everyone who, after conscientious consideration, believes himself entitled not to accept this teaching and considers himself not bound to obey it in practice, must be responsible before God for his attitude and way of acting.[9]

The Austrian and Belgian bishops express a similar view, although they seem to be speaking of dissidents whose knowledgeability in the matter is more than the average Catholic possesses.

Since the encyclical does not contain an infallible dogma, it is conceivable that someone feels unable to accept the judgment of the teaching authority of the Church. The answer to this is: if someone has experience in the field and has reached a divergent conviction after serious conviction, free of emotional haste, he may for the time being follow it. He does not err, if he is willing to continue his examination and otherwise affords respect and fidelity to the Church.[10]

Someone, however, who is competent in the matter under consideration and capable of forming a personal and well-founded opinion—which necessarily presupposes a sufficient amount of knowledge—may, after a serious examination before God, come to other conclusions on certain points. In such a case he has the right to follow his convictions provided that he remains sincerely disposed to continue his enquiry.[11]

Highly unusual is the explicit acknowledgment by the four hierarchies of the possibility of sincere and well-informed dissent and disobedience to the teaching of the encyclical, as well as their abstention from criticizing the dissent and disobedience on objective grounds. Equally significant is the positive encouragement: a dissident "may be safely assured that whoever honestly chooses the course which seems right to him does so in good conscience," "may for the time being follow his divergent conviction," "has the right to follow his convictions," should not "be considered a bad Catholic," but himself "must be responsible before God for his attitude and way of acting."

The bishops evidently feel that at least a good enough case can be made for disobedience to convince a fair number of sincere, well-informed, mature Catholics. It would follow that the grounds for disobedience are not purely subjective, but have a certain objective weight, whether or not they are fully adequate. This conclusion, which the rest of the present essay would explicate, may seem curious. What sense is it to speak of grounds for disobedience that are "objective," though they may not be "fully adequate." If one were trying to decide whether or not personally to disobey the encyclical, it would make little sense. But it makes excellent sense if one is trying to understand how the disobedience, in principle, fits in with being a Catholic, a loyal member of the Church. It is not only the Holy Father who speaks fallibly; so, too, do those who disagree with him. To recognize their stance as authentically ecclesial one does not have to hold that they are right. It is enough to see that the grounds they adduce are objectively serious in the context of the Church.

The point at issue is not whether the encyclical contains authoritative teaching of the Pope in his office as supreme teacher of the Church. Isolated voices have denied him the authority to speak on matters of natural morality, and, therefore, on contraception. But, on the whole, the liberal positions, whether of national hierarchies or of theologians, take into account the authority of the encyclical. There are good theological reasons for this. But it might suffice to note that no one has challenged the right of the Pope to speak out on nuclear warfare, peace, racism, starvation, etc.

Correspondingly, the point at issue is not whether the individual Catholic owes respect to the authority possessed by the encyclical. As the Dutch bishops expressed it, "A Catholic owes respect to the authority and the word of the Pope. The individual conscience cannot ignore such an authoritative declaration as this encyclical."[12] The Scandinavian bishops, who, like the Dutch, offered one of the more liberal statements, recalled approvingly the teaching of the Second Vatican Council that religious submission of will and mind must be shown in a special way to the authentic teaching authority of the Roman Pontiff even when he is not speaking *ex cathedra* (as the supreme teacher in an infallible manner).[13]

The point at issue, therefore, can be narrowed down. Is the respect due the authority of the encyclical such that a properly informed, objectively true conscience has no choice but to obey? Many in the Church, including Pope Paul VI, maintain the affirmative.

In the encyclical the Holy Father has given us the principles according to which Catholics are to form their consciences in this matter. The obligation of a Catholic to accept the teaching of the Church on any grave moral problem can never justifiably be regarded as an offense against the freedom of his conscience. Rather, the free acceptance of that particular obligation is implicit in the free decision, already made and still continuing, to accept the claim of the Catholic Church to speak with the authority of Christ.[14]

Those who maintain the negative, namely, that Catholics can respect the authority of the encyclical and still find objective grounds justifying their disobedience, premise, first of all, that the encyclical is not proposed as an infallible declaration of doctrine. No one contests the premise. As Msgr. Fernando Lambruschini observed when he presented the text at a Vatican press conference,

Attentive reading of the encyclical *Humanae Vitae* does not suggest the theological note of infallibility; this is also shown by a simple comparison with the "Profession of Faith" proclaimed on June 30, during the solemn rite in St. Peter's Square.[15]

He does not hesitate to affirm simply, "It is not infallible . . ."[16]

To say the encyclical is not infallible is to admit the possibility of its being in error. It is logical, therefore, as well as traditional, that a Catholic can legitimately come to disagree with such teaching. Of an authoritative, but not infallible declaration of the Supreme Pontiff,

> . . . one need not say: the Holy Spirit will never permit that this decree be published with erroneous content. . . . The presumption that it contains no error stands as long as the presumption is not brought down by a weighty reason to the contrary. Its authority demands a religious assent to the truth of its contents. The assent is, therefore, interpretatively conditioned, i.e., given with the tacit condition: "unless grave suspicion arise that the presumption is not verified."[17]

Not all those who insist on unconditional obedience to the encyclical have taken into consideration this traditional right of dissent from authoritative teaching. But no one of theological competence nor any national hierarchy has denied it. The conservative statement of the American hierarchy provides a clear vindication of it:

> There exists in the Church a lawful freedom of inquiry and of thought, and also general norms of licit dissent. This is particularly true in the area of legitimate theological speculation and research. When conclusions reached by such professional theological work prompt a scholar to dissent from noninfallible received teaching, the norms of licit dissent come into play.[18]

One sentence of the American bishops could well constitute the major premise of the reasoning of the present chapter:

> The expression of theological dissent from the magisterium is in order only if the reasons are serious and well-founded, if the manner of the dissent does not question or impugn the teaching authority of the Church and is such as not to give scandal.[19]

The rest of this chapter can be seen as an attempt to establish the minor premise of the syllogism: the expression of theological dissent from *Humanae Vitae* dissent not theoretical, but justifying contrary practice fulfills the conditions laid down by the American hierarchy.

As the first of their "serious and well-founded reasons," the dissenters submit that the argumentation offered in the encyclical is not convincing. It is easy to pinpoint the argumentation which the opposition finds unconvincing since the encyclical repeatedly grounds the prohibition of contraception on one basic premise. Only in number seventeen of the encyclical does Pope Paul adduce other arguments against contraception. "Upright men can even better convince themselves of the solid grounds on which the teaching of the Church in this field is based, if they care to reflect upon the consequences of methods of artificial birth control." But the first two consequences are not developed (in the English translation, less than 150 words for the two together), nor are they presented as decisively proving the immorality of all contraception. The third and final consequence is developed a bit (about 230 words), but appears to presuppose and merely confirm the one basic premise that runs through the encyclical:

> And such limits cannot be determined otherwise than by the respect owed to the integrity of the human organism and its functions, according to the principles recalled above and according to the correct understanding of the principle of totality illustrated by our predecessor Pius XII.[20]

It is rather this integrity of organism and functions that constitutes the one basic premise of the argumentation of *Humanae Vitae*:

> God has wisely disposed natural laws and rhythms of fertility that, of themselves, cause a separation in the succession of birth. None the less, the Church, calling men back to the observance of the norms of the natural law, as interpreted by her constant doctrine, teaches that each and every marriage act must remain open to the transmission of life.
>
> That teaching, often set forth by the magisterium, is founded upon the inseparable connection, willed by God and unable to be broken by man on his own initiative,

between the two significations of the conjugal act: the
unitive meaning and the procreative meaning.

. . . .

Hence one who reflects well must also recognize that an
act of mutual love that prejudices the openness to transmission of life that God the Creator, according to particular laws inserted therein, is in contradiction with the design
constitutive of marriage, and with the will of the author
of life. To use this divine gift, destroying, even if only
partially, its meaning and its purpose, is to contradict the
nature both of man and of woman and of their most intimate relationship, and therefore it is to contradict also the
plan of God and His will.[21]

This argumentation, the fulcrum of the reasoning of the
encyclical, is the chief target of the opposition, e.g., in the
motion submitted by the nine bishops of the Netherlands
and overwhelmingly adopted by the representative assembly
of the Dutch Church:

The plenary assembly considers the absolute rejection by
the encyclical *Humanae Vitae* of the artificial means of
birth control not convincing, on the basis of the argumentation given. The well-considered personal decision of conscience of married people should be respected.[22]

The operative principle of the encyclical, therefore, is that
natural reason can see in the very nature of marriage and the
conjugal act that God has willed that the act always be left
open to the transmission of life. What the opposition finds
unconvincing lies behind the word "always." The teaching of
the Church is based on, and the Holy Father is appealing
to, evidence not derived from revelation, but found in the
"natural law," accessible, therefore, to natural human understanding. Such evidence is said to show what is *always* God's
intention, i.e., for every single conjugal act regardless of consequences for the particular spouses and children and regardless of the general procreative tenor that their acts as a whole
may have.

To justify conjugal acts made intentionally infertile one
cannot invoke as valid reasons the lesser evil, or the fact

that such acts would constitute a whole, together with the fertile acts already performed or to follow later, and hence would share in one and the same moral goodness.[23]

God's intention, found in nature, makes every single act of contraception "intrinsically disordered and hence unworthy of the human person."[24] Those who share the contemporary understanding of man's responsibility before God cannot see how it is evident to human reason that such a divine intention governs every single act. They experience the opposite of what Pope Paul believed, "that men of our day are particularly capable of seizing the deeply reasonable and human character of this fundamental principle."[25] It is noteworthy that the encyclical makes no attempt to present this evidence that the divine intention bears on every single conjugal act without exception.

Obviously, the mere fact that one does not find convincing the argumentation of an encyclical does not justify disobedience or even disagreement. The authority of Church teaching is independent of its effectiveness in persuading or convincing by the reasons it gives. One of the purposes of the magisterium is to bring members of the Church to accept truths that for one reason or another they cannot come to by themselves, even after listening respectfully to the teaching. An example could be the authoritative teaching of the immorality of racial segregation. Consequently, to outweigh the authority of *Humanae Vitae*, powerful, positive reasons must be found showing it to be in error.

The positive reasons offered to this effect vary, but have, I believe, a common drift. Married people have indeed the responsibility, given them by God, of transmitting life. But it is their married life as a whole, and not necessarily each single conjugal act, that need meet the responsibility. Moreover, the responsibility of transmitting life must be coordinated with other responsibilities, such as those of rearing children or of their own mutual love and assistance. In regard to the procreative responsibility, the moral question is: have they over the years been generous in bringing life into the world? That every conjugal act be left open to procreation not only does not follow from this responsibility; it often runs counter to other responsibilities of the couple, such as bringing their children up well. In an ethics of responsibility, contraception can be of obligation for a married couple.

Convincing as the argument may be, an individual Catholic would be presumptuous to pit his own reasoning alone against the supreme teaching authority of the Church. But the exceptional character of the present situation is seen in the large number of Catholics, living actively their faith, educated in Catholic matters, and having competence in the matter in question, who have followed similar reasoning to similar firm conclusions concerning the legitimacy of contraception: theologians, philosophers, doctors, demographers, historians, sociologists, priests in pastoral ministry, and, last but not least, married couples. Typical were the 172 American theologians who by August 1, 1968 had signed a statement criticizing the encyclical and concluding "that spouses may responsibly decide according to their conscience that artificial contraception in some circumstances is permissible and indeed necessary to preserve and foster the values and sacredness of marriage."[26] Typical, too, were the six American lay members of the Papal Commission; within a week of the publication of the encyclical, all six were quoted in the press criticizing it.[27] Names like Donald Campion, editor of *America*, Bernard Häring, Karl Rahner, Richard McCormick, Avery Dulles and Walter Burghardt made it clear that the opposition was not simply a reaction of the far out left.[28] So, too, did the encouragement, mentioned above, given by certain national hierarchies to conscientious dissent and disobedience. Essential to the grounds of disobedience are these numerous respected voices, indicating in one way or another that the other grounds have objective weight.

The wide extent of open dissent has further force because it arises organically from the nature of the Church. Contrary to the use of the word "Church" in the encyclical, the Church is not to be identified simply with its teaching authority, but includes the whole people of God in their various roles. The witness of theologians, pastors and laymen, therefore, constitutes ecclesial evidence for truths about Christian faith and life. Karl Rahner has expressed well what is new in the present development in the Church and what is perfectly traditional, revealing the true nature of the Church.

What a Catholic and a theologian experience today in our question is really nothing absolutely new, for in the course of the history of the Church, there obviously have always arisen developments of doctrine as well as situations in which such a development was still open and one could not clearly predict its future history. The only thing new is that such developments of doctrine and such situations proceed or change more rapidly and thus force themselves more sharply on the individual, short-lived human being. New, too, is that this question affects more immediately the concrete life of countless men than other dogmatic questions. Whatever it may have been psychologically with the consciousness of the average Catholic in his relation to the Church, above all, in the last hundred years, it is not true that the Catholic Church has understood, or understands, itself as a Church in which everything important is always clear in advance and is held with absolute certainty, and in which every discovery of truth takes place uniquely and alone through the utterance of its supreme teaching office. The teaching authority in the Catholic Church—and especially when it gives no definitive declaration (and in many cases it is not even capable of doing it)—is an important, indispensable factor for the discovery of truth or the development of doctrine in the Church. But it is not a factor that alone, independently in every respect of other realities in the Church, determines totally this discovery of truth or development of doctrine. Even *ex cathedra* decisions of the Pope or the Councils were really always something like an underlining of a development that had been borne along by factors quite distinct from the teaching office and its formal authority. The authority of the teaching office in the Church and the respect due to it do not, therefore, demand that one so act in the Church as if all theological views in the Church were only the obedient repetition of a declaration of the teaching office. Properly understood, there is also in the Catholic Church an open "system," in which most diverse factors (the "sense" of the faithful, new acquisitions of knowledge by individual Christians and theologians, new situations of the time with new posing of questions, and many other things) work together to clarify the Church's consciousness of its faith and toward a development of doctrine. Nor would this total, open "system," in which the teaching office has its own proper and necessary place, be comprehensively and totally taken over and manipulated by this teaching office itself.[29]

Further ground for the opposition, according to some, would be signs that, in historical fact, the Church is nearing the end of a development of doctrine such as Rahner describes, and that therefore ecclesiastical authority will soon abandon the older position. Most of the theologians defending the encyclical, it is claimed, are about sixty years of age or older. Few of the younger theologians defend it. Moreover, many of those demanding absolute obedience to the encyclical do so exclusively because of its authoritative force; some of them admit privately that the natural law reasoning on which the encyclical is based would not convince them by itself. If this be true, it would seem likely that in a few years the vast majority of theological advisors to the Pope and the bishops will be critical of the present official position.

A sign pointing, by way of analogy, to this likelihood of change of the official position is the development that took place within the Papal Birth Control Commission after it was enlarged in June, 1964.

The papal commission now stood at about sixty-five members; all the human probabilities, as far as the composition of the group permitted, were that the result of discussions would be a basic confirmation of *Casti Connubii*—possibly with significant changes in the pastoral approach. At the start, only about three or four of the theologians were in favor of a new theological approach; the rest were known for their faithfulness to *Casti Connubii.* . . .

. . . .

However, developments in the Council, the absolute honesty of thought in the commission, and especially the presence of lay people, who were now assured that they could think and speak frankly, changed the situation, especially toward the end of the Council and right after it was over.[30]

Is it not likely that the similar honesty of thought and frank speaking and thinking now present in the Church will lead to an outcome similar to that of the commission?

The overwhelming majority of the commission of theologians and lay people and a sufficient majority of the bishops commission approved the majority report, which argued that the choice of methods of birth regulation be left to the discretion of the married couple, within the guidelines given in the *Constitution on the Church in the Modern World.*[31]

The convergence of all the above grounds for opposition suffices, in the eyes of some, to justify not only disagreement, but also disobedience. If the teaching is shown to be erroneous, what obligation remains for carrying it into practice? Others feel, however, that the encyclical does not merely teach, but also commands. Consequently, though evidently in error, it still possesses an authority analogous to that of positive ecclesiastical law. To justify disobedience, therefore, the individual married couple must be able to go a step further and find evidence (analogous to the "causes" that "excuse" from positive law) that obedience in their case would work proportionately grave harm to themselves and their family.

The disagreement on the necessity of establishing this further ground for opposition may be academic rather than important practically. Those who insist on the necessity admit that in the light of the other grounds for opposition the "proportionately grave harm" need not be very grave. And all those who oppose the encyclical recognize that the harm obedience could bring about for married couples is a principal motive for their opposition, regardless of the way in which they integrate it into rational argumentation.

The grounds of disobedience are various: against the authority of *Humanae Vitae* it is held that the encyclical is not infallible; that its argumentation is unconvincing; that an ethics of responsibility leads to a contrary conclusion; that many in the Church, having varied competence and experience, support contrary action; that in their support they are exercising their roles in the Church; that from an historical point of view there is evidence pointing to an imminent change in the official teaching and that obedience to the encyclical can concretely work grave harm to individual families. The case rests. Since the disobedience is well known, the individual Catholic has to give his verdict. Do the grounds of the disobedience fit in, in principle, with the reality of the Catholic Church in which he believes? Whatever his answer may be, he will be judging not only disobedience to the encyclical, but the Church and himself.

13 THE IMPORTANCE
OF BEING ROMAN CATHOLIC

American Catholics in the 1970s are experiencing thickening anxiety and discouragement, even despair. The mood is produced by the changes going on in the Church but, ironically enough, in two opposing ways. For some Catholics, the changes are going too far and too fast and look like they will go farther and faster. For other Catholics, the changes are too little and too late and there is no hope of stepping up the tempo.

The anxiety and despair engendered by either point of view can lead a Catholic to think of leaving the Church. He may think of it consciously and envision a departure that would have a certain punctuation and flourish. Or, on a practical, half-aware level, he may just gradually stop bothering about what has hitherto made up his Catholic practice. More commonly, the anxiety and despair induced by the changes tempt a Catholic, not to leave the Church or to give up his practice, but to mutter an embittered or confused "What's the use?" and to stop putting himself on the line and giving himself wholeheartedly to the life of the Church.

The question comes up painfully, "What is the importance of being Roman Catholic? What is its necessity, its value?" The question is all the more painful because the answer no longer comes easily. If a genuine theological question arises out of the lived experience of the Catholic people so, too, must the answer. The answer comes in understanding the experienced life of the faith of the people. The trouble is that in regard to the importance of being Roman Catholic (as in regard to many other things), the lived experience of the American Roman Catholic is in the process of hurtling transformation. The old theological answers are no longer pertinent. The new experience demands new theological understanding, new answers.

I would like to try to identify certain aspects of the new experience before offering a theological understanding of it. It already seems to have been in some dim, distant past that evermounting statistics of conversions and headlines about Clare Booth Luce and Thomas Merton and other famous converts symbolized wonderfully for us the value of Catholicism. What has happened since then is not so much that we have become less successful in converting (though that seems to be true, too), but that we are getting less and less interested in it. The entry of Tennessee Williams into the Church causes hardly a ripple and seems somehow anachronistic.

Even missionaries are caught up in the trend. At their gatherings, when they return temporarily to the States, they talk more and more of giving witness to Christ's love and improving the human condition of the people, and less and less of the number of conversions.[1] A Fordham theology professor remarked prophetically a few years ago: "Francis Xavier no longer serves us as a symbol or image to express our faith. We need a new symbol." That is obviously true today: as our Catholic experience has changed, it needs a symbol other than that of a man hastening about the world to save souls from hellfire.

For some centuries now, educated Catholics could explain why it was necessary to belong to the Church and still possible to be saved without being a member. But regardless of explanations, the day a Catholic stops being interested in conversions, something has happened. Something has gone from his concrete, lived understanding of his Church. This is why he is no longer satisfied with his old answer to the question, "Why is it important for me to be a Catholic?" The teaching authority of the Church has sensed the need to elaborate new answers.

A more recent example [of the Church reversing its teaching] would be Vatican II. In all honesty it is not possible to say that Vatican II speaks about the other Churches, the other religions, or religious liberty in the same way as earlier popes and councils had spoken. The ancient doctrine, "Outside the Church no salvation," has been so drastically reinterpreted by Vatican II that the meaning is almost the opposite of what the words seem to say. Modern Catholics take a very different view of this matter than their ancestors in the middle ages.[2]

In a document released by the Vatican Secretariat for Promoting Christian Unity, one reads:

Relations between Christians and Jews have for the most part been no more than a monologue. A true dialogue must now be established. The condition of dialogue is respect for the other as he is, for his faith and religious convictions. All intent of proselytizing and conversion is excluded.[3]

The growing loss of interest in converting is one aspect of the change we are noting in American Catholic experience. Another aspect is seen in a new phase of ecumenical dialogue. Several times in recent months, I have heard ecumenical groups ask, "Why is the excitement going out of ecumenism?" I think the reason is simple. Catholics, Protestants and Jews are getting to know each other. That's why. They are no longer acquaintances courteously respectful of each other; they are friends. When you get to know a man and his faith, not as it is outlined in propositions, even by himself, but as it is part of the man you have come to like and admire, then the differences between his faith and yours seem not less, but less important. The drama of men of different faiths getting together fades. Instead one realizes more keenly the sobering common task of religious men today.

I disagree, for example, with theses of Martin Luther concerning divine grace and fallen human nature. But when I lunch with my Lutheran colleague on the faculty and discuss, as I have many times in the past, religious matters of common interest, his Christian life and mine, it is simply impossible for me to say to myself interiorly, "Well, he's obviously sincere and invincibly ignorant, and God does not hold it against him, but of course, I, being Roman Catholic, have a better understanding of God and Christ and man than he does." If nothing else, my sense of humor prevents me from thinking this way. It might be that all the theses I hold are true, and that some of his are false, but now that I know the man, I cannot say that, objectively speaking, Christ is less understood and appreciated and lived by him than by me. The evidence arising out of our friendship is clearly the contrary.

One might object that the point is not to compare individuals, but Churches. But Vatican II has reminded us that the Church is nothing but the people of God, the living individuals who make it up. If coming to know certain Lutherans, I begin to suspect that all the individual Lutherans living in the United States understand and appreciate and love and live Christ more or less as well as all the individual Roman Catholics, I face anew the old question, "What is the importance of being Roman Catholic?" And I have to look for a new answer.

I believe that those of us who have come to know the personal faith of Jewish believers experience the same thing. That this rabbi is in error concerning Jesus Christ, and I am right—yes, I can hold that. But that he understands what God is basically doing with men less profoundly and perceptively than I do—this I could hold only until I got to know Rabbi X.

A third aspect of the change in Catholic experience that I am talking about could be identified by the now familiar label, "the anonymous Christian." The theology of the anonymous Christian is not new. It was worked out during the Second World War by thinkers as diverse as Karl Rahner, Jean Mouroux and Jacques Maritain. But only recently has the anonymous Christian become part of general Catholic experience, our imagination and feeling and apperceptive background. The incredible communication media have helped to bring about our increasing awareness of the rest of mankind on this dwindling earth, and therefore a keener sense of ourselves, the professed Christians, as a minority group. Then, too, we have come to know of men like U Thant and Albert Camus. We have left the ghetto and come to work side by side with agnostics, searching for truth with them, laboring with them for racial justice or peace or food for the starving. We have worked with them in Appalachia or some inner city or campaign headquarters or Peace Corps or theology department. And there is something in the air of our times—I do not know what it is—that makes it a little absurd for us to imagine that Christ is present in our minority group in a fuller, realer way than in the vast millions that press around us or in these men with whom we have shared ideals and labored to realize them.

Rather we cannot help seeing Christ working in all men so that all that is true (was it Saint Ambrose who first said it?) is said by the Holy Spirit, so that Christ (as Saint Justin insisted) is the light that enlightens *every* man that comes into the world, and that He is the light in which all human light is. The theological analyses of Rahner and Maritain and Schillebeeckx help us to understand how it is possible for these men to believe in Christ, to be enlightened by him, to be energized by him, and yet not know it. But the new vision contained in Catholic experience does not appear to depend on subtle theories. In fact, as far as theories go, the popularity of the synthesis of Teilhard may well be due to his expressing the new experience more faithfully than the neo-Scholastic analyses of Maritain and Rahner do.

In any case, our religious imagination now has Christ working in full redemptive efficacy in all men of good will. We are starting to talk of the Roman Catholic Church as the extraordinary means of salvation. As a vision of the world, it offers no practical problems to see Christ implicitly recognized and at work everywhere where men become more human, more loving. But it does pose in a new way the problem of the Church. What then is the Church doing? What is the value of being Roman Catholic? The old solutions no longer fit our experience.

And so, if my description is accurate, there is today in the onrushing transformation of American Catholic experience one current that can be discerned among the many. It shows itself in progressive disinterest in conversion, in high regard for the faith and wisdom of our Protestant and Jewish brothers, in a deepening sense of Christ's anonymously enlightening all men and fructifying all human endeavor, in a growing suspicion that those who have left the Church to marry a wife had honorable and good reasons for doing so. The core of the new experience is a dawning realization that Christ can be present as fully outside the institution of the Roman Catholic Church as within. The American Catholic has always realized that Christ can and presumably does save good people outside the visible structure of the Church. What he is now coming to realize is that Christ, His saving presence and gracious love, can be and presumably is *as fully* at work outside the visible Church as within. Consequently, he needs a new answer to the question of the importance of being Roman Catholic.

There are, I believe, at least two answers one might give. The first would be to explore what the Second Vatican Council proposed as the role of the Church in the world. The Church, as sacrament for all men, can be understood to communicate sacramentally God's saving grace even to nonbelievers. Although I may hold that Christ is as fully and effectively present outside the Church as within, I can still rejoice in belonging to this visible community which is the efficacious sign of all his presence, i.e., which, by signifying union with Him, effects it in all men of good will. The answer is probably a good one and reputable theologians today endorse it. But it has difficulties. How can the Church be a sacrament for those who do not see it as a sign of anything real? And does not the concept of an inexperienced instrumental efficacy follow only from scholastic metaphysics?

Without rejecting the above answer, I would like to suggest another reason that makes it important to be Roman Catholic, even in the problematic we have been discussing. It may be that other men have found their way to Christ as well or better than I, and their way was separated from Rome or was only implicitly Christian. It still remains true that *for me*, the way of finding Christ is in the Roman Catholic Church. It is *my* ordinary means of salvation.

I advance the thesis for human, pragmatic, empirical reasons, for I believe it is only in a human, pragmatic, empirical way that Christ comes to me and I go to Christ. This means that I meet Him in my personal human history and in my personal, human community. I also happen to believe it is the same visible community He founded 2000 years ago, but that is not key here. Christ undoubtedly speaks to the Lutheran in many concrete, human ways, and the Lutheran undoubtedly finds Him there, and in his response of faith and love, is enlightened and strengthened by His grace. But I have no reason to think it would be equally true for me, if I entered the Lutheran community. Christ speaks to me, not by mystical inspiration, not by injecting new ontological acts into my potencies, but through the events of my history and the contacts of my community. I cannot, like Descartes, reject my past and the human contacts I have had and have, and start all over again. Neither could Descartes, for that matter. You can't go home again, but you can't leave it either. H. Richard Niebuhr said that he was a Christian because he was fated to be one. The historical forces under which he had been placed had irrevocably made him that way. I would say the same of my Roman Catholicism, adding only that I see the "fating" as God's free choice to give me a Roman Catholic history and community instead of a Lutheran or Jewish or Buddhist one.

For example, I can, if so inclined, indulge in the contemporary fun-game of criticizing the nuns who taught me. The fact remains that their teaching is part of me (including, incidentally, many true and beautiful things about God and man) and will always be. Despite whatever flaws the teaching may have had, or whatever flaws my reception may have had, it remains within me in memory and imagination and habits of thought and feeling. It is one broadway where Christ speaks to me. Not mystically or ontologically. Not because of any authority of the nuns. But empirically, practically, Christ speaks to me through those human beings. Through them he gives me insights, feelings, impulses of action that mirror Him and His love. Much that He gives me through them is not what they intended to give. Often it is rather something that arises from my reaction to them, a reaction often negative. But part of my ongoing dialogue with Christ will always be in terms of my experience in grammar school under the Sisters.

That is only an example. One could speak of parental faith, liturgy, ways of private prayer, long conversations with friends, declarations of the hierarchy, apostolic enterprises, etc., etc. The point is that even if the hierarchy had made all the mistakes we subjects ascribe to them, even if the state of the liturgy were as regrettable as the worst critics claim, even if the visible Roman Catholic Church had all the defects of which its members have accused it—and the presuppositions cannot be true, since much of the criticism is mutually contradictory—it still would be true that Christ is speaking to me through this hierarchy, this liturgy, this Catholic Church.

He is speaking, as He has always done, through the human beings that make it up. Sometimes I find His Word in listening and receiving what they say and do. Sometimes I find it in reacting negatively and trying to change things. But this is where I find Him. And the fact that my Lutheran colleague finds Him as fully in his Lutheran faith, and my atheist friend finds Him implicitly in his lack of faith, is of little use to me. I do not doubt that men, like Charles Davis, were not only following their conscience in leaving the Church, but may well have found a more human life, greater maturity and therefore greater peace of soul, and therefore found Christ more fully on some implicit level. But I find it hard to believe that for men who have taken such a step, Christ remains, at least on the explicit, conscious level, as much the center and fullness of life as before. I say this partly because of my understanding of man as made up by *his* history and *his* community; there he finds himself and others and, consequently, Christ. But I say it also because of my acquaintance with individuals who have left the Catholic Church on the grounds that Christ was not lived there purely enough, not taken seriously enough. My experience is limited, and it is a hard thing to appraise. But I have the definite impression that the reality of Christ has subsequently paled and moved to the periphery of the lives of these individuals, for all their sincerity.

Most of us American Catholics do not face the dilemma of having to choose between active participation in the life of our Church and an adequately human life. A good number, however, as I mentioned in the beginning, are tempted presently to anxiety or discouragement. I would suggest that the reflections just offered on the importance of being Roman Catholic could counteract the temptation by revealing to us "the freedom of the Roman Catholic."

When Martin Luther vaunted "the freedom of the Christian man," he spoke of a freedom from anxiety and discouragement. When he looked at his persistent failings, anxiety and despair gripped him. But when he looked to Christ, he heard that God had chosen to love him, to accept him despite his weaknesses. And looking to Christ, he chose to believe His love for him, accept his acceptance, and thus he experienced the peace and joy that belongs to the Christian man. Since he had all that matters—God's love—he was at peace. And being at peace, with nothing to fear or worry about, he was free, too, to give to others, to love unreservedly. In fact, knowing now what Christ was for him, he spontaneously chose to be a Christ for others.

The freedom of the Christian man, described profoundly and eloquently by Luther, is also the freedom of the Roman Catholic of the last third of the twentieth century. It just takes a different concrete form. The anxiety and despair Luther and his contemporaries felt and from which Christ freed them arose from an oppressive experience of their humanness. The humanness that oppressed them was their personal sinfulness, their personal failure to love. The anxiety and despair American Catholics feel in 1969 arise, too, from an oppressive experience of their humanness. The humanness that oppresses them is the humanness of the whole Church (not excluding themselves), seen in the confusion wrought by the ongoing changes. The anxiety and despair, of both conservatives and liberals, come from their impotence to control the changes and an inability to see where they are going. The confusion makes it impossible at the moment to see how the Church is, and is going to be, an effective community of God's love.

What Karl Rahner wrote recently of the evolution of theology concerning birth control applies to many another current evolution in Catholic theology and life and experience. It is by no means new in the history of the Church that there be such evolution. What is unprecedented is the rapidity of the change. One suspects that 1975 may belong to as different an historical era from 1965 as the mid-sixteenth century did from the mid-fifteenth. In any case, it is the rapidity of the changes that has multiplied the confusion for the Catholic in 1969 and leaves him with a persistent tightening of the stomach along with a feeling of helplessness. One can imagine that the bark of Peter has run into stormier weather than this; what unsettles is that stars, compass and landmarks have disappeared and the old ship is rushing headlong into darkness.

The American Catholic today must remind himself of the freedom of the Christian man that is his as a Roman Catholic in this time and place. The only thing that matters is that God loves me and I have that. I believe and accept God's love as it comes to me concretely, i.e., through my history and my community, above all, through my Church today, the given individuals that make up this people of God, parents, colleagues, friends, old teachers, writers, superiors, Terence, Archbishop of New York, Paul, Bishop of Rome and Pope of my Church, etc., etc. However God's light and love may come to others, it is through these individuals around me and our interacting life that it comes to me, despite their limitations, and despite my limitations. If I look to the limitations, I am drawn to anxiety and despair. If I look to Christ, loving me through the history and community that make me what I am, through my Roman Catholic Church, then I am at peace, and free from fear and discouragement, and free to labor in love with Him, to try to be a Christ for others in this Church.

Indeed, the fact that the humanness of the situation presses down on me and limits all my endeavors can intensify my freedom as a Catholic. Sartre meant something analogous:

"We were never so free as under the Nazis." The limitations and frustrations imposed by the Occupation threw him back on what was the only thing that mattered, his inner freedom, his self-affirmation, the creative autonomy of his choice to be and do. Unlike Sartre, I believe myself not to be alone. The limitations and frustrations imposed by the situation in the Roman Catholic Church today, the night into which the bark of Peter is careening, throws me back on the only thing that matters, that through this human, sinful, confused Church God is loving me and I accept His love. Never have I been so free.

FOOTNOTES

Introduction

1. Eugene B. Borowitz, *Choosing a Sex Ethic. A Jewish Inquiry* (Schocken, 1969); Joseph Fletcher, *Situation Ethics. The New Morality* (Philadelphia: The Westminster Press, 1966).

2. "Faith and New Opinions," *America*, October 28, 1967, p. 479.

3. E.g., Robert Johann, *Building the Human* (New York: Herder and Herder, 1968), and *The Pragmatic Meaning of God* (Milwaukee: Marquette University Press, 1966); Charles E. Curran, *A New Look at Christian Morality* (Notre Dame, Ind.: Fides, 1968), and *Contemporary Problems in Moral Theology* (Fides, 1970).

4. Dulles, *loc. cit.*

1 No Absolutes

1. *Summa Theologiae*, II–II, qq. 47–56. Three good commentaries: Josef Pieper, *Prudence* (New York: Pantheon, 1959), the "Notes explicatives" and "Renseignements techniques" of T. H. Deman, O.P., in his edition and translation of the text (Paris: Éditions de la Revue des Jeunes, 1949), pp. 247–527; R. P. Sertillanges, *La philosophie morale de saint Thomas d'Aquin*, nouvelle édition (Paris: Aubier; in the copies available to me, the date of the edition is not clearly printed), pp. 157–166.

2. "A final word about self-assertion, initiative, or creativeness. Within the scope of traditional morality and asceticism there is ample room for personal responsibility for decisions of conscience. The key to this is found in the correct notion of Christian prudence, which supposes the knowledge of general norms and applies them to concrete situations. Thus in the sphere of obligation, there is much room for, and need of, individual mental activity in deciding how the principles concerning occasions of sin, cooperation, scandal, epikeia, and so forth apply to the individual situation; and the answers may differ from person to person, as well as for the same person in different situations. It was very likely to cases such as these that Pius XII referred when he distinguished between absolutely

binding precepts and cases in which there are no absolutely binding standards. Concerning these latter cases, he said:

> Where there are no absolutely binding standards, independent of all circumstances or eventualities, the situation which 'happens only once' demands, it is true, in its unicity, an attentive examination, in order to decide which rules are to be applied, and how. Catholic morality has always, and extensively, treated this problem of forming one's own conscience by first examining the circumstances of the case to be decided. The whole of its teaching offers a precious aid to the definite guidance of conscience, whether theoretical or practical. Let it suffice to mention the explanations of St. Thomas, still of value, on the cardinal virtue of prudence and the virtues connected with it. His treatise shows his understanding of a sense of personal activity and of actuality which contains whatever true and positive elements there may be in ethics according to the situation, while avoiding its confusion and wanderings from the truth. Hence, it will be enough for the modern moralist to follow the same line if he wishes to make a thorough study of the new problem."

John C. Ford, S.J., and Gerald Kelly, S.J. *Contemporary Moral Theology*, I (Westminster, Md.: Newman, 1958), pp. 139–140. Pius XII is cited from *Acta Apostolicae Sedis*, 44 (1952), 418; *Catholic Documents*, 8 (July, 1952), 19.

3. Joseph Fletcher gives the name "antinomian" to one who "enters the decision-making situation armed with no principles or maxims whatsoever. . . ." The true situationist does use principles; he "enters into every decision-making situation fully armed with the ethical maxims of his community and its heritage, and he treats them with respect as illuminators of his problems." *Situation Ethics* (Philadelphia: Westminster, 1966), pp. 22, 26.

Cf. also Daniel Callahan, "Do We Need a New Ethic?" *National Catholic Reporter*, December 18, 1970, p. 16. Callahan, if I understand him, goes further than I in depreciating, if not denying, the importance and extent of a distinction between "the new" and "the old" morality, once one "scratches under the surface." Cf. however my remarks toward the end of the present chapter on "traditional Catholic moral theology, as formed in the Middle Ages and in the sixteenth and seventeenth centuries" and the conclusions of Chapters 9 and 10.

4. H. Richard Niebuhr, *The Responsible Self* (New York: Harper and Row, 1963), e.g., pp. 51–54. I am not implying that there has ever been an individual thinking exclusively along the lines of the "citizen," or an individual thinking exclusively along the lines of "the new morality." But there have been, and are, many individuals whose moral thinking is more characterized by one approach than by the other.

5. *Summa Theologiae*, II–II, q. 57, a. 2, ad 1; cf. q. 120, a. 1, c.; also *In V Ethic. Aris. ad Nicomachum*, lect. xvi, 1085.

6. Perhaps the greatest contribution of Joseph Fletcher's *Moral Responsibility. Situation Ethics at Work* (Philadelphia: Westminster, 1967), is to work out specific moral principles, just as it was of *Situation Ethics* to spell out specific exceptions to principles. Critics of Fletcher for the stress he puts on the individual situation in *Situation Ethics* [e.g., Paul Ramsey, *Deeds and Rules in Christian Ethics* (New York: Scribners, 1967)] might have saved some of their polemic if they had read *Moral Responsibility*. As Bishop Robinson did, after *Honest to God*, in *Christian Morals Today*, Fletcher brings out more clearly in his later book the practical importance principles can have for moral decision, although he does it mainly by reprinting essays published before *Situation Ethics*.

Some of the principles Fletcher lays down open up perspectives, but are so general that they need other, more specific principles, based on practical experience, before they can "illuminate" adequately the moral problems that need illuminating. Examples are Fletcher's theses that sexual partners should treat each other as a subject, not as an object, and that no sexual act is ethical if it hurts or exploits others. Like every other contemporary ethicist, Fletcher suffers from the paucity of empirical data available in the matter of sexuality. Another principle that is helpfully suggestive, but can serve only as a generic orientation, is that technological civilization can and should be used for the enhancement of the individual and the creative powers of the independent personality. On the other hand, other principles that Fletcher advances are specific and practical, but of a familiar, perhaps overworked kind, i.e., permissive principles delimiting moral obligation. Thus Fletcher agrees with Pius XII that doctors are not obliged to use reanimation techniques on a patient hopelessly dying and already virtually dead. Similarly restrictive of obligation is a principle concerning sex laws: ". . . offenses should be restricted to (1) acts with persons under the legal age of consent; (2) acts in situations judged to be a public nuisance or infringement of public decency; and (3) acts involving assault, violence, duress or fraud" (p. 111).

Most valuably, Fletcher traces out principles that exemplify how demanding the new ethics can be, either in reinforcing traditional obligations or adducing ones that were rarely recognized in the past. Bribes in business are generally wrong, since the consumer pays the cost, the briber is soured, the bribee demoralized, the waters of relationship within their organizations are muddied and the practice spreads like a disease. On the other hand, a principle that may surprise, but is typical of the new morality, is the necessity of increased taxation, including a more carefully selective sales tax. Fletcher's development of this principle illustrates several aspects of the new morality. Poverty, in the sense of the original Franciscan destitution or of a voluntary poverty whose sole goal is self-surrender, lacks ethical value, because material wealth is a necessary means to love the neighbor. All wealth belongs to God. He gives it to all men, not as individuals, but as a family or community. Individual Christians holding wealth are only stewards acting in God's behalf and using the wealth for the good of the whole community. To be effective, such a use must keep in step with the collective structures and increasing organization of modern society. It must use social planning and public welfare, corporate and community-wide giving. Thus the Christian must administer stewardship on the level of law. His aim is not only to aid the materially poor, but to meet the spiritual and cultural needs of the community. Wealth must be used for educational grants and scholarships, art centers, the battle against juvenile delinquency, urban renewal, reforestation, medical care, etc. The foe is consumerism, the creation by high-pressure advertising of wants and needs of material goods, which arises from one's preoccupation with producing wealth instead of with distributing it. Influenced by John Galbraith, Fletcher calls for a new "macroethics." One corollary of the above reasoning is the necessity of an increased and more selective sales tax.

7. Probably, there has not been, nor will be, any specific moral condemnation by the Church that can be considered an expression of divine revelation or infallible. Any condemnation could, therefore, yield to exceptional circumstances or higher values. But once the Church issued a condemnation (e.g., of racial segregation or of contraception), a new factor confronts the Christian conscience. Graver reasons are needed to justify the kind of action condemned. In the concluding chapters of the book, I discuss the relationship between Church authority and individual conscience.

2   Sharing God's Dominion

1. The Church claims that it, and it alone, can dissolve the bond of legitimate marriage under certain conditions: when the marriage is not consummated or when the privilege of faith, of which the pauline privilege is only one form, applies (E. Genicot, S.J., and J. Salsmans, S.J., *Institutiones Theologiae Moralis*, seventeenth edition, II (Brussels, 1951), pp. 468–481, ## 672–693). "The bond of matrimony is dissolved by divine power under certain conditions. The Roman Pontiff possesses this power as God's vicar (*potestate vicaria*). The authors today call it 'the petrine privilege' and define it as the most extensive power of dissolving, for a good reason, all marriages that are not between Christians (*rata*) or have not been consummated as such . . .

. . . .

The Church became aware of this power only little by little through its practice." (p. 468).

2. Dietrich Bonhoeffer, *Letters and Papers from Prison*, ed. Eberhard Bethge, revised edition (New York: Macmillan, 1967), p. 188. The subsequent quotations in the paragraph are from pages 188, 196, 207, 202, 142.

3. *Summa Contra Gentiles*, III, 69.

4. Bonhoeffer, *op. cit.*, pp. 141, 193.

5. *Genesis*, I: 26–28.

6. Henry Davis, S.J., *Moral and Pastoral Theology*, I (New York: Sheed and Ward, 1943), p. 91. Similarly, Herbert Jone, O.F.M. Cap., and Urban Adelman, O.F.M. Cap., *Moral Theology* (Westminster, Md.: Newman, 1953), pp. 43–45. Probabilism is one of the two moral systems to which "most modern moralists give their allegiance." The other system is "equiprobabilism," somewhat more demanding than probabilism, but agreeing with probabilism "in holding that it is lawful to follow the less safe [i.e., the course of action less likely not to be sinful], if the safer is only equally probable, and the question is about the existence of the law." John A. McHugh, O.P., and Charles J. Callan, O.P., *Moral Theology. A Complete Course*, revised by Edward P. Farrell, O.P., Volume I (New York: Wagner, 1958), pp. 252–253. Properly understood and measured in terms of the possibilities for an ethics patterned on law, neither probabilism nor equiprobabilism are laxist. They do, however, provide excuses that do not hold for an ethics of responsibility.

7. C. H. Dodd, *Gospel and Law* (New York: Columbia University, 1951), p. 25.

8. C. Musonii Rufi, *Reliquiae*, ed. O. Hense (Leipzig: Teubner, 1905), Fragments 3, 12, 13A, 14. I am indebted to John P. Langan for permission to use his unpublished translation.

9. Albert Dondeyne, *Faith and the World* (Pittsburgh: Duquesne University, 1963), p. 23.

10. *Ibid.*, p. 22.

11. Peter J. Henriot, "Convocation on 'Pacem in Terris'", *America*, February 13, 1965, p. 224.

12. A survey of recent inquiries into the specificity of Christian morality is Richard McCormick, S.J., "Notes on Moral Theology: April–September, 1970," *Theological Studies*, March 1971, pp. 71–78. A magistral, though selective, historical survey of responses of Christian theologians to this question is James Gustafson, *Christ and the Moral Life* (Harper and Row, 1968).

3   Creative Activism

1. The chapter was written at the invitation of the editors of *Commonweal* to predict the state of ethics in the Church in the

year 2000. *Commonweal Paper 4: The Church in the Year 2000*, October 31, 1969, pp. 135–140.

2. *The Responsible Self* (New York: Harper and Row, 1963), p. 61.

3. Benjamin L. Masse, "On Campus the Encyclicals are Out," *America*, July 5, 1969, p. 5. The findings of Father Porter had appeared in the spring issue of the *Review of Social Economy*.

4. Cf. George E. Schreiner, M.D., "The Ethics of Human Experimentation," *The Pharos*, July, 1966, pp. 78–83. The code of Claude Bernard appeared in his *Introduction to Experimental Medicine*; the Nuremberg Code was formulated after World War II in response to a thesis done in the name of science by physicians and others as part of the experiment in national socialism under the Nazi regime; the Declaration of Helsinki is a recent code developed by the Eighteenth Meeting of the World Health Association; the code referred to of the British Medical Association is part of a code approved in 1963 by the Representative Body of the Association. A more recent example is the set of guidelines proposed for heart transplants by the American National Academy of Sciences' Board on Medicine. *The New York Times*, February 28, 1968.

5. Issued Oct. 14, 1966, by Rev. Gerard J. Campbell, S.J., President of Georgetown University. By the statement, I believe, Georgetown Hospital became the first hospital in the country to have a code governing experimental research on human beings.

6. I add these three paragraphs to the text of the original article in an effort to meet the criticism James Gustafson made of it in the same *Commonweal Paper* ("Responsibility and Utilitarianism," pp. 140–141). In "Objective Moral Evaluation of Consequences," *Theological Studies*, September 1971, I have undertaken to provide much more extensively the "careful analysis" Gustafson called for of the problems involved in discerning "the human values at stake."

7. Ira L. Reiss, "Introduction," *The Sexual Renaissance in America, Journal of Social Issues*, April, 1966, p. 1.

8. Lester A. Kirkendall, "Interpersonal Relationships—Crux of the Sexual Renaissance," *Journal of Social Issues*, April, 1966, pp. 47–48.

4 *Homosexuality and Love*

1. *The New York Times*, November 29, 1967, p. 1.

2. "The Homosexual in America," *Time*, January 21, 1966, pp. 40–41; "God and the Homosexual," *Newsweek*, February 13, 1967, p. 63; "The Sad 'Gay' Life," *Look*, January 10, 1967, pp. 30–33.

3. *Situation Ethics* (Philadelphia: Westminster, 1966), pp. 103–107.

4. C. Spicq, O.P., *Théologie morale du Nouveau Testament*, II (Paris: Lecoffre, 1965), pp. 481 ff.; C. H. Dodd, *Gospel and Law* (New York: Columbia University, 1951), pp. 42–45.

5. *Summa Contra Gentiles*, III, 122.

6. Isadore Rubin, Ph.D., "Homosexuality," *SIECUS*, Discussion Guide, No. 2 (New York, 1965), p. 3.

7. *Ibid.*, p. 4.

8. *Ibid.*, p. 1.

9. *Report on Homosexuality with Particular Emphasis on this Problem in Governmental Agencies*, formulated by the Committee on Cooperation with Governmental (Federal) Agencies of the Group for the Advancement of Psychiatry, Report No. 30, January, 1955, p. 2.

10. *Ibid.*, p. 3.

11. Philip H. Heersema, M.D., "Homosexuality and the Physician," *Journal of the American Medical Association*, September 6, 1965, pp. 159 and 160.

12. *Ibid.*, p. 1.

13. Cf. Martin Hoffman, "Homosexual," *Psychology Today*, July, 1969, pp. 43–45, 70; John McNeill, "Pastoral Counseling of the Male Homosexual," to appear in *Homiletic and Pastoral Review*. Studies cited by McNeill in support of the view that homosexuality is not of itself a serious emotional illness are Daniel Cappon, *Towards an Understanding of Homosexuality* (New Jersey: Prentice Hall, 1965); John R. Cavanagh, *Counseling the Invert* (Milwaukee: Bruce, 1966); H. Kimball-Jones, *Towards a Christian Understanding of the Homosexual* (London: SCM Press, 1967); Wainwright Churchill, *Homosexual Behavior Among Males* (New York: Hawthorne, 1967); Evelyn Hooker's study published in the New York Council of Churches report, *Foundations for Christian Family Policy* (1961); Michael Schofield, *Sociological Aspects of Homosexuality* (Boston: Little, Brown, 1965). Hoffman refers to a report by two London psychiatrists, Desmond Curran and Denis Parr, published in the British Medical Journal in 1957, and to the responses of a number of distinguished behavioral scientists asked by the Homosexual Law Reform Society, based in Philadelphia, their opinions on the relation of homosexuality to psychopathology.

Typical of the new evidence is that of the psychologist Evelyn Hooker: She found thirty homosexuals, not in treatment, whom she felt to be reasonably well-adjusted. She then matched thirty heterosexual men with the homosexuals for age, education and I.Q. Hooker then gave these sixty men a battery of psychological tests and obtained considerable information on their life histories. Several of her most skilled clinical colleagues then analyzed the material. They did not know which of the tests had been given to the homosexual men and which to the heterosexuals; they analyzed the tests blind. Hooker concluded from their analyses that there is no inherent connection between homosexual orientation and clinical symptoms of mental illness. She stated: "Homosexuality as a clinical entity does not exist. Its forms are as varied as are those of heterosexuality. Homosexuality may be a deviation in sexual pattern that is in the normal range, psychologically." This conclusion is based on the fact that the clinicians were unable to distinguish between the two groups. Nor was there any evidence that the homosexual group had a higher degree of pathology than the heterosexual group. Martin Hoffman, *op. cit.*, p. 43.

From a different point of view, the Catholic moral theologian Charles Curran concludes that homosexual acts might not always be wrong:

What about the cases where modern medical science cannot help the homosexual? In these cases it seems to me that for such a person homosexual acts might not even be wrong. I am not saying that such acts are ever a goal or an ideal that should be held up to others to imitate. Homosexual acts for such a person, provided there is no harm to other persons, might be the only way in which some degree of humanity and stability can be achieved. This would be a practical application of the theology of compromise. Compromise maintains that because of the existence of sin in the world a person might be forced to accept some behavior which under ordinary circumstances he would not want to choose.

Contemporary Problems in Moral Theology (Notre Dame, Ind.: Fides, 1970), p. 177; cf. "Dialogue with Joseph Fletcher," *Homiletic and Pastoral Review* 67 (1967), pp. 828–829.

14. John McNeill, who is impressed by the evidence that homosexuality is not necessarily a disease, nevertheless notes:

Practically all authorities agree that the first goal of counseling should be to guide the person with a homosexual problem to a heterosexual adjustment whenever this is possible.

The person who merely fears he may be a homosexual, or is attracted to the homosexual community, should explore every avenue toward the achievement of normal heterosexual capacities and relationships. This direction should be taken independently of what one's moral judgment may be concerning homosexual practices. Even the officers of the Mattachine Society, a homophile organization, agree with this aim: ". . . on the basis of our experience—the embarrassment, shame, and humiliation so many of us have known—we would definitely advise anyone who has not yet become an active homosexual, but has only misgivings about himself, to go the other way, if he can." The reason for this advice is the many problems the average homosexual encounters, which make a positive adjustment to such a life extremely difficult. McNeill, *Ibid.*

As a consequence, the first discernment a counselor should attempt to establish is whether or not a given individual is a true homosexual or merely suffering from "pseudo-homosexual panic" as a result of some experience or one of the many forms of conditional homosexuality mentioned earlier in the article. This discernment is especially important, as Hettlinger points out, in dealing with the adolescent or young adult. *Ibid.*

15. *Ephesians,* IV:11–15.

5 The Abortion Debate

1. According to *The New York Times,* in the last year or two a growing number of lawyers and judges have been predicting that the Supreme Court will recognize the constitutional right of an American woman to have an abortion, or that the courts will declare the nation's anti-abortion laws unconstitutional on less sweeping grounds, but with the same results. When, on November 10, 1969, Federal District Judge Gerhard A. Gesell ruled that the District of Columbia's abortion law, already more liberal than the law of most states, was unconstitutionally vague and probably an unconstitutional infringement of woman's private rights, the decision "illuminated a remarkable shift in attitudes towards abortion laws in two years. Opponents are now demanding abolition rather than reform; they are using litigation rather than legislation to get it; and they are coming to view abortion as a fundamental right that should be available to women who are poor and single as well as those who are well-off and married." Fred P. Graham, "Abortions: Moves to Abolish All Legal Restraints," in "The Week in Review," *The New York Times,* November 16, 1969, p. 9. Cf. Linda J. Greenhouse, "Constitutional Question: Is There a Right to Abortion?" *The New York Times Magazine,* January 25, 1970, pp. 30 ff.
However, since Graham wrote, there have been indications of a reversal of the "trend" he describes (the trend of attacking the constitutionality of any abortion law), e.g., the Supreme Court's rejection of Judge Gesell's ruling and the vigorous, successful campaign for a liberal abortion law in New York State.

2. John Noonan insists that the actual choice, practical and historical, now facing American law makers, is "between resisting the pressure for any change or, alternatively, permitting, in one guise or another, abortion on demand." A compromise such as a law tailored to meet permissively cases of rape, incest and mental instability is in fact ". . . a major step . . . toward abandoning the state's right to protect the fetus." For those "who accept the essential humanity of the fetus," "there can be no compromise, no

tolerance, no easy acceptance of legislation which destroys the most basic of human and civil rights for a class of children." "Amendment of the Abortion Law: Relevant Data and Judicial Opinion," *The Catholic Lawyer*, Spring, 1969, pp. 133–134. Mary Rosera Joyce, reviewing David Granfield's *The Abortion Decision*, agrees with the policy he urges: " 'It would be naive,' he says, 'for anyone to think that the compromise passage of a moderate abortion bill will do more than temporarily delay the fight for free abortion.' However, in order to avoid extreme permissiveness, those who are opposed to abortion ought to work for legislative *amendments* on a lenient statute when its enactment is inevitable, in order to contain its harm as much as possible." *The National Catholic Reporter*, October 15, 1969, p. 9. A recent *America* editorial urged, "Above all, Catholics must see for themselves and persuade others that the uterine person, the embryo, has inalienable human rights, chief of which is the right to live. This truth must be held to with tenacity during the long months of public debate ahead." (March 1, 1969, p. 240.)

3. Although his analysis of the situation differs in part from mine, Robert Drinan, too, affirms its critical nature: "It is painfully clear that Catholics confront in the abortion issue an agonizing question of public policy which could divide Catholics, weaken ecumenical relations and place Catholics and the Church in the years and decades ahead either in the position of having sinned by the use of its prestige and power against the sincerely held convictions of non-Catholics and non-believers or as a group which failed by silence to speak up when misguided men and women changed the law to permit the extermination of undesirable and unwanted human beings.

It seems self-evident that this challenge is unique in American Catholic experience, that it is awesome and that it is inescapable. Hopefully it is a challenge which, unlike any previous challenge, will arouse the minds and consciences of American Catholics to original, creative thought on a legal-moral problem of incalculable significance." "Catholic Moral Teaching and Abortion Laws in America," *Proceedings of the Twenty-Third Annual Convention of The Catholic Theological Society of America*, June 17–20, 1968, p. 130.

4. E.g., Mrs. N. Lorraine Beebe, State Senator of Michigan, arguing for a more liberal abortion statute and replying to critics' statements that abortion was tantamount to murder, "You do not have the right to impose your morals or religious convictions on us. We have religious freedom in this country." (*The New York Times*, June 13, 1969.)

5. E.g., Richard John Neuhaus, "The Dangerous Assumption," *Commonweal*, June 30, 1967, p. 412, as well as Joyce and Noonan in the articles cited above insist that the abortion question necessarily implicates the ethical question of infanticide and genocide.

6. Both men have written and spoken extensively to this effect,

e.g., André E. Hellegers, "Law and the Common Good," *Common-weal*, June 30, 1967, pp. 418–423. One thesis of Robert Drinan, if ever widely accepted, would ease a good deal of the debate, since it would defuse one of the most operative motives for the affirmative answer described in the following sentence above in the text. "If there is one thing which should be clear from the foregoing and from the state of the question regarding abortion and the law in America it is that there is no such thing as a 'Catholic position' on the jurisprudence of abortion laws. Catholics are free to advocate any of the three options available—strict legal prohibition of abortion, the Model Penal Code, or abortion on request." (*Op. cit.*, p. 129.) "It is submitted that episcopal statements going beyond the morality of abortion and entering into the question of jurisprudence or the best legal arrangements are inappropriate intrusions in a pluralistic society by an ecclesiastical official who wrongly assumes that he can pronounce on a legal-political question a moral and uniform position of his Church." (Pp. 124–125.) Cf. also "The Right of the Foetus to Be Born," *The Dublin Review*, Winter, 1967–1968, pp. 365–381.

7. For example, in 1967, members of the American hierarchy publicly opposed relaxation of abortion laws on the grounds of "a person's right to live" (Bishop Francis J. Green of Tucson), of "the right of innocent human beings to life . . . sacred and inviolable" (the bishops of New York's eight Catholic dioceses, led by Francis Cardinal Spellman), of the recognized immorality of "murder" (Richard Cardinal Cushing of Boston). *The Catholic Messenger*, February 16, 1967, p. 1. Richard McCormick, S.J., characterizes recent teachings of the magisterium (of Pius XI, Pius XII and the Second Vatican Council): "First of all, it developed and was nuanced merely as an application of a more general teaching, or at least hand in hand with it—the immorality of the direct killing of innocent human life." "Secondly, the teaching is presented with uncommon strength and insistence." "Thirdly, the teaching is presented without qualification. It is seen as absolute." "Past Church Teaching on Abortion," *Proceedings of the Twenty-Third Annual Convention of The Catholic Theological Society of America*, June 17–20, 1968, pp. 136–137. In the preceding pages, McCormick presents some important statements by pope and council and summarizes these and other pertinent magisterial documents.

"The stumbling block for those who reject abortion is the limit which the most humane, most libertarian, most autonomous of ethics must set: the right to life of another person. . . . If man can be recognized at all in the multiple forms of humanity, the notion of man necessitates respect for the human person's right to live. One person's freedom to obtain an abortion is the denial of another person's right to live." John T. Noonan, Jr., *The Morality of Abor-*

tion. Legal and Historical Perspectives (Cambridge: Harvard University Press, 1970), "Introduction," p. xvii.

Protestants opposing abortion often differ from Catholics in that the Protestants will permit abortion in certain exceptional circumstances. Nevertheless, in general, the foundation of the Protestant opposition is similar to that of the Catholic: the human fetus is essentially the same kind of being as the born child or adult. "How long can we meaningfully say that all men are created equal while the innocent unborn are sacrificed to personal whim, convenience or that new test of Americanism in our increasingly technologic and impersonal age: the qualification of being perfect, or being wanted, or being viable?" (Statement sponsored by the Value of Life Committee, signed by, among others, three Protestant theologians, J. Robert Nelson, George H. Williams, Albert C. Outler. *National Catholic Reporter*, February 26, 1971, p. 18. Cf. George H. Williams, "Religious Residues and Presuppositions in the American Debate on Abortion," *Theological Studies*, March, 1970, pp. 10–25. His essay, published in the volume edited by Noonan and cited above "constitutes in effect Part II of the larger essay" appearing in *Theological Studies*.)

Richard M. Nixon stated publicly on April 3, 1971:

"From personal and religious beliefs I consider abortion an unacceptable form of population control. Further, unrestricted abortion policies, or abortion on demand, I cannot square with my personal belief in the sanctity of human life—including the life of the yet unborn." (*National Catholic Reporter*, April 16, 1971, p. 5.)

8. E.g., in his presidential address to the Convocation of Canterbury, the Archbishop of Canterbury, Dr. Arthur Michael Ramsey, suggested that the line at which abortion was legalized should be drawn to cover cases where there was risk to the life and mental or physical health of the mother. He said that the "absolutist" position virtually equating abortion and infanticide could not be held today. Although the human fetus was sacred, he said it was unreal to identify a fetus with a human life. One was the prelude to the other. (Reported by *The Catholic Messenger*, February 2, 1967, p. 1.)

9. E.g., "Only one weighty objection to abortion remains to be discussed, and this is the question of 'loss.' When a fetus is destroyed, has something valuable been destroyed? The fetus has the potentiality of becoming a human being. A human being is valuable. Therefore is not the fetus of equal value? This question must be answered.

"It can be answered, but not briefly. What does the embryo receive from its parents that might be of value? There are only three possibilities: substance, energy and information. As for the substance in the fertilized egg, it is not remarkable: merely the sort of thing one might find in any piece of meat, human or animal, and there is very little of it—only one and a half micrograms, which is about a half of a billionth of an ounce. The energy content of this tiny amount of material is likewise negligible. As the zygote develops into an embryo, both its substance and its energy content increase (at the expense of the mother); but this is not a very important matter —even an adult, viewed from this standpoint, is only a hundred and fifty pounds of meat!" Garrett Hardin, "Abortion—or Compulsory Pregnancy?" *Journal of Marriage and the Family*, May, 1968, p. 250. Professor Hardin refutes with equal ease that the "information" might be "precious." The first step of his reasoning is an unsupported assertion simply denying the traditional position that there is in the embryo something besides his three possibilities, namely the principle of human life that makes a human being a human being. He makes no attempts to present and meet the arguments of the tradition. Professor Hardin, I am sure, is familiar with the traditional position and knows what he is doing in the article. But it is a typical incongruity in what one calls the "dialogue" or "debate" concerning abortion.

10. "Here the testimony of Dr. Arnold Gesell, founder of the Clinic of Child Development at Yale University, is of particular significance. In a chapter entitled 'The Nature of Mental Growth,' Dr. Gesell points out that from the point of view of a psychologist, 'mental growth is a process of behavior patterning.' He continues: '[e]ven in the limb bud stage, when the embryo is only four weeks old, there is evidence of behavior patterning: the heart beats. In two more weeks slow back and forth movements of arms and limbs appear. Before the twelfth week of uterine life the fingers flex in reflex grasps.'" John Noonan, *op. cit.,* p. 125, identifying the excerpt as Gesell, *The First Five Years of Life,* p. 11 (1940). It is to this testimony (along with a similar one by a fetologist) that Noonan presumably is referring when he concludes, "If you choose to resist all pleas and pressures for change [i.e., to legally permit more abortion], you will have the consciousness that you are acting in accordance with what is the converging testimony of those who have studied the womb both physiologically and psychologically" (p. 134). Noonan, like Hardin, may well be able to justify, in terms of the limits and purpose of the article, this abbreviated reasoning. But anyone who in advance disagreed with the anti-abortion position or had doubts about it would find that Professor Noonan had glided over the crucial question within the question: is the assertion of the "humanity" of the fetus in the humanistic, moral sense supported by evidence of "humanity" and "mental growth" in the sense of behavioral patterning such as heartbeat?

11. Hardin simply presupposes that the potential value of the fetus becomes actual at birth. "The *expected* potential value of each aborted child is exactly that of the average child born." (P. 250; italics his.) He reasons, "Analysis based on the deepest insights of molecular biology indicates the wisdom of sharply distinguishing the

information for a valuable structure from the completed structure itself." (P. 251.) But how does one determine when the information becomes the completed structure? How does one evaluate the intermediate stages? His own analogy of blueprint and finished house would raise the question, I would think.

12. E.g., at the International Conference on Abortion, held at Washington, D.C., September 6–8, 1967, sponsored by the Harvard Divinity School in cooperation with the Joseph P. Kennedy Foundation. Cf. the report of Richard A. McCormick, *America*, September 23, 1967, pp. 320–321.

The monumental essay of Daniel Callahan (*Abortion: Law, Choice and Morality*, New York: Macmillan, 1970) to respect both sides of this question (and others pertinent to the abortion debate) and to contribute to a basis for consensus (cf. pp. 15–21) has won merited accolades. What effect it will have on public debate and policy remains to be seen. Is it indicative that Callahan, who strongly criticizes "the Roman Catholic Christian position, prone to argue that the necessity of preserving all life, even potential life, is the single overriding value to be acted upon in abortion decisions" and rejects the position that "abortion is always wrong" (p. 19) was accorded the Thomas More Medal for "the most distinguished contribution to Catholic literature in 1970"?

13. *Grammar of Assent*, p. 413, and *Present Position of Catholics in England*, p. 261, cited by J. H. Walgrave, O.P., *Newman the Theologian* (New York: Sheed and Ward, 1960), pp. 122–123. Rev. John Whitney Evans, who had referred to the two passages in a letter to the editor of *America*, August 16, 1969, p. 79, pointed out to me an apparently analogous statement of Theodore Roszak: "There lurks behind our socially certified morality some primordial world view which dictates what reality is, and what, within that reality, is to be held sacred." *The Making of a Counter Culture* (Garden City, New York: Doubleday, Anchor Books, 1969), p. 80.

14. William Van der Marck, O.P., offers an epistemology of ethics that would justify the method. "Ethics" can mean, in the first place, "that complex of norms concretely in force in a particular community; it is the social language in actual use." It can mean, secondly, "a reflection upon, or science about the significance, various aspects, and implications of human actions, laws, norms, and the like." As reflective science, "it will aim, first of all, at an insight into all human activity, not being concerned with the particular how, or where, or according to what ethos this activity takes place. Secondly, this sort of ethics will extend its reflection to the actual ethos of a particular community, seeing in it a specification of the general ethical phenomenon." To the two aims correspond the two divisions of the science of ethics, "general" or "fundamental," and "particular" or "special." "The actual community, and thus also the

concrete ethos, comes before any reflexive attempt to establish the concrete ethic and, all the more so, comes before any establishing of the fundamental ethic. In other words, neither the concrete ethic nor the fundamental ethic is normative, unless and insofar as they are taken precisely to be the formulation and expression of the ethos proper to the community—an ethos which, besides finding expression in actual behavior and conditioning, is transmitted in definite formulas. Not ethics, but ethos and thus the community itself establish norms." *Toward a Christian Ethic* (Westminster, Md.: Newman, 1967), pp. 2–4.

15. E.g., "My feeling is that when we are becoming so sensitive about capital punishment, and are even debating whether wars are a proper instrument of public policy; when we're sensitive in so many areas to human life, to overlook this innocuous unprotected area just because it's invisible and inside the mother is to be retrogressive." George H. Williams, Professor of the Harvard Divinity School, *The New York Daily Column*, March 2, 1969, p. 2, quoting Professor Williams' remarks in a discussion broadcast by CBS on the same day. "Admittedly there are good and sincere people of other convictions who do not believe that an unborn child is human, or who believe that even if human it has no rights before birth, or that it is permissible to violate the right to life of the unborn when that right appears to conflict with another's welfare. . . . Indeed the increasing preoccupation with reverence for human life (e.g., proposed abolition of capital punishment) is clearly at variance with these beliefs." "Statement" of Cardinal Shehan of Baltimore, Archbishop O'Boyle of Washington, Bishop Hyle of Wilmington, March 6, 1967.

16. "Mentality A" is found conspicuously in the Roman Catholic tradition and has found technical expression in the works of moralists such as John Ford, Gerald Kelly, Thomas O'Donnell, and Henry Davis.

17. "Mentality B" is found conspicuously in the ethical thinking of many "liberals" and "situationists."

18. Concerning the same trio of questions, abortion, capital punishment and war, the anti-abortionists, too, draw the charge of inconsistency. The abortionists cannot understand how they exalt the value of human life in the face of abortion, and when the discussion turns to the Vietnam war or the executions of certain criminals, rather easily find reasons to justify the killing. The limits of the article prevent an adequate presentation of this position, but I believe it can be shown, as I will attempt to show for the opposing side, to be an organically consistent one.

19. For example, the obstacle course the moral theologians have to run, in connection with capital punishment, requires that they understand the sacredness and inviolability of human life in such a way that they can justify the killing by the state of certain criminals,

but can condemn the killing by the state of any innocent person, no matter how necessary for the essential ends of the state, and condemn the killing by a private person to punish a criminal, no matter how necessary or useful it may be. It is not surprising that the justification of capital punishment offered by one moralist varies and even conflicts with that of another. Cf. e.g., the article on "Todesstrafe" in the earlier and more recent editions of the *Lexikon zur Theologie und Kirche*; Thomas Aquinas, *Summa Theologiae*, II–II, q. 64; the commentary on this question by P. Spicq in the *Revue des Jeunes* edition, pp. 212–213; de Lugo, *De Iustitia*, disp. X, sect. ii, 56–75; cf. sect. iv, 102–110; Hürth-Abellan, *De Praeceptis*, II, pp. 46–50; Noldin-Schmitt-Heinzel, II, *De Praeceptis*, pp. 301 ff.; Davis, II, *Precepts*, p. 151; "Punishment, Capital," *Dictionary of Moral Theology*, ed. P. Palazzini.

20. E.g., according to reputable classical moralists, the pain and suffering a dying patient is undergoing can change what would normally be "ordinary means" of keeping him alive into "extraordinary means" and therefore make licit the discontinuance of the means and the allowing the patient to die immediately. Cf. Thomas J. O'Donnell, S.J., *Morals in Medicine*, second edition (Westminster, Md., 1960), pp. 61–74.

21. This is basically the methodology employed, I believe, by James Gustafson in "A Christian Approach to the Ethics of Abortion," *The Dublin Review*, Winter, 1967–68, pp. 346–364, though I am not sure Gustafson would agree. Certainly, his approach to abortion shows how one can approach the question without the principle of absolute inviolability of human life in the traditional Roman Catholic sense, and with a heavy reliance on experience both of men in general and this woman in particular, without proceeding along lines of an uncritical utilitarianism.

22. Some may find this an excessively benign interpretation of silences of abortionists. The interpretation in part is born of respect acquired in dialogue for the intelligence and moral seriousness of abortionists and in part is grounded in the historico-philosophical analysis of the concluding part of this chapter.

23. This is said without implying that modern culture is, like the barbarian, a lower one than the one it is succeeding.

24. One thinks, for example, of themes of John Dewey or Leslie Dewart.

25. Cf. "La norme morale," in Père Sertillanges' *La philosophie morale de saint Thomas d'Aquin* (Paris: Aubier, n.d.), pp. 11–13.

26. E.g., for Thomas Aquinas, "It appears that the boundary between sexual norms of natural law and sexual norms of divine, positive law is not precisely observed. In fact, one might ask whether the sexual norms of natural law are not simply placed here on the same level as positive law and treated as such: they are the law that

serves the common good and therefore knows no exception." Josef Fuchs, *Die Sexualethik des heiligen Thomas von Aquin* (Köln: Bachem, 1949), p. 175. Fuchs believes that in certain passages Thomas is appealing to divine positive law as complementing and determining natural law, but that often the distinction between the two seems to be denied. In either case, the perspective is that of the legislator ordering towards the common good. "The act of generation [unlike the act of nourishing oneself] is ordered to the good of the species, which is the common good. But the common good is subject to ordering by law . . . [Therefore] to determine of what sort the act of generation should be does not pertain to anyone, but to the legislator, to whom it belongs to order the propagation of children . . . But law does not consider what can occur in a particular case, but what has usually happened suitably. Therefore, although in a particular case, the intention of nature can be saved in regard to the generation and rearing of the child, still the act is disordered in itself and a mortal sin." Thomas Aquinas, *De Malo*, q. XV, a. 2, ad 12. Cf. my "Moral Absolutes and Thomas Aquinas" in *Absolutes in Moral Theology?* (Washington: Corpus, 1968), ed. Charles Curran, pp. 154–185.

27. E.g., Daniel C. Maguire, "Moral Absolutes and the Magisterium," *Absolutes in Moral Theology?* pp. 75–77. Father Maguire writes, "Thomas' realism about the nature of ethics is an extraordinary insight which has never had sufficient impact on Catholic moral theology." Neither did it have sufficient impact on Thomas' moral theology. Cf. the passage from *De Malo* in note 26. In *Summa Contra Gentiles*, III, 125, *sub fine*, Thomas recognizes that to any law there can be exceptions working against the common good, but that it is up to the legislators to grant the dispensation, in the case of the divine law, the divine legislator. The chapter of mine, referred to in note 26, presents Thomas' explanation of the cases he finds in Sacred Scripture of legitimate exception to moral laws, particularly laws concerning human life, sexuality and property. Never man on his own, but only God can authorize the exception.

28. Blaise Pascal, *Pensées*, 126 and 127 (Br.).

29. Renatus Des Cartes, *Meditationum de prima philosophia*, p. 28 (A.T.); cf. p. 34.

30. *Principia Philosophiae*, I, 22; t. VIII, p. 13, cited by Etienne Gilson, in his edition and commentary of Descartes' *Discours de la Méthode*, third edition (Paris: Vrin, 1962), p. 201. My translation.

31. *Ibid.*, I, 46; t. VIII, p. 22, cited by Gilson, p. 203.

32. *Ibid.*, I, 45; t. VIII, p. 222, in Gilson, *loc. cit.* For the sense of "praecisa," cf. *Med.*, p. 27, l. 13. An example of the continuation of Descartes' thinking in typically twentieth century philosophy: Edmund Husserl, *Cartesian Meditations. An Introduction to Phenom-*

enology, tr. Dorion Cairns (The Hague: Nijhoff, 1960), e.g., pp. 1-6, 152-157.

33. The five, like modern philosophers in general, have their differences in describing this primal context of man, nor do all prefer the word "experience" to designate it. But with the five, as with most modern philosophers, it is some form of direct and aware union of concrete subject and concrete reality grasped; for further understanding, the intellect can only probe and illumine the given union.

34. "Et haec quidem quae jam diximus, locum aliquem haberent etiamsi daremus, quod sine summo scelere dari nequit, non esse Deum, aut non curari ab eo negotia humana." *De iure belli et pacis libri tres*, Prolegomena, 11.

35. Vernon J. Bourke, *History of Ethics* (New York, 1968), pp. 131-135. Bacon makes his bow to religion and Hobbes does profess a crude version of the theological approbative theory, but in their essential and operative epistemology of ethics God plays no part.

36. Cf. Bourke, *op. cit.*, pp. 121-122; Viktor Cathrein, S.J., *Moralphilosophie*, I (Freiburg im Breisgau: Herder, 1911), pp. 194-195. Most of the scholastics of the period were merely emphasizing that to measure the basic goodness or badness of an act, human nature sufficed as a norm, and no reference to God was requisite. They admitted that to recognize the full and binding goodness of an act, one had to know there was a pertinent divine law, although the law, in turn, could never go contrary to the natural goodness and badness of the act.

Certain scholastics of the late sixteenth and the early seventeenth century went further and held that right reason could fully determine natural law, even if God did not exist or was not considered. Particularly influential was Gabriel Vasquez, *Commentariorum ac Disputationum in Primam Secundae S. Thomae Tomus Secundus*, disp. 150, c. 3, 22-26. Cf. Bourke, *op. cit.*, p. 152; Cathrein, *op. cit.*, pp. 394-395.

37. Carl J. Friedrich, *The Philosophy of Kant. Immanuel Kant's Moral and Political Writings* (New York, 1949), pp. xxii-xxiii. The passage of Kant is in *Fragmente* ed. Hartenstein, Bd. VII, p. 624. The translation is Cassirer's as presented in *Rousseau, Kant, Goethe*.

38. John Noonan seems to be criticizing this view, as advanced by some participants at the International Conference on Abortion sponsored by the Harvard Divinity School in Washington, D.C., Sept. 8-10, 1967. He writes, "This distinction is not serviceable for the embryo which is already experiencing and reacting. The embryo is responsive to touch after eight weeks and at least at that point is experiencing." "Abortion and the Catholic Church: A Summary History," *Natural Law Forum*, Spring, 1969, p. 127. Noonan's concept of experience is one with which I am not familiar. It is not the philosophic or humanistic one that involves consciousness or aware-

ness. It simply does not follow from physical response to touch (whether the response be of plant, fetus or human adult) that there is psychological awareness of the touch or response. Even the human adult is normally unconscious of many of his reflex reactions to stimuli.

6 Sin

1. Gerald Kelly, S.J., *Modern Youth and Chastity* (St. Louis: The Queen's Work, 1943).

2. John W. Glaser, S.J., "Transition between Grace and Sin: Fresh Perspectives," *Theological Studies*, June, 1968, pp. 260–274.

In "Conscience and Superego: a Key Distinction," *Theological Studies*, March, 1971, pp. 30–47, Glaser uses modern psychology to make a different, but equally suggestive crosscut study of human morality, guilt, and freedom. He concludes, "This article is meant to be a service to freedom, a service which does not relieve a man of all burdens, but hopes to locate the pain where it should be and where it can function creatively: in the context of love—the goal, reward and best name of all freedom."

3. Robert P. O'Neill and Michael A. Donovan, *Sexuality and Moral Responsibility* (Washington: Corpus, 1968), p. 42.

4. *Ibid.*, p. 43.

5. *Ibid.*, p. 39. A good presentation of the theology of the basic option and its implications for the rarity of mortal sin can be found in Charles E. Curran, *Contemporary Problems in Moral Theology* (Notre Dame, Ind.; Fides, 1970), pp. 14–23.

6. Bernard Häring, C. SS. R., *The Law of Christ*, translated by Edwin Kaiser, C. PP. S., I (Westminster: Newman, 1966), pp. 362–363.

7. *Ibid.*, p. 358.

8. J. Huizinga, *The Waning of the Middle Ages* (New York: Doubleday, 1954), pp. 23–24.

9. *The New York Times*, June 17, 1969.

10. I John I:8–10.

7 Becoming Free

1. The landmark is Immanuel Kant's *Metaphysical Foundation of Morals*. Like most philosophical landmarks, it represents not so much the first appearance of an insight as its first more or less clear conceptualization. Kant is indebted particularly to Jean-Jacques Rousseau and to the Pietism of his childhood.

2. Cf. *Acts* 17:23–24; *Romans* 8:19–21; *Galatians* 5:1; *II Corinthians* 3:17–18.

3. The sentence that provoked the sharpest criticism was my last ("The most important thing . . ."). I am grateful for the clarification and development offered by Robert O. Johann. "Wanting What We Want," *America*, November 18, 1967, p. 614, reprinted in Johann's *Building the Human* (New York: Herder and Herder, 1968), pp. 145–147.

4. April 30, 1966, pp. 622–624, reprinted in revised form as Chapter 11 of this book.

5. Cf. "Letters to the Editor," *America*, May 28, 1966, p. 760, and my reply, June 18, 1966, p. 844.

6. "Faith and Dogmatic Pluralism," *America*, May 13, 1967, p. 728.

8 *The Behavioral Sciences*

1. Behavioral scientists will hopefully pardon the oversimplification inevitable in an attempt to synthesize briefly the impact on ethics of the behavioral sciences in general. Under the label "attitudes" I will be including what at times might better be termed "tendencies" or "myths" or "cultural values" or "drives" or "compulsions" or "habits," etc. What is common to all the behavioral sciences is their effort to trace out empirically factors of human behavior that are only dimly conscious, if at all, but enjoy a certain consistency in affecting the person's decisions. This is what is meant, for convenience of terminology, by the word "attitudes" in the following pages.

2. Pioneering in this respect are the "Notes on Moral Theology" of Robert Springer, S.J., in *Theological Studies*, June, 1967, pp. 308–335; June, 1968, pp. 275–300; June, 1969, pp. 249–288.

3. The "basic option" theology owes its origin in part to the multilevelled view of the behavioral sciences, and this may be the route by which they will have their greatest impact on Christian ethics, since the theory of the basic option radically affects practical questions such as mortal sin and the state of grace. I have not presented the theory in the present book, partly because it is still a raw import (its main exponents, to my knowledge, are Europeans like Rahner, Monden and Metz) while the new morality I am concerned with is the American product, and partly because an adequate presentation of the theory, with its undergirding of transcendental philosophy and existentialism and its manifold practical ramifications requires a book in itself. A useful introduction in English is Louis Monden, *Sin, Liberty and Law* (New York: Sheed and Ward, 1965), pp. 19–72. Shorter, but much to the point is: John W. Glaser, S.J.,

"Transition between Grace and Sin: Fresh Perspectives," *Theological Studies*, June, 1968, pp. 260–274.

The theory is a good example of the fruitful blending of philosophy and behavioral science, frequent today also among secular thinkers. James Collins has reminded us that "the other existentialist," the late Karl Jaspers, devoted his life, in thought and action, to reconciling, on the one hand, human values and, on the other, "a world increasingly organized around scientific methods and technology." Jaspers' own self-professed philosophizing began when he realized that, as the kind of practicing and lecturing psychiatrist he was, he had been speaking philosophical prose all along, but that his discourse was set in a new register and hence had gone undetected even by himself." "Karl Jaspers. A Tribute," *America*, March 22, 1969, pp. 328–330. Younger psychiatrists, such as Erich Fromm, Viktor Frankl, and Rollo May, seem to have followed a similar itinerary.

9 *Criticism of Traditional Morality*

1. Richard A. McCormick, S.J., "Notes on Moral Theology: January–June, 1969," *Theological Studies*, December, 1969, p. 644. Chapter Twelve below discusses some of the analysis behind the dissent. The application of the principle in *Humanae Vitae* continues earlier papal teaching. Assembling passages of Pius XI and Pius XII, Fathers Ford and Kelly brought out in their analysis that "the principle stressed in all the papal texts is the principle of 'divine institution,' 'divinely established order,' 'divinely established design.' In other words: God has written a certain definite plan into the nature of the generative process, and human beings are not free to change it" (John C. Ford, S.J., and Gerald Kelly, S.J., *Contemporary Moral Theology 2: Marriage Questions* (Westminster, Md.: Newman, 1963), p. 286; the point is repeated throughout the analysis, pp. 286–291. Cf. Kelly's "Contraception and the Natural Law," *Proceedings of the Eighteenth Annual Convention of the Catholic Theological Society of America* [1963], pp. 28–33. My criticism of this traditional kind of principle (as developed in the original form of the present chapter, in *Theological Studies*, June, 1966) has drawn most recently a favorable echo from Nicholas Crotty, C.P., in "Conscience and Conflict," *Theological Studies*, June, 1967, pp. 229–230. Although I appreciate the earlier responses of Daniel Callahan ("Ethics and Evidence," *Commonweal*, October 21, 1966, pp. 76–78) and Richard McCormick, S.J. (e.g., "Human Significance and Christian Significance," in *Norm and Context in Christian Ethics*, ed. by G. H. Outka and P. Ramsey, New York, 1968, pp. 233–261), I find that Crotty most accurately reports what I was trying to say. My judgment, however, may not be unbiased, since Crotty also expresses the most extensive agreement with my position.

2. Or, if one prefer, the purpose of the object to be used. In this context one can speak indifferently of the purpose of speaking or of the purpose of the faculty of speech, the purpose of living a married life or the purpose of the institution of marriage.

3. Arthur Vermeersch, S.J., discussing his proof of the grave immorality of contraception, expressed well the first approach: "This argument is free from any consideration of the moment which that rightness [*honestas*, i.e., the essential order which man should observe in his use of the conjugal act] has for the private or the common good. True, the provident God himself, while he lays down the order to be kept, is the guardian and protector of the common good. But we should not weigh what advantage or harm each act may bring in order to determine from this that there is a serious or light fault. Mortal sin . . . is *formally* an act substantially *against order* laid down by divine law, but not *formally* an act against the common good." A. Vermeersch, S.J., *De castitate et de vitiis contrariis* (Rome, 1921), p. 256, n. 258; the italics are Vermeersch's.

4. Traditional ethicians have in recent years intensified their efforts to complement the argumentation from specific purposes with other approaches more congenial to contemporary thinking, e.g., from the symbolism or "sense" of a given act. However, since many still offer the first-mentioned argumentation as by itself decisive and since the new, complementary approaches are far from having attained universal acceptance, the dichotomy is, if only as a distorting epiphenomenon, widespread today.

5. "Further, if we consider the totality and complexity of the generative system—a complexity that is neural, glandular, vascular, muscular, with internal and external organs—what a small part of that whole system actually participates in the mere bodily union of intercourse, and what a small part of that whole system is the site of pleasure and bodily satisfaction. Surely, if God had envisioned the personal satisfaction of His individual spouses as the equal or primary purpose of the generative function in marriage, He would have fashioned man and woman in a different mold." Joseph S. Duhamel, S.J., *The Catholic Church and Birth Control* (New York: America Press, 1962), p. 16.

6. References to reasoning of this sort are given in notes 12, 16 and 18.

7. For example, Richard McCormick, S.J., in an article on "Abortion" (*America*, June 19, 1965, pp. 877–881), explains carefully *what* the absolute inviolability of any innocent man's physical life is. But he never indicates the reasons that prove there *is* an absolute inviolability, holding under all circumstances. He invokes the dignity and inviolability of the human *person*, but does not show that there follows from this an equally absolute inviolability of human *physical existence*. He does adduce pertinently the harmful consequences a

merely relative inviolability could entail. But he never makes clear whether it is these consequences that ground the absoluteness. If he would actually ground it on this basis, his solution could fit well into the general epistemological orientation that the present chapter is about to suggest. But such a grounding needs to be drawn into the clear and justified directly and fully. An analogous criticism could be made of the comments published in *America* concerning the killing of babies deformed by thalidomide (Aug. 18, 1962, p. 605; Sept. 22, 1962, p. 763; Nov. 10, 1962, pp. 1118 and 1128). The criticism would not be of the opposition to abortion and mercy killing nor would it deny the relevance of many points made. But the articles and comments neglect the epistemological question: What proves that innocent human life is inviolable under all circumstances? How do we know this?

8. It should be clear that the "human life" meant here is not the *vita hominis*, "life of man," mentioned above, the life of human understanding and love that alone constitutes formally the glory of God. The "human life" in question here is merely the physical existence of a human being on earth, which might be without any understanding or love and which is contrasted to any afterlife.

9. Gerald Kelly, S.J., "Contraception and the Natural Law," *Proceedings of the Eighteenth Annual Convention of the Catholic Theological Society of America* [1963], p. 30. J. J. Lynch, S.J., in "Notes on Moral Theology," *Theological Studies*, June, 1964, p. 234, refers to this argument of Father Kelly as one which "would appear to throw some new light on the teleology of the generative act." He also notes that J. L. Thomas, S.J., expressed the same thought a few years ago in *The Family Clinic* (Westminster, Md.: Newman, 1958), p. 186. Cf. also Ford and Kelly, *op. cit.*, pp. 286–291.

10. Recently an important study has treated this question extensively: Germain G. Grisez, *Contraception and the Natural Law* (Milwaukee: Bruce, 1964). The present chapter and Dr. Grisez's book are mutually independent, and though they follow a similar course in the first steps of the problem, are far from coming to the same solution. Cf. my "Contraception and the Natural Law: A Recent Study," *Theological Studies*, September, 1965, pp. 421–427.

11. Germain Grisez, *op. cit.*, describes well the epistemology of the new ethics. He points out that this sort of epistemology characterizes most of the contemporary attitudes that are hostile to traditional natural law and, in particular, refuse to condemn any particular external behavior unconditionally, i.e., under all circumstances. Without denying this, I try to develop in the following pages that the same kind of epistemology can be found also in the natural law tradition and that in the context of either new or old morality it can ground the general, if not unconditional, prohibition

of certain external actions, although the refinement and extension that empirical knowledge enjoys today may well diminish the number of actions that can be considered abstractly and condemned in a general way.

12. E.g., V. Cathrein, *Philosophia moralis* (2nd edition; Freiburg, 1895), pp. 309–311, nn. 448–449; E. Elter, *Compendium philosophiae moralis* (3rd edition; Rome, 1950), pp. 182–183; I. Gonzalez, *Ethica* (*Philosophiae scholasticae summa* III [2nd edition; Madrid, 1957]), pp. 754–760, nn. 931–942; V. Bartocetti, "Divorce," *Dictionary of Moral Theology* (Westminster, Md.: Newman, 1962), pp. 427–428.

13. Cf. E. Elter, *op. cit.*, pp. 149–151.

14. Thomas Aquinas, *Summa Theologiae*, II–II, q. 110, a. 3, c., and 4, ad 4; H. Davis, *Moral and Pastoral Theology* (New York: Sheed and Ward, 1952), p. 114; E. Elter, *op. cit.*, pp. 151–154; E. Genicot and J. Salsmans, *Institutiones theologiae moralis*, I (14th edition; Buenos Aires, n.d.), p. 340, n. 415; H. Noldin and A. Schmitt, *Summa theologiae moralis* II (27th edition; Barcelona, 1951), p. 578, n. 638; A. Sabetti and T. Barrett, *Compendium theologiae moralis* (34th edition; New York, 1939), p. 300, n. 312.

15. Thus Elter (although he does not believe that the empirical argument suffices to demonstrate that lying is by its very nature immoral and absolutely illicit in every case), Noldin-Schmitt, and Sabetti-Barrett, *loc. cit.*

16. L. Bender, "Lying," *Dictionary of Moral Theology*, pp. 720–721; V. Cathrein, *op. cit.*, pp. 212–213, n. 298; I. Gonzalez, *op. cit.*, pp. 598–599, n. 636; J. De Lugo, *De virtute fidei divinae* (Venice, 1718), 4, 1, 11; 4, 1, 9; 4, 4, 57; 14, 5, 74; *De justitia et jure* (Venice, 1718) 16, 2, 29; F. Suarez, *De fide theologica* (Paris, 1872), 3, 5, 8. One is tempted to put Thomas Aquinas in this group rather than in the one previously given (supra n. 14). True in question 110, article 3, he reasons purely from "neither natural nor owed," with no reference to the empirical. But in question 109, article 3, ad 1, he explains that the virtue of veracity "in a certain way takes into consideration the property of being owed [*rationem debiti*]," for ". . . one man naturally owes another that without which human society cannot be preserved. But men cannot live with each other unless they believe each other, as communicating the truth to one another." It is clearly an empirical argument. However, the context of question 109 is different from that of 110, and it is perhaps pressing the word *debitum* too much to conclude that Thomas is thinking of the same thing in both places.

17. This has been traditionally recognized, as the thesis of the knowability of miracles illustrates. The use the new morality makes of this kind of necessity has been discussed in Chapters One and Four.

18. E.g., C. Boyer, *Cursus philosophiae* 2 (Rome, 1939), 508; V. Cathrein, *op. cit.*, p. 203, n. 282.

10   *Thomas Aquinas and Exceptions to the Moral Law*

1. By "physical" here, as elsewhere in the book, is not meant "material" or "perceptible to the senses," but the objective effect not yet considered in any relationship to a norm of morality. By using consistently the phrase "as a means," I am, at the price of oversimplification and repetition, trying to avoid the necessity of a detour into the complexities of another traditional principle, the principle of double effect, which is not pertinent to the purpose of the present chapter.

2. E.g., *Dictionary of Moral Theology*, ed. P. Palazzini (Westminster, Md.: Newman, 1962), *sub voce*; Henry Davis, S.J., *Moral and Pastoral Theology* (New York: Sheed and Ward, 1943), I, pp. 62–63, and II, pp. 168–169; Marcellino Zalba, S.J., "The Catholic Church's Viewpoint on Abortion," *World Medical Journal*, Vol. 13, No. 3 (May–June, 1966), pp. 88–89, 92–93.

3. E.g., Joseph Sittler, *The Structure of Christian Ethics* (Louisiana State University Press, 1958), pp. 79–86; Dietrich Bonhoeffer, *Letters and Papers from Prison* (New York: Macmillan, 1962), pp. 17–19; Helmut Thielicke, *Theological Ethics. Volume I: Foundations* (Philadelphia: Fortress, 1966), pp. 578–647.

4. See Bonhoeffer's apparently absolute condemnation of abortion as murder in *Ethics* (New York: Macmillan Paperback, 1965), pp. 175–176. It shocked a more thoroughgoing situationist, Joseph Fletcher, as he states in his *Situation Ethics* (Philadelphia: Westminster, 1966), pp. 38, 74–75. Helmut Thielicke rejects the pragmatic slogan "to prevent something worse" as ethically destructive (*op. cit.*, pp. 624–625). Moreover, "although from the standpoint of justification 'all things are possible,' in human affairs there are from the human standpoint certain limits which cannot be transgressed" (p. 643). For example, there is no situation possible in which I would be justified in denying Christ or torturing a man to obtain some truth (pp. 643–667).

5. *Op. cit.*, p. 140.

6. Paul Lehmann, *Ethics in a Christian Context* (New York: Harper and Row, 1963); Joseph Fletcher, *op. cit.*, and *Moral Responsibility. Situation Ethics at Work* (Philadelphia: Westminster, 1967).

7. See John G. Milhaven, S.J., and David J. Casey, S.J., "Introduction to the Theological Background of the New Morality," *Theological Studies*, Vol. 28, No. 2 (June, 1967), pp. 224–244; also James M. Gustafson, "Christian Ethics," in *Religion*, ed. Paul

Ramsey (Englewood Cliffs, N.J.: Prentice-Hall, 1965), pp. 287–
354, especially, pp. 325–336, and "Context versus Principles: A Mis-
placed Debate in Christian Ethics," *Harvard Theological Review*,
58 (1965), pp. 171–202.

8. The genuine idea of natural law, Jacques Maritain recalls, is a
heritage of Greek and Christian thought. In listing those who have
contributed to its historical transmission and development, Maritain
notes that St. Thomas Aquinas "alone grasped the matter in a
wholly consistent doctrine . . . ." *Man and the State* (University
of Chicago Press, 1951), p. 85. Cf. Germain Grisez, *Contraception
and the Natural Law* (Milwaukee: Bruce, 1964), e.g., pp. 60, 71
(with note 29).

9. E.g., *S. Th.*, II–II, q. 64, a. 6 and 7; q. 154, a. 2; q. 66, a. 5.
The Marietti edition indicates parallel passages. To the point: "The
end of the act itself [fornication] by its nature is disordered, even
if the person acting could be intending a good end. The end intended
does not suffice to excuse the act, just as is clearly the case with
one who steals with the intention of giving alms." *De Malo*, q. xv,
a. 1, ad 3.

10. *Genesis*, XXII:1–14. The pertinent texts of Thomas will be
discussed below.

11. *Hosea*, I:1–3.

12. *Exodus* III:21–22; XI:1–2; XII:35–36.

13. *S. Th.*, q. 64, a. 5, and a. 3. Cf. a. 7.

14. *S. Th.*, Suppl., q. 65, a. 1 and q. 67, a. 2. In the present
study, the references will be to the original text of the *Supplement*
articles, the *Commentary on the Sentences*. In the case of the above
reference: IV, d. 33, q. 1, a. 1, and q. 2, a. 1.

15. E.g., Helmut Thielicke, *op. cit.*, pp. 664–667; Karl Barth,
Church Dogmatics, II, ii, *The Doctrine of God* (Edinburgh: Clark,
1957), pp. 672 ff.; John Macquarrie, *Twentieth-Century Religious
Thought* (New York: Harper and Row, 1963), pp. 222–223. Thie-
licke recalls the significance the Bible story had for Luther and
Kierkegaard.

16. Cf. André Thiry, S.J., "Saint Thomas et la morale d'Aristote,"
in *Aristote et saint Thomas d'Aquin* (Louvain, 1957), pp. 229–258.
Thiry could have indicated more clearly that it was ultimately from
the Stoics that the medieval theologians inherited the notion of a
science of ethics based on natural first principles and oriented toward
purposes imposed on man by his nature and by God. Cf. Max
Pohlenz, *Die Stoa* (Göttingen: Vandenhoeck and Ruprecht, 1959),
pp. 243–245; also Heinrich Rommen, *The Natural Law* (St. Louis:
Herder, 1947), pp. 16–40. Along lines similar to Thiry's: Etienne
Gilson, *The Christian Philosophy of St. Thomas Aquinas* (New
York: Random House, 1956), pp. 291, 302–305.

17. Although his theological problematic never exactly coincides with the one we are considering, the research of Dom Lottin provides valuable material on the development of our question in the medieval period before Thomas. Especially useful are "La loi naturelle depuis le début du XIIe siècle jusqu'à saint Thomas d'Aquin" and "Le problème de la moralité intrinsèque d'Abélard à saint Thomas d'Aquin," in *Psychologie et Morale aux XIIe et XIIIe siècles* (Louvain: Abbaye du Mont César, 1948), II, i. pp. 71–100 and 421–465. Both studies incorporate previously published work of Lottin. Much remains to be done. For example, there is still lacking, to my knowledge, a comprehensive, scholarly study that would analyze how Thomas' integration of the newly translated Aristotelianism differed from that of his mentor, Albert the Great.

18. Cf. O. Lottin, "La valeur des formules de saint Thomas d'Aquin concernant la loi naturelle," in *Mélanges Joseph Maréchal*, II (Paris: Desclée de Brouwer, 1950), p. 345.

19. Harry V. Jaffa's thesis is that, although Thomas generally interprets or explains statements of Aristotle in terms of other statements of the Greek philosopher nonetheless, in so doing, he imputes non-Aristotelian principles to Aristotle. *Thomism and Aristotelianism* (University of Chicago, 1952), pp. 167–188. Jaffa (pp. 189–193) invokes for his support Frederick Copleston, S.J., *A History of Philosophy, Volume II, Medieval Philosophy: Augustine to Scotus* (Westminster, Md.: Newman Press, 1950), Chapter XXXIX. Maritain admits that Thomas' doctrine on natural law "unfortunately was expressed in an insufficiently clarified vocabulary" and his respect for the stock phrases of the jurists causes some trouble, particularly when it comes to Ulpian (*loc. cit.*). Cf. M.-D. Chenu, O.P., *Towards Understanding St. Thomas* (Chicago: Regnery, 1964), pp. 126–149.

20. Some brief studies of Thomas' thought patterns in dealing with the cases: R. P. Sertillanges, *La philosophie morale de saint Thomas d'Aquin* (Paris: Aubier, 1946), pp. 110–113; Josef Fuchs, *Die Sexualethik des heiligen Thomas von Aquin* (Cologne: Bachem, 1949), pp. 170–178; Hans Meyer, *The Philosophy of St. Thomas Aquinas* (St. Louis: Herder, 1946), pp. 493–499. A longer and, unfortunately, unpublished study has been of assistance to me: John W. Healey, S.J., *The Mutability of the Natural Law in Selected Texts of Saint Thomas*. For a present day Thomistic discussion of the question, see M. Zalba, S.J., *Theologiae Moralis Summa*, I, 2nd edition (Madrid: Biblioteca de Autores Cristianos, 1957), pp. 232–236.

21. *S. Th.*, II–II, q. 64, a. 5, c. For the Latin text of this and subsequent translations from Thomas, see the corresponding footnotes of the original form of the chapter, "Moral Absolutes and

Thomas Aquinas," *Absolutes in Moral Theology?*, ed. Charles E. Curran (Washington: Corpus, 1968), pp. 282–297.

22. ". . . as Augustine says, in the First Book of *The City of God*, when Samson crushed himself along with the enemy in the ruin of the building, he was excused only by the fact that the Spirit, who was working miracles through him, secretly commanded this. And he assigns the same reason for certain holy women who killed themselves in time of persecution and whose memory is celebrated in the Church." *S. Th.*, II–II, q. 64, a. 5, ad 4.

". . . Augustine, in the First Book of *The City of God*, says that Samson is excused because it is believed that he did it on God's command. A sign of this is that he would not have been able to bring down so great a building by his own strength, but by the strength of God, who does not give assistance to the evil." *Ad Hebr.*, c. XI, 1. 7, 629 (Marietti).

In "De Quinto Praecepto," *Duo Praecepta Caritatis et Decem Legis Praecepta*, 1261 (Marietti), the case of Samson and the holy women is recalled by way of objection to argue that the prohibition to kill forbids the killing of another, but not the killing of oneself. Thomas quotes Augustine's reply, "Who kills himself certainly kills a man," and concludes, "If, therefore, it is not permitted to kill a man except by the authority of God, it is, consequently, not permitted to kill oneself except by God's command or the instinct [*instinctu*] of the Holy Spirit, as is said of Samson."

"In reply to the sixth objection, it should be said that according to Augustine in the First Book of *The City of God*, no one is permitted to lay hands on himself for any reason unless perhaps it is done by divine instinct to give an example of courage in contemning death. Those concerning whom the objection has been made are believed to have brought death on themselves by a divine instinct. Wherefore their martyrdom is celebrated by the Church." *In IV Sent.*, d. 49, q. 5, a. 3, sol. 2, ad 6.

By "instinct" Thomas means that motion of the Holy Spirit in which, unlike prophecy, the human agent does not know what he is seeing or saying or doing; see *Ad Hebr.*, c. XI, 1. 7, 631 (Marietti).

23. *S. Th.*, II–II, q. 154, a. 2, ad 2.

24. Cf. *Situation Ethics*, pp. 57–58.

25. *De Malo*, q. 3, a. 1, ad 17; *In I Sent.*, d. 47, q. 1, a. 4 c, and ad 2. I am translating *dispensare contra* and *dispensare in*, wherever they appear, as "dispense from." But an analysis of the context is needed in each case to determine whether or not Thomas means dispensation in a strict, legal sense. For our purpose, it suffices that he means, as he himself says, that what otherwise a man may not do because of natural law or the decalogue, he may now licitly do in virtue of the divine command or permission.

26. In translating or paraphrasing, I am rendering all Latin words

of the stem "ord-" (e.g., *ordo, deordinationem, ordinatae*) by English words of the stem "ord-" (e.g., order, ordering). It makes for clumsy English, but seems the best way to convey the unity, nuances and ambiguity of Thomas' expressions.

27. *De Potentia Dei*, q. 1, a. 6, ad 4.

28. *In III Sent.*, d. 37, a. 4; *S. Th.*, I–II, q. 100, a. 8. The phrase is *sint dispensabilia*.

29. The cases of Hosea and the Israelites in Egypt ground the third objection raised in the *III Sent.* article and discussed in the corresponding reply. The same cases plus that of Abraham are discussed in the reply to the third objection in the *Summa* article.

30. *Loc. cit.*, ad 3.

31. Here, as in some other passages, Thomas takes "justice" in a broad sense, as regulating whatever is due to another. In the reply to the third objection, he treats adultery as a violation of justice. In *Summa Contra Gentiles*, III, 128, Thomas takes "justice" in the same wide sense and applies it to each of the precepts of the second table of the decalogue. In other places, Thomas understands "justice" in a narrow sense, distinct from virtue in general and chastity in particular, e.g., in the passages quoted below in notes 36b and 51.

32. *Loc. cit.*, ad 2.

33. *Loc. cit.*, ad 3. The sentence and its context will come in for discussion subsequently.

34. The text of Aristotle that Thomas had before him, at least in later writings such as the *Summa*, is the version of Grosseteste as revised by William of Moerbeka. It can be found, for example, in the Marietti edition of Thomas' commentary on the Nicomachean Ethics, *ad locum*.

35. *S. Th.*, I–II, q. 100, a. 8, 1; similarly *In III Sent.*, d. 37, a. 4, 2.

36. *Loc. cit.*, ad 2.

37. *S. Th.*, I–II, q. 9a, a. 4, 2 and ad 2.

38. *In Decem Libros Ethicorum Aristotelis Ad Nicomachum Expositio*, lib. V, lectio xii, 1018; cf. 1023.

39. *Loc. cit.*, 1026; cf. 1027.

40. 1029.

41. *Loc. cit.*, 1018.

42. *S. Th.*, I–II, q. 100, a. 8, *corp.*

43. Implied in *In V. Eth.*, 1028.

44. *Loc. cit.*, 1018.

45. *S. Th.*, *loc. cit.*, ad 3.

46. *Loc. cit.*, ad 1.

47. *In III Sent.*, *loc. cit.*, ad 2.

48. *Ibid.*

49. *S. Th.*, I–II, q. 94, a. 4, c.

50. *In V. Eth.*, 1018, 1023 and 1029.

50a. "And therefore whatever follows, as a conclusion, from what is naturally just must be naturally just, as from the fact that one should harm no one unjustly it follows that one should not steal, and this indeed pertains to natural justice." *In V Eth.*, 1023; cf. 1029 quoted above.

51. *S. Th.*, II–II, q. 104, a. 4, ad 2. One sees how two approaches of Thomas that seemed to conflict are here united: the apparent nominalism according to which God's will is the sole determinant of what is moral (cf. *S. Th.*, II–II, q. 154, a. 2, ad 2, cited in note 23) and the insistence that God can will only what is just and virtuous (cf. *S. Th.*, I–II, q. 100, a. 8, and parallel passages quoted above).

52. *Ad Heb.*, c. XI, 1. iv, 604. Thomas uses an almost identical formulation in *S. Th.*, II–II, q. 64, a. 6, ad 1: ". . . God has dominion over death and life, for both sinners and just die by his ordination. And therefore he who kills an innocent man at the command of God does not sin, just as God does not, whose executor he is. And he is shown to fear God in obeying his commandments."

53. *S. Th.*, I–II, q. 100, a. 8, ad 3; q. 94, a. 5, ad 2; the objection was that the incidents concerning Hosea, Abraham and the Jews in Egypt prove that the natural law can change.

54. *De Pot.*, q. 1, a. 6, ad 4.

55. In three other passages Thomas describes God's command to Abraham as an unusual precept of God (*S. Th.*, II–II, q. 154, a. 2, ad 2, quoted in note 23), as a direct and miraculous ordering of the killing to God as man's final end (*I Sent.*, d. 47, q. 1, a. 4, c. and ad 2), and as a dispensation from a primary precept of the natural law (*In IV Sent.*, d. 33, q. 2, a. 2, sol. 1, which will be discussed shortly). But in none of the three passages does he make an attempt to show how this fits in with inviolable principles of morality and justice.

56. *S. Th.*, II–II, q. 104, a. 4, ad 2. Similarly *De Malo*, q. XV, a. 1, ad 8.

57. *S. Th.*, I–II, q. 94, a. 5, ad 2. Similarly *In III Sent.*, d. 37, a. 4, ad 3. In two other passages, it is not clear whether Thomas is appealing to God's universal dominion in order to justify his command: ". . . it was not stealing because it was due the Egyptians by God's sentence" (*S. Th.*, q. 100, a. 8, ad 3); ". . . that something belong to another be taken, secretly or openly, in virtue of the authority of a judge who decrees it is not stealing, for it becomes due to one by the very fact that it has been granted him by judicial

sentence. Wherefore much less was it stealing when the children of Israel took spoils of the Egyptians at the command of the Lord who was decreeing it for the afflictions the Egyptians had brought on them without cause." *S. Th.*, II–II, q. 66, a. 5, ad 1.

58. *S. Th.*, II–II, q. 104, ad 2. Similarly in the *De Potentia* passage, Thomas justifies the action of God by his being "the orderer of all human generation" (q. 1, a. 6, ad 4).

59. *S. Th.*, I–II, q. 100, a. 8, ad 3.

60. *De Malo*, q. 15, a. 1, ad 8.

61. *S. Th.*, I–II, q. 94, a. 5, ad 2.

62. *In III Sent.*, d. 37, a. 4, ad 3.

63. *In IV Sent.*, d. 33, q. 2, a. 2, sol. 1 and ad 2.

64. The entire second article is devoted to the question.

65. There are three other passages in which God's command to Hosea is discussed, but is not justified in terms of moral principles: *S. Th.*, II–II, q. 154, a. 2, ad 2; *De Malo*, q. 3, a. 1, ad 17; *In Matth.*, c. XIX (p. 255, Marietti, 1925). In the light of analysis made earlier in our inquiry, it is not surprising that in the first passage Thomas offers no specific moral justification for God's command, and that in the second passage he merely applies the principle that "the good of the neighbor is a particular given good" and therefore God can bypass it, still ordering the man to his final good, God himself. In the third passage, it is not clear to me in exactly what sense Thomas is comparing God's command to Hosea to the Mosaic dispensation for divorce, but in any case there is no reference to specific moral principles.

66. The textual evidence concerns only the disposing of human generation. It says nothing of the possibility of God's authorizing non-generative sexual activity, e.g., contraceptive or homosexual.

67. *S. Th.*, II–II, q. 66, a. 1, c. and ad 1, 2 and 3.

68. *In III Sent.*, d. 37, a. 4, ad 3. Similarly, in *S. Th.*, II–II, q. 66, a. 5, ad 1, Thomas compares God's authority in changing the ownership of the Egyptians' property to that of a human judge.

69. *Duo Praecepta Caritatis et Decem Legis Praecepta*, "De quinto praecepto," 1260 (Marietti); cf. *S. Th.*, II–II, q. 64, a. 2, c. and ad 2. Thomas uses the identical argument here that he did for God's command to Abraham; cf. the passages quoted in note 52.

70. Pertinent parts of the paragraph are quoted in note 22.

71. *S. Th.*, II–II, q. 64, a. 3, c. and ad 1; cf. a. 4, ad 1.

72. *S. Th.*, I–II, q. 100, a. 8, ad 3. A similar comparison of divine and human authority is made in *De Pot.*, q. 1, a. 6, ad 4.

73. *S. Th.*, II–II, q. 64, a. 6, c.

74. *S. Th.*, I–II, q. 100, a. 8, ad 3. In *S. Th.*, II–II, q. 154, a. 2, ad 2, Thomas quotes Augustine and places Hosea's act in the hier-

archical network of authorities: "For as in the powers of human society the greater stands above the lesser to be obeyed, so God above all."

75. *Summa Contra Gentiles*, IV, 78, second paragraph in the Leonine edition.

76. *S. Th.*, I–II, q. 100, a. 8, ad 3. Similarly *III Sent.*, d. 37, a. 4, ad 3, and *Summa Contra Gentiles*, III, 125.

77. Josef Fuchs, *Die Sexualethik des heiligen Thomas von Aquin* (Köln: Bachem, 1949), p. 175. Fuchs believes that in certain passages Thomas is appealing to divine positive law as complementing and determining natural law, but that often the distinction between the two seems to be denied.

78. *De Malo*, q. XV, a. 2, ad 12. Cf. ad 14 and *Summa Contra Gentiles*, III, 125, *fine*.

79. M.-D. Chenu, *Towards Understanding Saint Thomas* (Chicago: Regnery, 1964), p. 271.

80. *In IV Sent.*, d. 33, q. 1, art. 2, sol. What Thomas means by "primary" and "secondary" precepts is brought out in the solution of article 1.

81. Q. 1, a. 3, sol. 3 and replies; q. 2, a. 2, sol. 2 and replies. Cf. above the summary of Thomas' position on the Mosaic permission for divorce.

82. Cf. J.-M. Aubert, *Le droit romain dans l'oeuvre de saint Thomas* (Paris: Vrin, 1955), p. 111; J. Fuchs, *Die Sexualethik des heiligen Thomas von Aquin*, p. 177; J. Maritain, *Man and the State*, p. 85; O. Lottin, "La valeur des formules de saint Thomas d'Aquin concernant la loi naturelle," *Mélanges Joseph Maréchal*, II, pp. 351 ff.; O. Lottin, *Psychologie et Morale aux XIIe et XIIIe siecles*, II, i, p. 96.

83. *Summa Contra Gentiles*, III, 125; cf. *De Malo*, q. 15, a. 2, ad 12.

84. *In IV Sent.*, d. 33, q. 2, a. 2, sol. 1. Cf. q. 1, a. 2, sol. and ad 1, 2 and 3, where Thomas develops further, *a propos* of polygamy, how dispensations of this sort are possible where natural sequences hold only for the most part. On the other hand, the prohibitions of polyandry and of concubinage in the strict sense, i.e., of fornication, are primary precepts of the natural law and not subject to dispensation of this sort (q. 1, a. 1, ad 8; q. 1, a. 3, sol. 3 and ad 1).

85. Joannis de Lugo, *Tractatus de iustitia et iure*, disp. X, sect. I, 2.

86. *Loc. cit.*, 9.

87. Cf. R. P. Sertillanges, *La philosophie morale de saint Thomas d'Aquin* (Paris: Aubier, 1946), p. 95; Dietrich Bonhoeffer, *Letters and Papers from Prison* (New York: Macmillan Paperback, 1962),

e.g., pp. 190–191, 194–197; H. Richard Niebuhr, *The Responsible Self* (New York: Harper and Row, 1963), e.g., pp. 66, 131.

88. *Loc. cit.*, 2.

89. Classic expressions of the contemporary vision are H. R. Niebuhr, *The Responsible Self*, e.g., pp. 47–68, and Dietrich Bonhoeffer, *Letters and Papers from Prison*, especially the pages cited in note 87. In a sense, all of Niebuhr's book is an attempt to clarify the twentieth century vision of man before God by putting the image of man-the-responder in a place of prominence over that of man-the-maker and that of man-the-citizen. Niebuhr observes that even the word "responsible" seems to have acquired its current moral sense only in the nineteenth and twentieth centuries (p. 47). It is interesting that there is no exact verbal equivalent in classical Greek and Latin for "responsibility" just as there is none for "loneliness."

90. Max Müller, *Existenzphilosophie im geistigen Leben der Gegenwart* (Heidelberg: Kerle, 1958), p. 140. In translating, I have availed myself of the context in order to make clear Professor Müller's meaning in the brief quotation.

11   Loyal Opposition in the Church

1. *The Making of a Mind*, tr. René Hague (New York: Harper and Row, 1965), pp. 268–269. Teilhard wrote the letter to his cousin, Marguerite Teillard-Chambon, on December 13, 1918.

12   Responsible Disobedience in the Church

1. *Human Life in Our Day*, issued November 15, 1968, by the National Conference of Catholic Bishops. I am using the text published in the *Baltimore Sun*, November 16, 1968, pp. A12–A13. The present quotation is on p. A12, Column 3. The emphasis is added.

2. Statement issued, September 24, 1968, by the bishops of England and Wales, section 8. The text is of the *Documentary Service* issued by the Press Department, U. S. Catholic Conference, on September 26. Both this and the preceding quotation have been deliberately chosen from statements that offer little, if any, encouragement to the opposition to the encyclical as it is understood in the present article.

3. *Op. cit.*, p. A12, Col. 5.

4. *Ibid.*

5. *N. C. News Service*, issued by the Press Department, U. S. Catholic Conference, August 2, 1968.

6. *The New York Times*, November 9, 1968, p. 16.

7. Besides the French and Dutch bishops and the four hierarchies about to be cited, the German and British bishops fail, in their official statements, to declare erroneous a conscience that would lead a Catholic to disobey the encyclical. Furthermore, while recognizing the authoritative force of the encyclical, they fail to endorse its teaching.

8. Statement issued September 27, 1968, numbers 17, 25 and 26 (*Documentary Services*, September 30).

9. *The National Catholic Reporter*, October 30, 1968, p. 3.

10. Statement of the Austrian bishops issued September 23, 1968, toward the end of section II (*Documentary Service*, October 4, 1968).

11. Statement of the Belgian bishops issued August 30, 1968, section 2, number 4 (*Documentary Service*, September 7, 1968).

12. *Ibid.*

13. *Ibid.* The quotation, without the parentheses, is from *Lumen Gentium*, 25.

14. Statement of the bishops of Scotland to be read in all parishes, October 13, 1968, number 6 (*Documentary Service*, October 11).

15. *The Catholic Mind*, September, 1968, p. 54.

16. *Op. cit.*, p. 55.

17. L. Lercher, S.J., *Institutiones Theologiae Dogmaticae*, fourth edition (Barcelona: Herder, 1945), no. 499 (my translation). I am grateful to Rev. James A. Sadowsky, S.J. for drawing attention to this paragraph of a traditional theology manual.

18. *Op. cit.*, p. A12, Col. 6.

19. P. A13, Col. 1.

20. *Humanae Vitae*, 17 (*Catholic Mind*, September, 1968, pp. 41–42).

21. *Ibid.*, 11, 12 and 13 (*Catholic Mind*, pp. 39–40).

22. *The New York Times*, January 9, 1969, p. 28.

23. *Op. cit.*, 14 (*Catholic Mind*, p. 40).

24. *Ibid.*

25. *Op. cit.* 12 (*Catholic Mind*, p. 39).

26. *The New York Times*, August 2, 1968, p. 1.

27. *Ibid.*

28. "An Editorial Statement on 'Human Life,'" *America*, August 17, 1968, pp. 94–95; cf. D. R. C.'s "Of Many Things," *ibid.*, on the back of the cover; Bernard Häring, "The Encyclical Crisis," *Commonweal*, September 6, 1968, pp. 588–594; Karl Rahner, S.J., "Zur Enzyklika 'Humanae Vitae,'" *Stimmen der Zeit*, September, 1968 (an English translation was published by *The National Catholic*

Reporter, September 18, 1968, p. 6); Richard A. McCormick, S.J., "Notes on Moral Theology: January–June, 1968," *Theological Studies*, December, 1968, pp. 707–741; Avery Dulles, S.J., "Karl Rahner on 'Human Life,'" *America*, September 28, 1968, pp. 250–252. Walter Burghardt, S.J., was one of the signers of the theologians' statement just mentioned. The attitude of the six theologians in regard to opposition to the encyclical varies, but they all make the point that whether the encyclical be right or wrong, opposition should not be regarded as an unfounded, deplorable, though sincere, delusion, but can be respected as an objectively serious and authentically Catholic attitude.

29. *Op. cit.*, pp. 209–210 (my translation).

30. Bernard Häring, *op. cit.*, pp. 589–590.

31. *Ibid.*, p. 590.

13   The Importance of Being Roman Catholic

1. Cf. Francis Hezel, S.J., "Peace Corps Volunteer or Missionary—Does It Really Make a Difference?" *The Catholic World*, pp. 205–207.

2. Avery Dulles, S.J., *Delmarva Dialog*, May 31, 1968.

3. In an advance notice given by Cardinal Shehan of Baltimore, reported in "The Week in Review," *The New York Times*, December 14, 1969, p. 10.

OTHER IMAGE BOOKS

OTHER IMAGE BOOKS

B 76 – 2

R45